THE POLITICS OF
JAMES
BOND

From Fleming's Novels to the Big Screen

JEREMY BLACK

UNIVERSITY OF NEBRASKA PRESS
LINCOLN AND LONDON

First Nebraska paperback printing: 2005

Library of Congress Cataloging-in-Publication Data
Black, Jeremy.
The politics of James Bond: from Fleming's novel to the big screen / by Jeremy Black.
p.   cm.
"Published in paperback by arrangement with Greenwood Publishing Group."
Includes bibliographical references and index.
ISBN 0-8032-6240-X (pbk.: alk. paper)
1. Fleming, Ian, 1908–1964—Characters—James Bond.   2. Politics and literature—Great Britain—History—20th century.   3. Fleming, Ian, 1908–1964—Film and video adaptations.   4. Fleming, Ian, 1908–1964—Political and social views.
5. Spy stories, English—Film and video adaptations.   6. Spy stories, English—History and criticism.   7. James Bond films—History and criticism.   8. Spy films—History and criticism.   9. Bond, James (Fictitious character)   10. Politics in motion pictures.
11. Espionage in literature.   12. Spies in literature.   I. Title.
PR6056.L4Z585   2005
823'.914—dc22   2004029696

For Armstrong Starkey, a good friend

Contents

Acknowledgments

I am most grateful to Nigel Aston, John Bourne, George Boyce, Grayson Ditchfield, Paul Doerr, Robert Johnson, Keith Laybourne, Stewart Lone, Don MacRaild, Robert Pearce, Nigel Saul, David Sturdy and Andrew Thorpe for their comments on earlier drafts, and for the opportunities to develop ideas offered by invitations to speak to the Staff Seminar of the History Department at Exeter University, the Undergraduate History Society at Exeter and at Georgia State University. I would like to thank Heather Staines, Rebecca Ardwin and Geoffrey Garvey at Praeger for seeing this book efficiently and helpfully into production. Most of all, I'd like to thank my father for taking me to the early Bond films.

Introduction

"The Name's Cook—Robin Cook!" Garland's cartoon in the *Daily Telegraph* of 29 August 1997 need say no more. The decision by the British Foreign Secretary to order MI6, the foreign intelligence service, to step up its drive against the international drug trade landed his cartoon figure among four swim-suited nymphets. The elegance and suavity of the black-tied Bond pose, pistol at the ready, contrasted with the wild eyes and hirsute features of the foreign secretary, as yet not widely known as an admirer of the opposite sex. This gentle mocking of pretentiousness reflected the iconic potency of Bond, a figure of style as well as intent, and, perhaps with Diana, Princess of Wales, the most famous Briton of the twentieth century.

This study approaches Bond through the politics of his creators, specifically their geopolitics, although domestic politics, attitudes to class and gender, and the demonology of the works are also considered. Ian Fleming's novels and the subsequent films are discussed in order to try to re-create the international world within which Bond was supposed to operate. This is presented as more complex than might be envisaged. Bond may have been a creation of the Cold War, but the Cold War of the novels and, still more, films was far from clear-cut. Both novels and films drew on current fears, but did so in offering a form of escapism from the politics of the age that reassured the public that their future was in good, gentlemanly hands, and that good (us) would always win in the end. This was tempered in Fleming's case by a strong pessimism that was largely ignored in the films. They were more upbeat in mood as well as content, generally offering, for example, a sense of humor and lightness of tone that he did not seek.

The setting and dynamics of the adventures changed, as the cultural, historical and political environment in which the Bond character operates altered. Part of the interest of the sequences of novels and films rests in the manner in which they reflected shifts in the global situation and in Britain's part within it. The decline of Britain, and the changing British world role and view of the world, can all be approached via Bond. Alongside the apparent timelessness of the icon, there is a timely awareness of historical change. This affects also both the presentation of the British Secret Service and, more clearly, the demonology of the works, one in which Nazis and Communists were replaced by more universal threats. Aside from being a mixture of Cold War warrior and a medieval knight rescuing maidens from modern dragons, even at risk to his mission, Bond was also a conduit through whom Fleming explored the ambivalent relationship between a declining Britain and an ascendant United States.

The novels and films also present potent images of national character, which connect to wider stereotypes, and are counterpointed by the villains. The images include M, father figure or sexless old school tie; attractive English roses exploited by callous foreigners; and Bond, cold-hearted but warm, a consummate gambler, society man, rock-hard war hero–type, and the all-British version of Romeo. He was, and is, an image of toughness, sharpness, cleverness and male sexuality, a national and class stereotype, that Fleming sought to identify anew with the British after the disruption of World War II and the Labour governments of 1945–51. Part of the strength and appeal of the Bond character, however, was that it was capable of different interpretations by particular audiences. Looked at more critically, this was an aspect of the description of Bond as "the ultimate prostitute" by the master of spy fiction, John Le Carré.

Bond's character was displayed in his actions: he represented and defined a notion of gentlemanliness understood as action, not as a set of empty conventions. Thus his gentlemanly virtues were seen to include sportsmanship and being an all-rounder. This ability, and the active nature of his gentility, were necessary because Britain was presented as under threat. Furthermore, with his combination of gentlemanly values and decisiveness, Bond represented the values and self-image of manly courage of the officer class in the British armed forces: he was like a stylish commando able to set his own rules but guaranteed to do so in a fair fashion and to worthwhile ends.

In contrast to Bond, women were accorded only a secondary place in the stories. This was borne out in the films by the failure of the starlets who appeared in them to amount to much thereafter. There were actresses and entertainers such as Honor Blackman and Grace Jones who were already established when they appeared in the Bond films, but the budding actresses whose first break was a Bond film tended thereafter to sink without a trace.

Imaginative literature is an important guide to overt and covert attitudes that shape and are shaped by the world. The Bond novels were best-sellers in their day, both within Britain and abroad. The films have been even more popular, becoming the most enduring and successful film franchise in history. Individual films have not done as well as, say, *Star Wars*, but the series as a whole has been more profitable than any other. For nearly a decade, it has been claimed that half the world's population has seen a Bond film, ensuring that billions of people have viewed an image of global struggle through Western eyes, offering a particular perception of Britain. Bond therefore has been a world star, one successfully played by a series of actors and thus able to maintain his persona. Millions of people who have never read one of the books have seen all the films. When regularly shown on Christmas Day television in Britain from 1975 (although not in 1997), the films were so popular that there were many surges in demand for electric power on the National Grid when large numbers of electric kettles were switched on during the advertising intervals. *GoldenEye* (1995) earned $350 million in the cinema alone. Opening in the United States on 19 December 1997, *Tomorrow Never Dies* had earned $115.5 million by 24 January 1998. By then, the total box-office gross earnings of the films were estimated as more than $2.6 billion.

Such popularity is born of their success as gripping adventure stories. They are not read or seen as political texts. Furthermore, much within them is treated as implausible by readers and viewers, especially the plans of some of the psychotic troublemakers whom Bond overthrows. Yet there is a limit to this implausibility. The plots are not those of science fiction. As Kingsley Amis pointed out in an introduction to the reprint of his 1968 Bond novel, *Colonel Sun* (1991), "the matter of setting, of where [is] so important in all Bond's adventures." There is a tactility, indeed precision, in many of the books that reflects Fleming's strong concern with verisimilitude, although this verisimilitude was less apparent in the films. In the novels, it was seen most powerfully in Fleming's description of underwater flora and fauna, guns and cars. Yet it also affects the politics of his plots. This worldview played a major role not only as context, but also in providing both a dynamism and a morality in the plots. It is time to turn to the start of Bond's world.

PART I

FLEMING'S BOND: THE SECRET AGENT IN THE NOVELS

1

Cold War Stories

Bond was not a free spirit or an independent force. Instead, he was a British agent and Fleming's was very much an account of Britain. That it was idealized did not detract from his presentation of Britain at a particular moment. This was late-imperial Britain, as the decades of defense took their cumulative toll, and the tide of empire ebbed under the pressure of a hostile world. Yet this pressure was resisted. Britain was one of the victorious powers at the close of World War II and her success in resisting Nazi aggression was a matter of great pride. Furthermore, signs of the cost of the struggle were still around Fleming's readers in the bombed townscapes of Britain.

Postwar Britain was still a major imperial power, and she sought to act like one in the late 1940s and 1950s in Africa, Malaya and the Middle East. The limited decolonization of the late 1940s—India and Pakistan (1947); Burma, Ceylon and Palestine (1948); and Newfoundland (1949)—was part of a strategy designed to ensure the maintenance of Britain's position as a great power. Conscription—seen as a measure necessary to show national resolve in the Cold War—was continued with the National Service Act of 1947 and was not phased out until 1957–63. Britain became a nuclear power in 1952.

This is the background to Fleming's novels, the first of which appeared in 1953. It is interesting that none are set in parts of the British empire recently granted independence; or, indeed, in the "Dominions" that had earlier gained independence: Australia, Canada, South Africa and New Zealand. Instead, it was a still-active empire that Bond was called upon to defend, as indeed were the young men of the country who were conscripted. This, however, was an empire and a world that were at risk, and this may be a reason why the novels were so popular. In the 1950s, indeed, a series of crises— the Abadan crisis of 1951, the Suez crisis of 1956, and the overthrow of the pro-British Iraqi government in 1958—revealed the limitations of British strength and encouraged a new attitude toward empire that was to lead to rapid decolonization.

Bond is a figure designed to resist the threat to empire. Possibly increasing problems and rising decadence, across the world and even at home, is the sole setting in which Bond and the global villains can truly operate. It makes both appear sufficiently probable to carry the plots. Fleming had Bond join the Secret Service in 1938 and, having seen off the Nazis, he was to resist the Communists. Indeed, Bond can be seen, at least initially, as a central figure in the paranoid culture of the Cold War. The novels and early films charted a period when Britain was making adjustments to her world status in uneasy alliance with the United States against Communism, and, increasingly, offering skill, brains and professionalism, instead of mere might. Even when in the stories Britain's opponents were not Communist, the plots encouraged a sense of Britain as being in great danger, and the foreign character of the villains underlined this point. The extent to which the Soviet Union was indeed a threat is controversial. Fleming certainly did not underrate it. He also created a character whose role, in a series of adventures in which he would be greatly outnumbered and faced with sinister foes, served to dramatize the threat to Britain.

CASINO ROYALE: THE GUN IS PRIMED—THE POLITICS OF COLD WAR

> History is moving pretty quickly these days and the heroes and villains keep on changing places.
>
> —James Bond in *Casino Royale*

Casino Royale was finished on 18 March 1952, the first book by the forty-three-year-old Ian Fleming, a *Sunday Times* executive whose varied earlier career had included a period with Reuters and, more significantly, service as personal assistant to the director of Naval Intelligence during World War II. This had been the most enlivening and assured period of Fleming's life. More generally, Fleming's well-connected and wealthy background and circumstances, especially his love of travel, stylish disdain for what he saw as the commonplace and quest for adventure, helped to shape the Bond novels.

Published in April 1953, *Casino Royale* was, like the other early Bond works, a novel of the Cold War produced in the shadow of World War II. Winston Churchill, the war leader in that conflict, was prime minister again in 1951–55 and the Conservatives under Churchill had fought the 1950 election by urging the electors to "make Britain great again." Returned to power in October 1951, Churchill was determined to defend British interests and for several months in 1953 he assumed direct control of foreign policy. British assertiveness included in late 1952 Royal Air Force overflights of Buraimi oasis, an oil-rich part of the Arabian peninsula then in dispute between the British-backed Persian Gulf rulers and Saudi Arabia, which looked to American support. More generally, Britain sought to act as a great power. The accession (1952) and coronation (1953) of Queen Elizabeth II led to talk of a "New Elizabethan Age," and the ascent of Mount Everest in 1953 contributed to this excitement.

The politics of *Casino Royale* followed hard on the mood setting of the arrestingly written opening scene introducing the world of the casino at Royale and linking it to the far-flung scope of the British Secret Service. They were outlined, in the second chapter, in the form of a dossier for "M," the head of the Secret Service. This concentrated on the target, Le Chiffre, a loathsome individual with one English and two German aliases, who was paymaster of the Communist-controlled trade union in the heavy and transport industries of Alsace, the most vulnerable part of France to Soviet attack. The trade union was presented as an important fifth column in the event of war with "Redland," the Soviet Union. Indeed, in 1947 "Wild Bill" Donovan, the former head of OSS (the American Office of Strategic Services), had helped persuade the American government to fund anti-Communists in the French trade unions that, he claimed, were a Communist fifth column.

There was considerable sensitivity in Britain at the time about the extent of Communist influence in the trade unions. In 1949, the Labour government had sent in troops to deal with a London dock strike that it blamed on Communists. The following year, Hugh Gaitskell, the minister for fuel and power, and later the lover of Fleming's wife Ann, claimed that a strike in the power stations was instigated by Communist shop stewards and served for them as a rehearsal for future confrontation. The accuracy of such views was a matter for controversy. Critics argued that they reflected Cold War paranoia, but the belief that Communists were encouraging agitation both in the trade unions and the empire was widespread. Fleming both contributed to such attitudes and derived benefit from their popularity.

Without the permission of his superiors, the fictional Le Chiffre had invested in the Cordon Jaune, a network of Norman and Breton brothels, in January 1946, but, that April, a new law against brothels ruined his investment. Encouraged by the British and by the French Deuxième Bureau (Secret Service), the French police then turned the heat up by closing down as many of the brothels as they could find.

To recoup the original investment, fifty million francs of trade union funds, Le Chiffre proposed to win at baccarat at the casino in Royale-les-Eaux, a fictional spa which was based on Fleming's prewar visits to Deauville and Le Touquet, glamorous French casino resorts on the Channel. Le Chiffre's plan was grasped as an opportunity, to wreck a potential fifth column that might otherwise control much of France's frontier in wartime, by the head of Station S of the Secret Service, the station concerned with the USSR. He proposed that Le Chiffre be out-gambled by the Secret Service's best gambler. The Cold War was at its height and had to be fought; and it was best not to remain on the defensive. Seeking to convince M of the value of the scheme, S presented British intelligence as in competition with the secret services of her allies. His remark that the Deuxième Bureau and the Central Intelligence Agency would doubtless be delighted to take over the scheme was intended to highlight the question of whether Britain had a role.

Not only a role, but a hero. Bond is chosen and dispatched to Royale. Cleaned out by Le Chiffre, Bond is rescued by Felix Leiter, the CIA observer, who loans him 32 million francs, with which Bond subsequently beats the villain. In both novels and films, Bond's gambling skills were to be repeatedly employed. They are a measure of skill and style. He is put under pressure, but not contaminated, by gambling, just as he is not by killing. Skill at gambling and knowledge of how to behave at a casino were seen by Fleming as attributes of a gentleman that were important to Bond's success. This was an aspect of Bond's character that was taken up in some of the films but that can now appear dated.

Bond's need for the American money at Royale reflected the central role of the United States in the defense of the West. Leiter provides it without difficulty and is happy to rely on Bond's skill, suggesting a far smoother working of the Anglo-American alliance than was in fact the case. The two powers cooperated, having recently fought as allies against the Chinese in the Korean War (1950–53), and being partners in the UK-U.S. Security Agreement covering signals espionage, and in the North Atlantic Treaty Organization—NATO (1949–   ). America provided Britain with Marshall Aid to aid postwar reconstruction, and American B29 Superfortress atomic bombers were based in East Anglia, able to strike from there at Moscow.

However, there were also serious differences of opinion between Britain and America, especially outside Europe. For example, the Americans pressed the British to accept their views on the liberalization of trade and air routes, followed a different line on Palestine, and helped to undermine Britain's position in Persia (Iran). In January 1954, Sir Roger Makins, the British ambassador in Washington, expressed the concern that "the Americans are out to take our place in the Middle East." The British desire to preserve and strengthen empire, seen by both Labour and Conservatives as the basis for Britain's international and economic position, clashed with American interest in a new world order of capitalist democracies, a world order that challenged imperial rule as much as Communism. For example, the CIA-supported "Asia Foundation" produced anti-imperialist propaganda in Singapore on the model of the anti-Soviet "Radio Free Europe."

Fleming did not press this Anglo-American clash in his novels, but he was aware of it and at times his plots can be seen as efforts to create an impression of the normality of British imperial rule and action, with Bond as a defender of empire. This is not, however, the issue in *Casino Royale*. The harmonious relationship of Bond and Leiter concealed a more troublesome reality. Indeed, American concern over the British spy system had risen greatly after the defections of Guy Burgess and Donald Maclean in 1951. The Americans firmly, and correctly, believed that Kim Philby, the Secret Service's liaison officer in Washington, was a traitor, and in 1952 the director of the CIA insisted that he not return to Washington.

After the card game at Royale, Vesper Lynd, Bond's assistant, is kidnapped by Le Chiffre, and the pursuing Bond ambushed, captured and tortured. The torture, however, is cut short as an agent of SMERSH secretly arrives and shoots Le Chiffre. SMERSH had already been introduced at the outset of the novel as the fearsome Soviet counterintelligence network, "the efficient organ of Soviet vengeance . . . SMERSH is short for SMYERT SHIPIONAM—Death to Spies." With his tormenters dead, Bond is told of the devastation of Communist morale caused by the exposure and collapse of Le Chiffre's system.

However, he then reveals a degree of reflectiveness and ambiguity that gives his character some depth. Bond tells his French contact, René Mathis of the Deuxième Bureau, that "this country-right-or-wrong business is getting a little out-of-date." He points to the mutability of political divisions: "If I'd been alive fifty years ago, the brand of Conservatism we have today would have been damn near called Communism and we should have been told to go and fight that," a reference to the Conservative government's willingness to maintain the welfare state created by their Labour predecessors.

Mathis is appalled, criticizing Bond as an anarchist, only to receive the rejoinder that Bond would be willing to kill Le Chiffre were he alive, but for personal revenge, not "high moral reason or for the sake of my country." This tension between introspection and duty was to recur in the novels, and Mathis tackles it by telling Bond he must personalize the struggle and surround himself with human beings, who "are easier to fight for than principles," the last an argument that reflected Fleming's views.

The personal approach is given flesh in the character of Vesper. Bond has an affair with her at L'Auberge du Fruit Défendu. This idyllic hotel was owned by a Monsieur Versoix, who, in an echo found throughout the novels, but not the films, is located with reference to World War II, the defining test of character. He had lost his arm fighting with the Free French in defeating the Vichy French on Madagascar when the British invaded in 1942, and therefore is a "good" Frenchman.

Vesper, however, commits suicide, revealing in a letter to Bond that she was a Soviet double agent. Her boyfriend, a decorated ex-RAF Pole, had been a British agent, captured in Poland, tortured, and kept alive in order to force Vesper to cooperate. Again, this is a reference to the continuation between World War II and the Cold War. For Fleming and Bond, the Soviets had replaced the Nazis, a worldview convincing to those who all along had opposed the Russian Revolution and had been uncomfortable about the wartime alliance with Stalin, the position of much of the British right.

In love with Bond, Vesper renounces Soviet control by killing herself. This leads Bond to resolve to fight and destroy SMERSH, which he sees as the terror behind Soviet espionage. The book closes with Bond's cold utterance "The bitch is dead now," a reference to Vesper and her betrayal of him, but, in a way, also to Bond's doubts.

The gun is now primed. Although this resolution is not reached until the end of the novel, indeed it is its conclusion, there were earlier hints both of Bond's internal struggle and of the brutality of SMERSH. At dinner with Vesper at Royale, Bond explains the meaning of his Double O. This is self-depreciatory and at the same time an insight into his doubts: "I've got the corpses of a Japanese cipher expert in New York and a Norwegian double agent in Stockholm to thank for being a Double O. Probably quite decent people. They just got caught up in the gale of the world," a phrase that echoes that of Draza Mihailovic, the leader of the Chetniks, the anti-Communist Yugoslav resistance, accused of making deals with the Germans, and executed in 1946 on the orders of the Communist leader Tito after a show trial. Bond continues by pleading orders and deploying style: "It's a confusing business but if it's one's profession, one does what one's told. How do you like the grated egg with your caviar?"

In fact, the plots of both books and films are designed to free Bond from this dilemma about violence. He is not shown fighting decent people, but, instead, people who are trying to blow up a gale to bring down the world. Bond might like to present himself as a stylish cog, but he is given purpose, not by his profession, not by the machine of which he is part, but by the morality of the wider struggle in which he figures. Fleming's was in many senses a Manichean world. Evil was afoot, and while the sense of evil was not that of one of Denis Wheatley's black magic novels, it was more atmospheric than in the subsequent Bond films.

While waiting for the hot toast necessary to enjoy their caviar, Vesper tells Bond about the details of the plot to kill him on the streets of Royale. Le Chiffre sought to devour his own people as well as his opponents: the killing of Bond was left to three Bulgarians, "part of a pool held in France for this sort of job—saboteurs, thugs, and so on," a comment, like many others, intended to suggest that Fleming was particularly knowledgeable about the world of espionage. The smoke-grenade behind which the Bulgarians were supposed to escape was in fact a high-explosive device intended to kill them as well, and Le Chiffre's plan was only thwarted because the Bulgarians set it off first, instead of, as instructed, at the same time as they threw the other bomb at Bond.

This was to be a repeated theme of the books. The evil of Bond's opponents not only justified his actions, but also helped to thwart their very purposes, a stock device in fiction. Thus, in *Thunderball* (1961), the killing of the traitorous Giuseppe Petacchi by SPECTRE after he has delivered the hijacked plane loaded with atomic bombs to them, gives Bond his opportunity to alienate Petacchi's sister from SPECTRE. Evil in short thwarted itself. Bond was the beneficiary, deliberately or unconsciously exploiting the weaknesses inherent in evil.

The most obvious manifestation of these was the repeated failure of villains who had seized Bond to dispatch him forthwith, and their preference for "clever" deaths. Bond's death was delayed so that he could be the intended victim of a giant squid in *Dr. No* (1958) and of a rocket's after-burn in *Moonraker* (1955). Such delays helped to provide Bond with a chance to escape, while they also served the plots by providing apparently victorious villains with opportunities to reveal their dastardly schemes. This was a common device. Sax Rohmer's villain, Dr. Fu-Manchu, made the same mistake. Bond's flaw—his conscience—was thus secured and more than compensated for by his opponents' flaws—the foolish deceit, self-deceit, and over-confidence integral to evil.

This pattern, of the hubris and callousness of evil, providing opportunities for the bravery and integrity of Bond, was set at the outset of the series, but so, also, was a more specific aspect of the politics, the divisiveness of the opposition. In *Casino Royale* this serves to save Bond. Le Chiffre is killed by SMERSH while in control of Bond. Such a resolution does not recur in other novels and was not repeated when the story was televised for CBS in 1954. Instead, elsewhere Bond is responsible for the villains' deaths and this indeed is the dramatic culmination of the plot, but he is frequently the beneficiary of divisions within the opposition, as on the streets of Royale when the Bulgarians' refusal to obey their instructions is fatal to them, but not to Bond.

If *Casino Royale* sets the pattern for the series, that owed much to the response when it was published. The book was rapidly reprinted and the publishers, Jonathan Cape, offered Fleming a contract for three further books. Bond was set. The money was there. Now the plots had to follow.

LIVE AND LET DIE: A HOT WIND FROM JAMAICA

> Dexter: Our policy with Mr. Big is "live and let live."
>
> Bond: When I come up against a man like this one, I have another motto. It's "live and let die."

The second book followed in 1954. Indeed, before *Casino Royale* was published, Fleming had already researched and written what was originally to be called *The Undertaker's Wind*, but which was published as *Live and Let Die*. Far from repeating the formula of his first success, this was a world away from the sinister style of a luxurious European gambling resort, a classic location in interwar novels. Instead, Bond was sent to the New World, the United States, his target not the deracinated European Le Chiffre—described as part Jewish with some Mediterranean, Prussian or Polish blood added into the mix—but the more exotic Mr. Big, an intimidatingly large Negro and a figure that focused American anxieties.

In place of the tired, cloying opulence of the casino at Royale at 3 AM, the story opened with the movement, energy and luxury of a welcomed arrival at Idlewild (now JFK) airport in New York, a scene based on Fleming's arrivals in 1941 and 1953. Thanks to the airplane, Bond is able to travel at will and at speed across the globe, an idea that was increasingly seductive as air travel became easier and more popular after World War II. Fleming enjoyed such travel.

But even while Bond observes the pace of the city for the benefit of the British readers—most of whom knew little of the United States other than through American films but saw it as interesting and glamorous—he is also aware of New York as threatened. Driving in, Bond notes "the Civil Defence warnings: IN CASE OF ENEMY ATTACK—KEEP MOVING—GET OFF BRIDGE" and he tells his American escort "this must be the fattest atomic-bomb target on the whole face of the globe," a remark that serves to underline the degree to which both the United States and Britain are threatened by Soviet nuclear weaponry and thus by the traitors who provide the USSR with nuclear secrets.

As Bond arrives at his hotel, the best in town, he catches sight of Mr. Big scrutinizing him. His cover has been blown. Thus, along with the wealth and vigor of New York, readers were shown the tensions and fears, and the enemies, in the midst of the leading city of the United States.

M had already explained Bond's task. Sixteenth- and seventeenth-century gold coins were turning up in the United States and then being melted down into the "black bullion market." Just as the Soviet Union used Le Chiffre's network in France, so another network was in place in the United States. Negro workers in the transportation industry would distribute the money across America.

Mr. Big is revealed as "the most powerful negro criminal in the world. . . . the head of the Black Widow Voodoo cult," and also a known member of SMERSH. This allows M and Bond to offer their views on the ethnicity of crime, views that reflected ignorance, the inherited racialist prejudices of London clubland, and a sense of change:

"I don't think I've ever heard of a great negro criminal before," said Bond. . . .

"Our man's a bit of an exception," said M. "He's not pure negro. Born in Haiti. Good dose of French blood. Trained in Moscow too. . . . And the negro races are just beginning to throw up geniuses in all the professions. . . . It's about time they turned out a great criminal. . . . They've got plenty of brains and ability and guts. And now Moscow's taught one of them the technique."

This exchange suggests that Fleming's approach to ethnicity was more complex than some passages in his works might imply. The frequency of his references and his willingness to offer racial stereotypes, typical of many writers of his age, jars on the modern consciousness and are ignored or understated in the films. The Black Power activist Eldridge Cleaver claimed in *Soul on Ice* (1968) that "The 'paper tiger' hero, James Bond, offering the whites a triumphant image of themselves, is saying what many whites want desperately to hear reaffirmed: 'I am still the White Man, lord of the land, licensed to kill, and the World is still an empire at my feet.' " This was an image of Bond as colonial adventurer, the upholder of empire and, thus, the defender of white control.

The comments by M in *Live and Let Die*, nevertheless, reveal both admiration for the abilities of the "negro races" and a sense of fluidity. He was the mature and impressive source of much wisdom in Fleming's novels, certainly more so than in the films. Similarly, Felix Leiter admires their self-improvement and thinks only some are "stinkeroos." Such remarks are nevertheless patronizing. They are certainly uncomfortable for the modern reader.

As with many individuals in the novels, Mr. Big's career reflected the impact of World War II. His ability in French led him to be called up by the Office of Strategic Services and sent to Marseilles to act against the Vichy regime and to provide naval intelligence. In these tasks, Mr. Big operated closely with a Soviet spy, preparing the ground for his recruitment by SMERSH. The Mediterranean port cities were to produce another villain in Emilio Largo from Naples in *Thunderball*, and later Kristatos in "Risico," one of the short stories in *For Your Eyes Only*. As in *Casino Royale*, there was in *Live and Let Die* an emphasis on the threat to the West's communications, and thus security.

The black population having been presented as varied and generally law-abiding, it was next portrayed as open to manipulation by Mr. Big. When Lieutenant Binswanger of the New York Police Department criticizes FBI caution and suggests arresting Mr. Big and then giving him a violent questioning, Captain Dexter of the FBI warns that this would lead to a race riot. Thus the Soviet military threat from without was apparently matched by that of subversion from within, the very pluralism of politics in the West providing an opportunity for Soviet power with its apparently inexorable monolithic and global power. Bond "felt his spine crawl at the cold, brilliant efficiency of the Soviet machine." Black power is the threatening tool of Soviet malice, an argument frequently made by racists in the 1950s.

Public concern about Soviet espionage was then at a high level in both Britain and the United States. In Britain, it was heightened in 1954 by the Petrov case, the defection of the Soviet consul at Canberra and the Soviet attempt to prevent his wife from defecting, an unsuccessful attempt played out in public. The suggestion of a remorseless multifaceted Soviet espionage offensive seemed steadily more credible.

There was also concern about black neighborhoods in Britain. On 14 September 1953, for example, the headline of the *Daily Sketch*, a British popular newspaper, proclaimed GUNMEN AT LARGE: DOPE, DAGGERS AND TERROR IN THE STREETS. THE FACTS. This introduced an exaggerated account of the problems of Tiger Bay in Cardiff, the leading city in Wales, and a misleading attempt to link them to the black population of the area of Butetown, also in Cardiff. The former was emblematic of poverty and crime. Ironically, Shirley Bassey, the most famous *chanteuse* of Bond theme songs, came from Tiger Bay and was herself black.

Bond did not visit Tiger Bay, but his search for Mr. Big leads him to cross boundaries, especially by visiting Harlem—an aspect of the novel as travel story. Superficially there are similarities between Harlem and Manhattan where Bond is staying. Bond, listening to a conversation reported in the local dialect, remarks "Seems they're interested in much the same things as everyone else—sex, having fun, and keeping up with the Jones's [*sic*]."

However, the signs of the occult in the shops, of charms and superstition, leads to an awareness of difference, of clashing worlds within New York itself. These worlds also involve control: Mr. Big dominates Harlem and Bond is not safe there. When Bond is seized by Mr. Big, he is brought up against the symbols of the voodoo Baron Samedi. Mr. Big's followers believe him to be the Zombie (living corpse) of Samedi, and, as he is therefore already dead, he can't be killed. For him, the barrier between life and death had been overcome.

Having shot his way out of Harlem, Bond then takes the Silver Phantom train to Florida to investigate how and where Mr. Big's treasure enters the United States. Bond foils an attempt to kill him on the train, but Leiter is badly injured by a shark when investigating Mr. Big's warehouse, the Ourobouros Worm and Bait Company, which was based on a live worm warehouse in St. Petersburg, Florida, that Fleming had visited in 1953. Bond takes revenge by killing, as he has not done in *Casino Royale*, only to find the FBI keen to get him out of the country and reluctant to act against Mr. Big.

By this stage, there has been a break from the world of espionage, but that theme is reintroduced with a reference to Cuba and the information that "Cuba comes under Harlem and runs red agents all through the Caribbean." It is taken further when Bond travels to Jamaica and is briefed by Commander John Strangways, the chief Secret Service agent for the Caribbean, about the Isle of Surprise, an offshore island recently purchased by Mr. Big. Readers were offered a defined sense of strategic threat:

Since 1950 Jamaica had become an important strategic target, thanks to the development by Reynolds Metal and the Kaiser Corporation of huge bauxite deposits found on the island. So far as Strangways was concerned, the activities on Surprise might easily be the erection of a base for one-man submarines in the event of war, particularly since Shark Bay was within range of the route followed by the Reynolds ships to the new bauxite harbour at Ocho Rios, a few miles down the coast.

Bauxite was necessary for the manufacture of aluminum, a strategic metal, not least for the aircraft infantry. One-man submarines had been used to great effect for sabotage missions in World War II. Ordered to penetrate the island, Strangways is thwarted when his two divers are killed by sharks and barracuda.

Bond already knew Jamaica, again because of a political connection. He had spent time there assigned to protect local labor unions from infiltration by Communists based in Cuba shortly after World War II, again a reminder of the swift transition from fighting Nazis to combating Communism and of the vulnerability of the unions to hostile, specifically Communist, penetration. In fact, as part of the empire, Jamaica for intelligence purposes came under E Branch of MI5, so the fictional Bond was presumably seconded from MI6.

After Bond is briefed by Strangways, the book becomes an adventure story, shorn of politics. Bond is captured and a lurid death is prepared for him, in which he will be eaten by fish after being pulled across a reef. According to Mr. Big, shark and barracuda play a role in Voodooism, thus satisfying his followers, while Bond's death would give him an opportunity to continue his experiments with carnivorous fish, an aspect of the perversion of science that

Fleming was to associate with several of his villains. Bond, instead, escapes when Mr. Big's boat is blown up, thanks to a bomb he has already planted. Mr. Big falls victim to a leopard shark. At the close, Bond is left to enjoy "passionate" leave with Solitaire, the Creole beauty with the power to read minds whom he had freed from Mr. Big. She is part of the occult world that Bond is able both to free (from Mr. Big) and to convert to benign purposes.

The precariousness of empire revealed by Mr. Big's possession of the Isle of Surprise was a theme Fleming later returned to. In *Dr. No* (1958), he observed of the bastion of colonial rule in Kingston: "Such stubborn retreats will not long survive in modern Jamaica. One day Queen's Club will have its windows smashed and perhaps be burned to the ground." This sense of the empire under threat matched the portrayal of Britain. The two were not separable, a characteristic of the politics of Fleming that ensures that the geopolitics of the novels were totally different from those of today. To Fleming, Britain had to be defended throughout the empire, whether in Jamaica or the Seychelles.

The wide-ranging nature of the imperial state indeed provides the context for Fleming's Secret Service. In *Casino Royale*, for example, Fawcett is described as follows: "One of the men from the Caymans who had volunteered on the outbreak of war, he had ended up as a Paymaster's clerk in a small Naval Intelligence organization in Malta." After the war, he had been recruited by the Secret Service and found a job on the *Daily Gleaner* of Jamaica, ready to serve the empire. Although precarious, the empire was still effective. Once in Jamaica, Bond was not dependent on American resources or approval.

In practice, British intelligence in these years did cooperate closely with the Americans, both against the Soviet Union and elsewhere. The British sought American assistance against Mohammed Musaddiq, the anti-British prime minister of Iran who was overthrown in 1953 after domestic opposition had been stirred up by the CIA. Winston Churchill, then prime minister of Great Britain, actively encouraged the operation, which revealed the continued importance of skillful agents on the ground. Kermit Roosevelt of the CIA was the crucial figure. Having met Roosevelt at the White House, President Dwight Eisenhower, another supporter of covert operations, recorded in his diary, "I listened and it seemed more like a dime novel than a historical fact." President John F. Kennedy was to be similarly impressed by the Bond stories.

MOONRAKER AND ROCKETS: FROM JAMAICA TO KENT

He is almighty—the man in the padded cell who is God.
                                                    —Bond, of Drax

The world of rockets was to play a major role in the Bond opus, both in the novels and in the films. Leaving aside the possible phallic significance of rockets, "this pastel column, so incredibly slim and graceful," to quote Fleming, there is also a political dimension to rockets. The rocket symbolized modernity, a real departure from the clubland setting of many works, including the opening of *Moonraker* (1955). It did more than that, however. Like air power, but even more vividly, the rocket meant the end of British invulnerability. No longer could the nation rely on the traditional defenses of seapower, on heroes of the type of Francis Drake and Horatio Nelson. Like Fleming, Bond's own background was naval, but he had to face a very different challenge.

It was necessary for Britain to consider a forward defensive perimeter. With airpower and the German V-1 and V-2 rockets of World War II, Britain could be and was attacked from northwest Europe. In *Thrilling Cities* (1963), Fleming referred to a "recurrent waking nightmare" of a surprise German rocket attack on Britain (he in fact refers to England). The novel *Moonraker* was set in this newly exposed world. During his research, Fleming sought information about V-2 rockets, although the rocket intended for the destruction of London in his novel was to be fired from Kent. The villain's explanation for his use of a German workforce is that they worked on the V-2 and, therefore, had the necessary experience, being the experts the Russians were not able to seize.

Moonraker was a variant on the "traitor within" idea, a theme already employed with Le Chiffre and Mr. Big, but now more powerfully so, as the traitor within was a prominent figure who was not suspected by the police; in short, he was like the villain in such interwar works as John Buchan's *The Three Hostages* (1924). In the films, including the film of *Moonraker* (1979), the idea of rockets was to serve a different purpose. The availability of intercontinental rockets and, in the case of the film *Moonraker*, of satellite-to-earth rockets, provided the theme of the vulnerability of the whole earth and of the exposure of mankind itself to the schemes of dangerous megalomaniacs. This increased the stakes dramatically and made Bond a very different figure: in the film *Moonraker*, as the savior of the species. This taxed credibility. Whereas one man's activities might be seen as helping to save a nation, it was less plausible to think of them as saving the world. Such a portrayal also served to underline the possibility of, and need for, cooperation between different secret services.

The novel *Moonraker*, written in 1954 and published in 1955, was very different. It was both specific, rather than global, and about Britain, not Jamaica, the United States, or the casino world of Royale. This location in Britain was both an opportunity and a problem. Fleming would not be able to interest his then predominantly British readership, and permit the story to proceed, by guiding the reader through the unfamiliar, as in his accounts of the Silver Phantom train or Harlem nightspots.

Setting the plot in the familiar world led Fleming to make the challenge more immediate. Indeed, whereas Le Chiffre was a threat only in time of war, a foe with potential, and Mr. Big was financing a network, the villain of *Moonraker*, Sir Hugo Drax, was planning to destroy London, and very soon. This was far more directly a problem for Britain than the schemes of Le Chiffre and Mr. Big, both of whom threatened foreign, albeit allied, powers: France and the United States. The threat to Britain was also one in which the crucial initiative was taken by the opponent. The pace of the book is set by the preparation for the rocket's launch, due to be fired less than four days after M gives Bond the job. Bond had to be a savior. The grand, even apocalyptic, scenario of *Moonraker* was less credible than that in the earlier novels and, thus, put pressure on the plot. Fleming indeed suggested to the film producer Alexander Korda that the story would make a good basis for a film.

To add weight to his new super-villain, the novel *Moonraker* brought together the two foes of Fleming's world, the Nazis and the Soviets. Drax was working for the latter, but he was also a Nazi. As with Le Chiffre and Mr. Big, and later Ernst Blofeld (the villain first introduced in *Thunderball*), his origins were crucial and the war played a major role in them. Drax was a wealthy tycoon and a member of Blades, a fictional leading London club, very different in its membership from the louche world of French casinos, and a "sparkling scene" described with great reverence by Fleming, who was an enthusiastic clubman. Drax had also, however, been one of the Werewolves, German commandos sent behind Allied lines as saboteurs, a group that was to cause trouble for Biggles's counterpart Gimlet in one of Captain W. E. John's adventure stories for boys. Found badly injured and without papers on the battlefield of the Ardennes at the close of 1944, Drax was an outsider; yet he gained vast wealth and became a social figure. He had cornered the market in colombite, a metal crucial for the manufacture of jet engines. This outsider who had made his way into the establishment had been entrusted with his nation's defense, in a way that was not possible for either Le Chiffre or Mr. Big. In Kent, he was constructing a nuclear rocket, the core of the Moonraker plan. This was designed to provide Britain with, as M puts it, "an independent say in world affairs," a major aspiration of British politicians, both Labour and Conservative, in the late 1940s and 1950s. The plot thus reflected the possibility that Britain could develop the technology to overcome the economic and military gap with the superpowers. Britain indeed became the third atomic power in 1952, and the third power with a hydrogen bomb in 1957. The Joint Intelligence Committee warned that war with the USSR would lead to serious rocket attacks on Britain.

Drax had invested £10 million of his own money on the rocket project, a commitment that had made him very popular. Although a social outsider, "a bullying, boorish, loud-mouth vulgarian," who sweated "rather freely" and bit his nails, Drax was a "public hero." This might imply a criticism of mass society and its heroes, which might seem ironic in view of the subsequent mass popularity of Bond. The plot revealed how misguided the public could be, but also how vulnerable the British establishment was to new men. It also bridged two eras with its discussion of Blades and rockets. Contrasting settings were successfully combined in a story that presented Britain as on the cusp of change and sought to reconcile change and continuity, an issue at once focused and endangered by Drax's role and character.

Drax's Nazi origins and his scheme for a rocket attack on London ensured that the theme of the villain within was not extended to any notion of class war. Drax wants to destroy London, not stir up revolution. The plot is therefore different from those of the interwar novels that suggested that sinister conspiracies lay behind political and industrial problems. That had been the theme of *Bulldog Drummond: The Adventures of a Demobilized Officer Who Found Peace Dull* (1920), *The Black Gang* (1922) and *The Third Round* (1924) by Lieutenant Colonel Herman Cyril McNeile under the pseudonym of Sapper. As with *Moonraker*, they were postwar adventures suggesting that the war was not over. John Buchan (1875–1940), a Scottish writer who served in intelligence during World War I before becoming an MP (Member of Parliament) and governor-general of Canada, had discerned in *The Three Hostages* (1924) "wreckers on the grand scale, merchants of pessimism, giving society another kick downhill whenever it had a chance of finding its balance, and then pocketing

their profits. . . . they used the fanatics . . . whose key was a wild
hatred of something or other, or a reasoned belief in anarchy."
Buchan was apt to see the "hidden hand" of a Jewish/Communist plot
to take over the world. According to Agatha Christie's *The Big Four*
(1927), "The world-wide unrest, the labour troubles that beset every
nation, and the revolutions that break out in some. . . . [T]here is a
force behind the scenes which aims at nothing less than the disinte-
gration of civilization. . . . Lenin and Trotsky were mere puppets."
Technology was seen by Christie as at the service of this force: "a
concentration of wireless energy far beyond anything so far attempted, and capable of focusing a beam of great intensity upon
some given spot . . . atomic energy," so that the Big Four could become "the dictators of the world." In Buchan and the genre of the
gentleman spy, patriotism was given a markedly right-wing character. The "hidden hand" of the Jewish/Communist plot to take over
the world was very important. Similar themes were developed in
interwar films, such as those of Sapper's stories, although the Alfred
Hitchcock/Robert Donat film version of Buchan's *The Thirty-Nine
Steps* (1935) changed the villains to the Nazis in the climate of im-
pending war.

Although the opponent in *Moonraker* was within and planning to
employ new technology, Fleming's account did not propose a politics
of paranoia or focus on domestic threats. Britain and her empire
were under threat, but, whereas trade unions in France and Negro
workers in the United States could be seen as dangerous, there was
nothing comparable to the demonology of Buchan and Christie: it
was individuals and the foreign power they represented that posed
the challenge, not the openness of British society and its fanatics to
manipulation.

Fleming did not use class enemies for his villains, instead relying
on physical distortion or ethnic identity to locate them, as in his
portrayals of Le Chiffre, Mr. Big, Drax, Dr. No, Goldfinger and Blofeld. This reflected the role of ethnicity and racialism in his politics
and a disinclination to look for evil among the British. The ordinary
people were not heroes, but their role went no further. Lacking great
wealth and megalomaniacal pretensions, they could not be the villains. Fleming was not interested in them. Furthermore, in Britain
foreign villains used foreign servants and employees: Drax used Germans, Goldfinger Koreans. In the empire, Dr. No employed Chinese-
Negroes who were British subjects but distanced, by their ethnicity,
from the ordinary population. This racism reflected not only a pronounced theme of interwar adventure writing, such as the novels of
Buchan, but also wider literary culture. It was incessant and occurred in the depiction of minor as well as major characters. Thus,

for example, in Patricia Wentworth's detective novel *The Clock Strikes Twelve* (1945), the very unheroic jewel thief Albert Pearson is in league with "Izzy," clearly a Jew.

There was also, however, in *Moonraker* a sense of capitalism and social change as solvents of traditional values. Drax is not only a traitor; he is also "new money," adding a class element to the story. Throughout the book, the conduct of this wealthy, public new "hero" is contrasted with the true hero, Bond. Drax is repeatedly revealed as callous, cruel and arrogant. He deliberately drives another car off the road, and, when he has Bond and Carla Brand at his mercy, threatens them with "The Persuader," a blowtorch. Aside from being a sadist, Drax is also a perversion of gentility: "To me a gentleman is just someone I can take advantage of." Bond, in contrast, is presented as a gentleman. Drax is also without any girlfriend, an indication that he is abnormal in the Bond world.

Drax was a Nazi, and World War II frequently echoed in the book. It bonded the good. The liftman at the Secret Service's headquarters had only a stump of his left arm thanks to the war. The brandy at Blades was a gift from the Rothschild estates at Cognac, a yearly barrel hidden there during the war. Bond is told "The Germans don't seem to be able to forget the bloody word 'Heil,' " and he recalled the traitorous Cicero, the valet of the British ambassador in Ankara, who had betrayed secrets to the Germans. Drax compares his Mercedes with Bond's Bentley, which, he claims, was once a good car, but now was "only built for going to the theatre." In the headlamps of the Mercedes, the beauty of the Kentish wood flowers makes Krebs, one of Drax's Nazis, happy: "Der Tag [the day] had been a long time coming, but now it was here . . . At last the cheering crowds, the medals, the women, the flowers," references to the scenes of Nazi expansion that had been broadcast in German propaganda films, for example the annexation of Austria in 1938. Drax refers to the Moonraker rocket as a "great arrow of vengeance" for his conquered fatherland. Krebs was the name of Hitler's last chief of staff in the Berlin bunker.

When Drax is defeated, M reflects that Nazism is not dead and this meant that the British government will proceed more cautiously on the issue of German rearmament. This was a slur by Fleming on the Germany of the mid-1950s, and Drax's plan had scarcely revealed widespread Nazism. However, the statement reflected Fleming's concerns about German rearmament, concerns born from his distrust of the Germans and his belief in national stereotypes. Fleming also represented a widely held fear of Germany as the "eternal enemy." Many newspaper articles and politicians of the period referred to the apparent dangers posed by German rearmament.

In the early 1950s, the British were less enthusiastic than the Americans about rearming the West Germans and integrating them into NATO, although they overcame their doubts in order to please their allies. Hostility to German rearmament was particularly a Labour party theme. In August 1950, Ernest Bevin, the Labour foreign secretary, asked, "How could [I] go down to [my] constituency— Woolwich—which had been bombed by Germans in the war, and tell [my] constituents that the Germans would help them in a war against Russia?" Germany finally joined NATO in January 1955.

Drax may also have represented broader contemporary concerns about the survival of Nazism, concerns that periodically appeared in the press. The idea of another "der Tag" reflected deep-seated fears of a possible Nazi revival. In the short story "For Your Eyes Only" (1960), Bond is sent to kill an ex-Gestapo agent and M warns him that certain "banana republics" harbored many Nazis who had slipped out of Germany at war's end. Furthermore, the recurrence of German militarism in the 1930s so soon after World War I encouraged an anxiety that the same situation might repeat after World War II. For Fleming, the past was not dead.

The exposure of Drax and the revelation of his true schemes was a bigger challenge for Bond than Le Chiffre or Mr. Big had been. They were both clearly known as villains, their nature outlined in the intelligence briefings provided at the start of both books. There was no real surprise or exposure in either book. The twists and turns of the plots had included many surprises, such as the arrival of the SMERSH agent in *Casino Royale* and the descending nightspot table in *Live and Let Die* that permits Mr. Big to capture Bond and Leiter, but there was no real mystery to unravel. Neither villain would have been invited to play cards at Blades.

In that sense, *Moonraker* contained some of the atmosphere of John Buchan's world, more particularly of *The Three Hostages*, with its influential villain Sir Richard Medina, an MP. Drax, however, cannot sustain his role. He cheats at Blades, thus proving he is no gentleman and inviting suspicion. Bond then beats Drax in a high-stakes bridge game by cheating himself: the cheat deserves to be cheated. Drax tells him to "spend the money quickly," closing a piece of sustained writing in which Fleming offers clubland as a vital world populated by glittering individuals, not anachronisms. Bond is sent to check security at Drax's factory in Kent, where the British security officer has been killed, eventually uncovering a nest of Nazi scientists intent on using their rocket against London.

The politics of the book are provided by the need for Britain to have an independent say, and, as the prime minister [in real life Churchill] puts it, "a long era of peace," and by the role of the Soviet

Union in supporting Drax. Throughout, the USSR is assumed to be a threat, but, initially, when there is trust in Drax, this threat is assumed to be against him and his project. M tells Bond that Russian sabotage of the Moonraker would be a "colossal victory." The Soviets could easily threaten the German workers with possible harm to relatives still being held in Russia, a reference to an established Soviet technique.

The Soviets provide the atom bomb for Drax's rocket, as well as the rocket expert, Walter, and the submarine that takes Drax and his men away into the North Sea. Drax gives the Soviets the "cherished instruments" designed by the British for rocket navigation. However, if the USSR is clearly hostile, Fleming's view of the United States is not free from ambivalence. Bond observes American jet planes criss-crossing the sky above Manston aerodrome, a testimony to their role in the protection of Britain. Drax despises the British, "Useless, idle, decadent fools, hiding behind your bloody white cliffs while other people fight your battles. Too weak to defend your colonies, toadying to America with your hats in your hands." M, however, is also concerned about American Cold War zeal, a widespread fear in British policymaking circles in the 1950s, although this theme is not stressed in the book. He supports the cover-up after Drax is thwarted: "What's the alternative? Trouble with Germany? War with Russia? Lots of people on both sides of the Atlantic would be only too glad of an excuse." Freedom of information is definitely not on the agenda. M promises the " 'biggest cover-up job in history.' "

The horror of the atomic bomb is captured in a way that was not to be attempted in the films, which were generally lighter, and less reflective, in tone. Gala envisages the rocket landing on London:

Dropping fast as light out of a clear sky. . . . The nursemaids in the park. The birds in the trees. The great bloom of flame a mile wide. And then the mushroom cloud. And nothing left. Nothing.

At the close, Bond reflects on

how nearly there might be nothing now but the distant clang of the ambulance bells . . . the stench of burning, the screams of people still trapped in the buildings. The softly beating heart of London silenced for a generation. And a whole generation of her people dead in the streets amongst the ruins of a civilization that might not rise again for centuries.

Gala and Bond are given an understanding of the significance of a nuclear attack, and the threat is presented in inclusive terms. In contrast, in Raymond Benson's Bond continuation novel *Tomorrow Never Dies* (1997), the villainous Elliot Carver presents Bond with the prospect of an H-bomb attack in which Bond is associated with an exclusive concept of nationhood: "Will you sneer when the fireball vaporises Buckingham Palace? Will you sneer when the shock wave mows down your private clubs, your Saville Row, your high-and-mighty banks? Will you sneer when the firestorm roasts those pink-cheeked boys at Harrow?"

Moonraker was the most British of the Bond novels, in terms of both setting and context. The setting in Kent not only reflected Fleming's knowledge of the county, but also the totemic significance of the White Cliffs of Dover. Furthermore, there was a sense that, in Kent, Britain was most exposed. The landscape contains other defense installations referred to in the story, such as Swingate radar station and Manston aerodrome, and visible remains of past defenses, most prominently Dover Castle, now, thanks to technology, only a "wonderful cardboard castle." Bond and Drax were therefore combatants in a timeless struggle. The foe was foreign, but he was operating in a British disguise and in Britain, "in May, in England, in peacetime." This dramatized the message of threat, underlined the role and importance of Bond as a savior, and led M to reflect that Drax's scheme would make the job of the Special Branch and the Secret Service easier by showing politicians that in a nuclear world the deadliest sabotage threat now fell to "the little man with the heavy suitcase," a theme that was to recur at the close of the millennium. In fact, M's clearly authoritarian view of the need for the politicians to accept the consequences of the call for vigilance was not taken up.

A British setting for Bond's adventure placed a burden on readers' credulity. It was possible to imagine and locate many convoluted or sinister plots outside Britain. This was especially so in places exotic to the bulk of Fleming's readers, for example Tangier, where Drax made his money, and anything was possible. It was harder to do so in Britain. Realism would have to play a greater role. This was a problem for Fleming. He took great pains with his research and prided himself on the accuracy of his details, but the plots were inherently implausible, a dilemma that proved even greater in the films. This gap was harder to overcome in a domestic setting, providing a rationale (again, most obviously in the films) for overseas and particularly remote or exotic settings.

DIAMONDS ARE FOREVER: "SUPERSONIC JOHN BUCHAN"

Published in 1956, Fleming's fourth Bond novel, *Diamonds Are Forever*, returned to a foreign setting and offered a lesser threat to Britain than that in *Moonraker*. The subject was "the richest smuggling operation in the world," a pipeline that began in "the great diamond mines around Sefadu" in Sierra Leone, "part of the powerful mining empire of Africa International, which in turn is a rich capital asset of the British Commonwealth." Diamonds were stolen from the diggings by the miners, taken away in their mouths, and collected by the mine dentist. The dentist then crossed the nearby border into French Guinea on his motorbike, and the diamonds were collected by helicopter. With the usual echo of World War II, the pilot was a German Luftwaffe veteran who despised other people.

Smuggled out of Africa, these diamonds hit the sales carried out in London by the Diamond Corporation, "the biggest dollar-earner we've got" according to M. Government concern over at least £2 million worth of diamonds being smuggled out leads to orders to intervene. The Treasury and the Board of Trade argue that "the thing's too big to be handled by a lot of separate mining companies, however efficient they are." This was the first example in the novels of an attempt to disrupt markets and economic links. In *Goldfinger* the villain focuses on gold, while in *On Her Majesty's Secret Service* and in *The Man With the Golden Gun* there are threats to food products. This aspect of the plots reflects the greater interconnectedness of the world economy and the importance to Britain of trade and the honest operation of markets. Their disruption provides opportunities for villains both to make money and to threaten British interests.

Rather than simply hit the carriers, the government decides to follow the pipeline to the biggest diamond market, America. Britain is only a stage, an entrepot whose profits are being purloined. The pipeline leads through the House of Diamonds, big New York jewelers with an office in Hatton Garden, London, who are no longer buying through the Diamond Corporation. They are Bond's target.

This is small fry compared to Drax, but the chief of staff builds up the challenge by explaining to Bond that the Mafia is probably behind the diamond smuggling. His explanation provides an opportunity to sketch out the threats in M's world:

There aren't many things that worry M . . . SMERSH of course. The German cypher-breakers. The Chinese opium ring—or at any rate the power they have all over the world. The authority of the Mafia. And, and he's got a damned healthy respect for them, the American gangs. The big ones. That's all. Those are the only people that get him worried.

Bond is unimpressed, resorting to some crude ethnic abuse that is updated "Sapper": "There's nothing so extraordinary about American gangsters," protested Bond. "They're not Americans. Mostly a lot of Italian bums with monogrammed shirts who spend the day eating spaghetti and meat-balls and squirting scent over themselves," the last a clear sign of contemporary British views on masculinity while the comment on food reflected the then limited use of foreign cuisine. The chief of staff, however, emphasizes the threat. He accepts Bond's ethnic abuse, but not his overall assessment: "those are only the ones you see. There are better ones behind them . . . gambling's the biggest single industry in America."

Indeed, the House of Diamonds turned out to be owned by the Spangled Mob, one of the leading gangs. On a visit to Los Angeles in 1954, Fleming had been extensively briefed on the Mafia by Captain James Hamilton, the head of the Los Angeles Police Department's intelligence service. As in *Live and Let Die*, his plot reflected American anxieties and Fleming's interest in American organized crime. In *Live and Let Die*, Mr. Big's curriculum vitae includes working "for a hi-jacking team in the Legs Diamond gang." The plot of *Diamonds Are Forever* both appealed to British interest in the United States and had something to offer American readers.

The journey across the Atlantic was described more fully than in *Live and Let Die*, providing Fleming with an opportunity to show his skill as a travel writer. Like his wife's friend Evelyn Waugh, the author of three travel books, and his own older brother Robert, Fleming could have been a successful travel writer.

The flight itself would have been exotic to most of his readers. This is difficult to appreciate in the modern age of mass travel. Now the details of a flight across the Atlantic are of scant interest. Instead of being an adventure, it has become a chore. Indeed, in John Gardner's Bond novel *Nobody Lives Forever* (1986), Bond flies Pan Am first class from Zurich to Miami: "The food was reasonable, the flight boring, the movie violent and cut to ribbons." That is it. In 1956, the situation was very different. Weekly flights to New York had begun only in 1946.

In the 1950s, the mystique of America as a land of wealth and excitement held great sway in a Britain still in the grips of austerity. Furthermore, as Britain became more prosperous, it increasingly turned to America as a model for a consumer society. This was unwelcome to many commentators. There had long been concern about

American populism, but American links, a positive image of the United States, and a habit of looking at Britain through an American prism had all been greatly accentuated by World War II, when Britain had been more obviously saved and supported by the Americans than in World War I. This remained the case after the war. Truman's Democratic administration (1945–53) was far from identical to Attlee's Labour governments (1945–51), with their nationalizations and the creation of a welfare state, but it was possible, and necessary, to stress common language and values, certainly in comparison, and in confrontation, with the Soviet Union. Furthermore, American cultural "hegemony" was stronger in Britain than in the other major West European countries. Through popular music and the increasingly ubiquitous television, American influence grew rapidly in the 1950s. It became the currency of the affluence that replaced the austerity of the 1940s. There was criticism on the left, and, in addition, traditionally minded Conservatives were challenged by many aspects of American culture and society, not least the fluidity and democratization of the society. Fleming's notion of the appropriate equivalence of territory and ethnicity, of a proper spacing, of what, to him, were clearly distinguished racial groups, was questioned by the success of the deracinated United States.

Once in America, Bond goes to Saratoga Springs at the instruction of the Spangled Mob, for whom he is supposedly working, and then to Las Vegas, near where he kills one of the Spangs:

one of the brutal, theatrical, overblown dead-end adults who made up the Spangled Mob. He had been a stage-gangster, surrounded with stage properties, but that didn't alter the fact that he had intended to kill Bond.

Gangsters were personally degenerate and yet menacing. Felix Leiter, now working for the Pinkerton Detective Agency, told Bond: "Now the hoodlums don't run liquor. They run governments. State governments like Nevada. . . . Maybe you can strike a blow for Freedom, Home and Beauty with that old rusty equalizer of yours." The threat from organized crime was to be taken up in Fleming's discussion of America in *Thrilling Cities*. In some respects, he was as interested in crime as in espionage, and Bond was to be used as much against the former as in more conventional spying.

Having killed the two assassins sent to get him when he recrossed the Atlantic on the *Queen Elizabeth*, a symbol of British continuity and excellence, Bond then pursues "ABC," Rufus B. Saye, in reality Jack Spang, head of the Spangled Mob, to West Africa. In a display of imperial military range, he is able to fly by RAF Canberra from

Boscombe Down to Sierra Leone, still a British colony, and then to obtain the support of a truck from the Freetown Garrison Force with a Bofors gun and a crew of two. Using the Bofors, Bond shoots down Spang's helicopter when he tries to evade arrest.

The shooting down of Spang was the last of the story's set pieces. The novel lacked the intensity of several of the others, in part because the villain was not a dominant figure. Indeed, the division of the villainy between the two Spangs, one of whom, Jack, was presented as little more than an effective hood, weakened the novel. There was no megalomaniac fervor, no weird self-obsession, at the dark center of the plot.

In terms of place, *Diamonds Are Forever* also lacked a focus. The individual sites of the action were either well realized—Saratoga Springs and Las Vegas—or presented without any particular interest—London and New York. There was no stage equivalent to Royale in *Casino Royale*, Istanbul in *From Russia, With Love*, and Jamaica in *Dr. No*. Lastly, the book lacked a true sense of malevolence or even threat, partly because neither Britain's place in the world nor ideas of Britishness were challenged. The Mafia did not equal SMERSH in terms of secrecy, menace or sophistication. This failing was to be remedied in Bond's next adventure.

FROM RUSSIA, WITH LOVE: HOT WAR IN THE BALKANS

[Bond] reflected briefly on the way the Russians ran their centres—with all the money and equipment in the world, while the Secret Service put against them a handful of adventurous, underpaid men. . . . Yet Kerim had the run of Turkey. Perhaps, after all, the right man was better than the right machine.

Included in President John F. Kennedy's list of his ten favorite books that he publicized in March 1961, *From Russia, With Love* was probably the most fluent of the Bond novels. Described in the *Times Literary Supplement* as "most brilliant," the book was a great commercial success and helped to launch Fleming as a best-selling novelist. It also received extensive attention in the press. In 1958 the *Daily Express* launched Bond in a daily cartoon strip that ran until 1963. Jacqueline Kennedy was to give a copy of the book to Allen Dulles, the head of the CIA.

Published in 1957, the book returned Bond to the intelligence beats of Europe and to the struggle with SMERSH. In place of a psychopath or a master criminal, Bond's opponent was Soviet power. In *From Russia, With Love*, unlike *Casino Royale*, the initiative was taken by

the Soviets. SMERSH attempted to weaken the British and take revenge on Bond by tricking him into a mission to Istanbul, the unlikely bait being an apparent Soviet defector, Tatiana Romanova, and
the Spektor cipher decoder.

The novel included a lengthy SMERSH discussion in which the
British Secret Service is praised and contrasted with the allegedly
less proficient Americans, in terms that reflected British unease
about the relationship between the two. General Vozdvishensky offers an account of British ability, professionalism and honesty. Despite paltry pay, both MI5 and MI6 have achieved success—due in
part to devoted agents who serve because of their love of adventure.

The novel reflected current public interest in East-West espionage,
interest that had arisen from the outbreak of the Cold War, with a
series of spy scares, including the defection of Guy Burgess and Donald Maclean in May 1951. Public awareness of the espionage aspect
of the Cold War had risen in 1956. In April, the Soviets broke into
and publicly exposed the American tunnel built to intercept their
cable traffic in Berlin. The same month, Commander Crabb's unsuccessful and fatal attempt, on behalf of MI6, to study the hull of a
Soviet cruiser then in Portsmouth led to Soviet complaints, press
discussion and the replacement of the head of MI6. A realistic review
of British intelligence in 1956 would have been less complimentary
than Vozdvishensky's fictional account, which owed more to the assumptions expressed in interwar British adventure fiction.

More generally, the Cold War had heated up in 1956. Soviet control of Eastern Europe was brutally demonstrated when a popular
attempt to bring Hungary independence was brutally repressed in
November 1956. Security forces had suppressed a workers' uprising
in Poznan in Poland in June. *From Russia, With Love* was carried
forward in a moment of rising tension in the Cold War and at the
same time provided a sense of humor and of relief from the real
world. There was both a feeling of moment and one of unreality.

The plot gave Fleming an opportunity to use his knowledge of the
hotter aspects of the Cold War, specifically of the nature of Soviet
intelligence. SMERSH had in fact been replaced in 1946, but Fleming
continued to use it, as it fulfilled the need for a duel between Bond
and his opponents, a need later to be served by SPECTRE.
SMERSH's head of operations in the story, Colonel Rosa Klebb, was
Fleming's first female villain, a fatal woman rather than a femme
fatale. She was based on a Colonel Rybkin whom Fleming had written about in the *Sunday Times* and was portrayed as an ugly and
sadistic lesbian.

Fleming took a strongly anti-Soviet position in the novel and pressed for a firm British stance. There was no sense that the Soviets had moved toward "peaceful coexistence," as was indeed the objective first of Georgi Malenkov, chairman of the Council of Ministers in 1953–55, and then of Nikita Khrushchev, Stalin's successor as general secretary of the Communist Party from 1953 to 1964. Kerim Bey, the likable head of the British station in Istanbul, justifies killing Soviet agents:

They are hard people. With them, what you don't get from strength, you won't get from mercy. They are all the same, the Russians. I wish your government would realize it and be strong with them.

Bond agrees. The Russians "simply don't understand the carrot. Only the stick has any effect."

The use of Istanbul as a locale for much of the action both presented the reality of a location of East-West intelligence operations and confrontation and offered the opportunity of describing a place that could be at once gritty and exotic. It was in Istanbul in 1945 that Konstantin Volkov had proposed to defect from the NKVD to the British, only for the case to end up with Kim Philby, then head of Section IX, the Soviet Department of MI6. Philby informed his Soviet controller and a stretcher-bound, unconscious Volkov was taken back to the USSR on the excuse of requiring medical treatment.

Turkey was crucial to the Baghdad Pact, a British-backed attempt to create a northern layer of states in the Middle East opposed to southward expansion by the USSR. It was one of the two original members of the pact, which was signed on 24 February 1955. The other was Iraq, a state then very close to Britain. The Pact was joined later that year by Britain, Pakistan and Iran. The pact exaggerated British power but was part of an assertive British policy in the Middle East directed against the Soviets and against Arab nationalism, which included plans for intelligence operations designed to overthrow the governments of Egypt, Syria and Saudi Arabia, plans that culminated with the unsuccessful Suez invasion of November 1956.

Exotic Istanbul was more the world of Eric Ambler than of Le Carré's Bonn or Deighton's Berlin. Indeed, Fleming read *The Mask of Dimitrios*, an Ambler thriller, as a guide to the city when he visited it for the Interpol Conference in 1955. He also praised Ambler in *Thrilling Cities*. Istanbul both provided a new setting for Fleming's sub-Chandleresque writing and allowed Bond unusual sights, such as the female wrestling match, without any apparent departure from reality.

The same was true of the return from Istanbul on the Simplon-Orient Express, where Bond grapples for his life with the SMERSH killer "Red" Grant. In fact Fleming had found the train very drab when he had traveled on it in 1955: it lacked a restaurant car. Nevertheless, it was real and thus could be made more exciting than an invented train, such as Spang's Cannonball in *Diamonds Are Forever*. As was the Silver Phantom in *Live and Let Die*, the Simplon-Orient Express is a reminder of the role of long-distance train travel in the 1950s. This dates the novels, and also films from the period, such as Hitchcock's *North by Northwest* (1959). Nevertheless, trains also helped provide an opportunity for set pieces, as with the shootout on the train in *The Man With the Golden Gun*. Of these four trains, only that in *From Russia, With Love* survived in the film version, although the train transporting the circus played a role in the film *Octopussy* and the villain's armored train in *GoldenEye*.

From Russia, With Love was published to great critical acclaim and was a major commercial success. It ended with Bond seriously wounded by Rosa Klebb and nearly killed, as was to be revealed in *Dr. No*, by fugu poison from the sex organs of the Japanese globefish, a method that might have been expected from Dr. Fu-Manchu but that also reflected the interest of Soviet spy agencies in poisons. While the ending was not quite Sherlock Holmes and his apparently fatal last struggle with evil at the Reichenbach Falls, Fleming had provided himself with an opportunity to remove his hero. He was not, however, to take it. There was public agitation when 007 was reported dead. Bond had become irreplaceable.

DR. NO: BIRDS IN THE CARIBBEAN

Bond returned to the Caribbean in *Dr. No*, written in 1957 and published in 1958. This was the work that inspired the most famous attack on Fleming's work, Paul Johnson's essay "Sex, Snobbery and Sadism," published on 5 April 1958 in the *New Statesman*, then a respectable British literary journal with wide appeal. Condemning *Dr. No* as "badly written to the point of incoherence" and "the nastiest book" he had read, Johnson anatomized it, describing its essential contents, "all unhealthy, all thoroughly English—the sadism of a schoolboy bully, the mechanical two-dimensional sex-longings of a frustrated adolescent, and the crude, snob-cravings of a suburban adult." "Thoroughly English" was then a term that Johnson would have employed as an insult. More generally, Bernard Bergonzi, writing in the March 1958 issue of the *Twentieth Century*, referred to "a strongly marked streak of voyeurism and sado-masochism" and "the total lack of any ethical frame of reference."

These, and other attacks, reflected disquiet about the popularity of Bond, his violence, sexual drive and lifestyle, but Johnson offered a less than complete description of what was an accomplished adventure story. There were weak moments in the book, not least the bizarre, or, as Bond put it, "grotesque," hotel-type reception in Dr. No's mountain fastness. Dr. No's testing of Bond was improbable, the "Bond girl" Honeychilde Rider's survival of her ordeal surprising, and some of the dialogue lacked subtlety:

"Oh Honey, Honey. Are you all right?" Desperately, unbelieving, he strained her to him.

"Yes, James! Oh yes!" He felt her hands at his back and his hair. "Oh James, my darling!" she fell against him sobbing.

"It's all right, Honey." Bond smoothed her hair. "And Doctor No's dead. But now we've got to run for it. We've got to get out of here. Come on! How can we get out of the tunnel?"

Weak, but the novel had started in a more promising fashion, and much of it was well paced and exciting.

Dr. No was a novel of discovery, the uncovering of a major conspiracy behind the guano-digging activities of Dr. No on the Caribbean island of Crab Key, a dependency of Jamaica. Bond is led to this by another discovery. Sent to Jamaica to investigate the disappearance of Commander John Strangways, the representative of the Secret Service already introduced in *Live and Let Die*, and his secretary, Mary Trueblood, a significant choice of name, he rapidly ascertains that this is unlikely to be a lovers' flight and instead is linked to Dr. No.

The link is made through the roseate spoonbill, a rare wading bird resembling a stork. The Audubon Society, an American body for the protection of rare birds, had established a sanctuary for the spoonbills on Crab Key, but the island had then in 1943 been purchased by Dr. Julius No as a source for guano.

The British Secret Service became involved as a result of the society's pressure on the British ambassador. The sanctuary's keepers had been mysteriously killed, and, when two of the Audubon Society's officials went to investigate, they died when their Beechcraft apparently crashed on landing. Strangways was ordered to investigate and had then disappeared. Indeed, Strangways and Trueblood were shot and their bodies dumped in the reservoir.

His investigations lead Bond to Crab Key where he initially evades attempts to kill him but is finally captured by Dr. No's "dragon," a diesel-engined, tracked marsh buggy equipped with a flamethrower. Taken to Dr. No's mountain fastness, Bond is provided with all the answers when the Doctor, described in *Time* as "one of the least forgettable characters in modern fiction," tells him his secrets. He traces his own evil to his birth, the unwanted son of an illicit relationship between the son of a German mercenary and "a Chinese girl of good family." In some respects, Dr. No echoes the sinister orientalism of Dr. Fu-Manchu, the creation of the British crime reporter Arthur Sarsfield, who wrote under the pseudonym of Sax Rohmer. Fu-Manchu, "the greatest genius which the powers of evil have put on earth for centuries," and the foe of British civilization in *The Mystery of Dr. Fu-Manchu* (1913) and *The Devil Doctor* (1916), combined great cruelty with advanced scientific research. In his account of Macao in *Thrilling Cities* (1963), Fleming referred to his "Doctor Fu-Manchu days . . . the adventure books of one's youth."

Unloved, Dr. No joined the Shanghai Tongs who "represented revolt against the father figure who had betrayed me." Joining the Hip Sings, one of the two great Tongs in New York, Dr. No stole their treasure, only to be captured, tortured and shot. However, Dr. No is "the one man in a million who has his heart on the right side of his body," as, indeed, is possible, an instance of Fleming's use of generally unknown information about unusual circumstances. Dr. No survived and set out to achieve power, "the power to decide, to judge, the power of absolute independence from outside authority."

Isolating himself from the world on Crab Key, Dr. No built a base hidden within the mountain on which the guano birds laid his wealth. The base is "to be developed into the most valuable technical intelligence centre in the world." Dr. No reveals that he has been overriding the instructions sent to test rockets launched 300 miles away from the American missile-testing base on Turks Island, a British colony the use of which is an important aspect of Anglo-American cooperation. Dr. No's intervention leads the rockets to go off course or destroy themselves. Churchill indeed had feared Soviet sabotage of the testing of the first British atom bomb in 1952.

Rockets were a major issue in 1957 when Fleming was writing the book. The Soviet Union launched the first satellite, Sputnik I, into orbit that year, revealing a capability for intercontinental rockets that brought the whole of the world within strike. Investment in expensive rocket technology appeared an option thanks to the strategic threat posed by nuclear-tipped, long-range ballistic missiles. American rocket programs, however, encountered serious initial setbacks, leading to widespread concern that the Soviet Union was winning the space race, a race that had obvious military consequences for the security of the United States and Britain. The United States literally came within range.

Dr. No is in partnership with the Soviet Union, which both trains his men and provides advice on how best to penetrate the American controls. Although also prepared to negotiate with China, to see if it is willing to pay more, Dr. No is preparing for a last major fling, "a priceless victory in the armaments race," for which he intends the Soviet Union to pay. The American rockets are to be brought down near Crab Key, the prototypes sold to the Soviets, and, if the Americans discovered the hostile radio signals and started looking for Dr. No, their rockets would go wildly off course to hit Havana (not then in Communist hands), Jamaica or Florida. The resulting public outcry would force closure of the Turks Island base.

This was not the limit of Dr. No's ambition. He also plotted an ingenious end for both Bond and Honey, designed to test the length of their endurance. With his knack of bringing in the Nazis as a measure of horror, Dr. No remarked "The German experiments on live humans during the war were of great benefit to science." Bond survives, defeats the giant squid that is the last test, a creature straight out of the world of interwar adventure stories, and kills Dr. No by burying him beneath a mound of guano from a conveyer belt.

As with *Diamonds Are Forever*, the crisis is brought to an end with a display of imperial power, a display organized in King's House in Kingston, Jamaica, after a disagreement between the petulant acting governor, who disliked Bond, the Secret Service and action, and his advisors. The brigadier in command of the Caribbean Defence Force, "a modern young soldier of thirty-five . . . unimpressed by relics from the Edwardian era of Colonial Governors, whom he collectively referred to as 'feather-hatted fuddy-duddies,' " pressed for immediate action without waiting for approval from London. He would provide a platoon that would be embarked on HMS *Narvik*, a warship whose name recalled a World War II British naval success at a stage in the conflict before America joined the war. The youthfulness and vigor of the brigadier suggests that the empire is not moribund. Thus, the American missile tests had been saved without any need to rely on American force. This was a book without Felix Leiter, the CIA or the American military, ironically so as the story had originated as a screenplay by Fleming for a projected American television series designed to star an American, Commander James Gunn. The series, however, was not to Hollywood's liking.

If, in the eventual novel, the British in the person of Bond had sorted out the mess themselves, Fleming made it clear, nonetheless, that British culture made a solution more difficult. In part, this was a matter of a failure of vigilance. Besides the fact that the complacent acting governor was inclined to dismiss all problems, confident that Strangways had done "a bunk with the girl," and was ready to dispense with any intelligence presence in Jamaica, the likable colonial secretary, Pleydell-Smith, had no office security. His secretary, Miss Taro, was an agent of Dr. No, no Miss Trueblood, and Pleydell-Smith showed little concern about missing files. More generally, there was the problem of a state fighting evil with its hands tied. Dr. No tells the captured Bond that if the government sends forces to search for Bond he will reply by denying that he had met him, by asking them for their evidence and by drawing attention to the strictness of English law. Indeed, Dr. No's very position on the island reflected the immunity of private property from effective surveillance.

Pleydell-Smith captures a shift in imperial control. Comparing contemporary Jamaica with the situation when Bond had visited it in *Live and Let Die*, only four years earlier as far as the book sequence was concerned, "four, five years ago," according to Pleydell-Smith, he draws attention to interest in self-determination. Pleydell-Smith's "wish you'd start another bonfire like that here. Stir the place up a bit" is, in part, a call for distraction from the pressures and frustrations of a weakening imperial grasp.

Dr. No tells Bond that the latter has "been reading too many novels of suspense. Your little speech reeked of grease-paint and cardboard." At times, this description may seem particularly apt for the novel. The conversations between Bond and Dr. No seem especially contrived. However, Bond's attempt to escape his hunters on Crab Key is vivid, and, more generally, Fleming's personal experience of the Caribbean enabled him to paint convincing portrayals both of Jamaica and of Crab Key, which was based on Inagua, the most southerly island in the Bahamas. Fleming had visited it in 1956, noting the mangrove swamps and extensive birdlife, which included the green cormorant bird, a source of guano. The novel indicated the increasing hold of the tropics on Fleming, a hold that was of great importance in the development of his writing. This was a matter of his personal life, not a response to the degree to which the Cold War was increasingly being played out in the Third World. Indeed, in 1958 Jamaica was still part of the empire, and Fleming's own regular residence there for part of the year after World War II was made possible as a result. The West Indies were close to Fleming, but attractively exotic to his readers.

GOLDFINGER: FORT KNOX UNDER THREAT

> [R]egard history as a train speeding along through time . . . I am like
> the hawk that follows the train . . . ready to pounce on anything that
> may be flushed by the train's passage.
>
> —Auric Goldfinger to Bond

SMERSH reappeared in the next novel, *Goldfinger*, which was published in 1959. The target was again American. The villain, Auric Goldfinger, a fabulously wealthy member of SMERSH, originally from Latvia, who is fascinated by gold, planned to seize the gold in the American reserves at Fort Knox, Kentucky.

The novel's settings were more varied than in *Dr. No.* Bond first meets Goldfinger in Miami, where, on behalf of the wealthy Junius Du Pont, he outplays the cheating Goldfinger at cards. Returning to Britain, Bond finds that M is interested in Goldfinger as potentially responsible for bullion leaks. Bond then plays golf against him at Royal St. Mark's, Sandwich, a club based on Fleming's Royal St. George's, and a sequence that reveals Fleming's knowledge and love of the game. He would have made a good golfing correspondent. Similarly, the recurrence of cards and gambling in the books reflected not only Fleming's interest in and knowledge of them, but also his ability to write about them in an exciting fashion. Thanks to this, cards and gambling did not lose their drama on the printed page.

Bond followed the villain to Coppet in Switzerland, where Goldfinger had a factory in which he removed the gold he had smuggled out of Britain in the bodywork of his Rolls-Royce. Bond is seized by Goldfinger, and, somewhat improbably, used by him as an aide for the plan to seize Fort Knox, a device that both brings Bond into proximity with the villain and enables him to act under cover. Bond wrecks the scheme by giving prior notice of the plan to poison the water supply, and, eventually, strangles Goldfinger.

Due to Goldfinger's membership in SMERSH, the novel was securely located in the Cold War. He planned to transport the gold to Norfolk, Virginia, and load it on a visiting Soviet cruiser. This time it was Russia against America with Goldfinger taking the lead. This was also war, but, before the last stage of the book, the plot proceeded via a series of scenes from the lives of the super-rich. Near the beginning of the story staying, thanks to Du Pont, at a suite in the luxurious Floridiana, Bond calculates that if he was paying the bill, a stay of only three weeks would take his entire year's salary.

Yet the golf match is different from the Miami prelude because, by then, Bond is on duty, not taking a diversion while delayed by a plane connection. Unlike the Miami restaurant, to which Bond is taken by Du Pont, and the Floridiana, the golf club is a scene from the life of the wealthy where Bond's ability to conduct himself properly and successfully is important to the defense of his country. The theme of responsibility is introduced earlier by a passage in which Bond is on night duty at the headquarters of the Secret Service. A military note is struck. The building at night "gave you the impression of being in a battleship in harbour."

Bond then moves to another building, the Bank of England. Again, this is a repository of secret knowledge and power, but it is also under challenge. Just as Bond, on night duty, had arranged the dispatch of limpet mines to destroy Communist spy junks intercepting British freighters off Macao—M's effort to let the enemy know that the service in Hong Kong was still in business—so Colonel Smithers at the bank had to try to protect the currency and prevent the loss of bullion. Smithers's military background is significant. The threat was driven home to the reading public by reference to the new £5 notes, necessary to prevent Soviet forgeries, and to the interest rate. Bond is told to bring Goldfinger to justice and to return the gold to England, which suffered from a currency crisis and a high bank rate. In short, Goldfinger was partly to blame for high interest rates.

This was economic war. The idea of forging British banknotes had indeed been considered by the Comintern and the British Communist party in the early 1920s, only to be rejected. The interest rate had been under pressure in 1957, and this was politically sensitive for 1957 was also the year of the Bank Rate Tribunal dispute. The Macmillan government raised the bank rate by 2 percent in September. It was alleged by the opposition, and, in particular, by Harold Wilson, that the decision had been leaked in advance by government sources. A tribunal of inquiry was set up and ultimately exonerated the government.

By linking the financial crisis to SMERSH, Fleming domesticated the international conflict. He did it in characteristic fashion, with an emphasis on the secret enemy within, with the characterization of this enemy in terms of hubris, ambiguous sexuality, and non-English racial background, and also with a stress on the role of chance and personal resolve. Who would guess that Goldfinger, a respected member of Society—an insider:

was one of the greatest conspirators of all time. . . . How often in his profession had it been the same—the tiny acorn of coincidence that soared into the mighty oak whose branches darkened the sky. And now, once again, he was setting out to bring the dreadful growth down. With what? A bag of gold clubs.

The last captured the sporting metaphor in the stories, a metaphor also much employed by Buchan and other interwar writers. Bond was a good sportsman (in both quality and morality), who hunted down cheats, punishing them if necessary by cheating himself, as in the card game with Drax and the golf match with Goldfinger. The role of the match, as of the jousting with cards in *Casino Royale*, *Moonraker* and *Goldfinger*, captured the element of personal competition—repeated in both novels and films in the car chases—but it also helped to date, or at least locate, the stories. The stories were recognizably 1950s in style and setting, but the nature of the plots, as personal struggles between Bond and wealthy evil individuals acting on their own behalf—albeit also representing larger, sinister corporations and conspiracies—ensured that such a setting, or at least a location amidst the leisured rich, was necessary. Bond was interested in big crooks, and Fleming gave narrative structure and lent a moral dimension to his plots by personalizing the world of adventure and espionage. Indeed, far from there being any equality between the two sides, this world was slanted, because those opposed to Britain were crooks, spiritually bankrupt and morally without bearing. The conflation of crime and espionage focused on sinister individuals, and their personal failings condemned their cause.

Goldfinger was personally disordered, with a misproportioned body, not English, a "Balt" with possible Jewish blood, and psychologically warped—in part, Bond feels, due to his short man's inferiority complex. "Napoleon had been short, and Hitler. It was the short men that caused all the trouble in the world." Such characterization reflected both racialism and crude psychology. Like much imaginative literature earlier in the century, Fleming had been influenced by the popularity of eugenic assumptions. Ironically, in *Live and Let Die*, although the villain's first name was Buonaparte, Mr. Big had "huge height and bulk."

Goldfinger is also a killjoy, although his views are now the orthodoxy in the West. He does not smoke or drink, characterizing smoking as "entirely against nature. Can you imagine a cow or any animal taking a mouthful of smouldering straw then breathing in the smoke and blowing it out through its nostrils? Pah!"

Such views are condemned because they come from Goldfinger. So also is the provision of "some curried mess [in fact shrimps] with rice." Fleming and Bond are both conservative in their eating habits, and in his visit to Hong Kong in 1959, recounted in *Thrilling Cities*,

Fleming was surprised by the delicious quality of the food. The tension between established eating practices and the new possibilities offered by cosmopolitan influences was increasingly felt by the Western diner in general from the 1950s.

Goldfinger's ruthlessness is established by words as well as conduct, and this provides an opportunity for Fleming to sketch out his own views, including those on racial stereotypes and wealth, with World War II again serving as a frame of reference. Goldfinger explains to Bond that his handpicked staff of Korean servants has no respect for human life: "They are the cruellest, most ruthless people in the world." Goldfinger provides them with prostitutes from London to fulfill their need "to submit the white race to the grossest indignities." Some of the women die.

Bond reacts to Oddjob and the other Koreans with great hostility throughout the story, and racialism is overt in the novel. Jews are not allowed at the Floridiana, and, indeed, this was a period when such anti-Semitic exclusion was common in the United States and Britain. Bond regarded Koreans as "rather lower than apes." Crude, but it is Goldfinger who is shown to be truly callous toward his fellow mortals. He plans to poison about 60,000 people in Fort Knox, unsurprisingly so, as he regards most people as worthless.

Goldfinger employs Germans, three of whom were with the Luftwaffe, and Japanese, and is also able to recruit American gangsters for his attack on Fort Knox. Thus, the gangsters are placed by their willingness to associate with opponents from World War II. For the attack, Goldfinger proposes to use the most terrifying of modern weapons: an atomic warhead in order to blast open the bullion vault, and a nerve poison perfected by the Wehrmacht in 1943, captured by the Soviets, and supplied to Goldfinger. The pedigree of this poison recalls the Nazi-Soviet combination in *Moonraker*. Pussy Galore, the head of the Cement Mixers, a lesbian gang of American criminals recruited by Goldfinger, looks "like some young S.S. guardsman" but, in her case, looks are deceptive. The echoes of World War II help to locate this story in the 1950s.

The Cold War is strongly present, as is a sense of America under threat. One of the gangsters asks Goldfinger about fallout, while the superintendent at Pennsylvania Station tells Goldfinger that travelers from Louisville report being sprayed from the air by the Russians. Britain itself is in decline. The pound and the bank rate are under pressure. Bond warns Goldfinger not to "underestimate the English" (he omits to say British); but national security is dependent on American Super Sabres based at Manston "toting a hydrogen bomb round the skies over Kent," and the Americans had only a limited interest in Britain. With America's gold once again safe and sound, who in America would care about the Bank of England's gold or that Goldfinger remained at large?

This reflection would have struck a powerful echo with readers. The American refusal to support the pound at the time of the Suez invasion in November 1956 had played a major role in wrecking the Anglo-French action against President Gamal Abdel Nasser of Egypt. The American action had also revealed the fragility of British power: the Americans had refused to extend any credits to support sterling, undersold the pound on the New York Stock Exchange, condemned the invasion in the United Nations, blocked Britain's access to the Independent Monetary Fund until she withdrew her troops from Suez, and refused to provide oil to compensate for interrupted supplies from the Middle East. These actions led to a brief burst of anti-Americanism on the British right and to renewed concern about American attitudes to the British empire.

In the event, Bond thwarts Goldfinger and gets Pussy, although the gold goes to the bottom of the Atlantic in the BOAC Stratocruiser hijacked by Goldfinger. The last scene, in which Bond strangles Goldfinger on the plane, is implausible, and the ending hurried and unsatisfactory; but novels of this type are not easy to end. One-man heroism is forced to achieve too much in *Goldfinger*.

Yet the absence of any substitute for Bond also has a darker message. Britain is vulnerable and threatened, its richest citizen none other than Goldfinger. If Bond saves the American gold reserves in *Goldfinger*, the old world coming to the aid of the stronger new, he is also all that Britain can rely on. The conscientious Smithers could not stop Goldfinger from exporting his bullion, and both MI5 and the Secret Service had failed to track him down as the SMERSH paymaster, and that despite his prosperous presence in the country since 1937. So it was all down to one man, a latter-day St. George, again an English, rather than British, image.

To a certain extent, by this novel, Bond was a representative of the post-Suez shift in Britain's position, one from brawn to brains, resources to skill. Harold Macmillan, Conservative prime minister in 1957–63, held a summit conference with President Dwight Eisenhower on Bermuda in April 1957 that was designed to re-create the appearance of partnership after Suez. That October, he claimed to have regained the special relationship with the United States. However, the British position was precarious. Macmillan later had to charm Kennedy, rather than speak as an ally from a position of military power, let alone equality. This was a reflection and result of Britain's failure to develop its own rockets, and the resulting dependence on the Americans for British defense. Rockets played a role in several of Fleming's novels.

Bond was presented as a complex figure in this novel. The gravity and depravity of the threat posed by Goldfinger justified Bond's use of violence. The major plot thus served as an extended working out of the clash of values Bond experienced while waiting at the Miami airport at the start of the story—over his recent killing of a Mexican thug. As in *Casino Royale*, there are, however, no doubts at the close, and indeed, in Fleming's terms, the end of ambiguity is sealed with Bond's conversion of Pussy. Patriotism, bravery and Tender Loving Care provide an uncomplicated close, one that can hardly be praised for subtlety. "I never met a man before," says Pussy, and the lack of resolution of the start is replaced in the two short concluding paragraphs by a "passionate rather cruel mouth . . . fiercely slitted grey eyes," the last sentence, "His mouth came ruthlessly down on hers." This was all instantly forgettable, a contrast to the duel with Goldfinger that gave the remainder of the novel form, drive and bite, but it also reflected Fleming's sexual politics. Bond's heterosexuality converted the unambiguously named Pussy Galore. This was the crude end of the book, a form of Happy Ending in which Bond got his reward, but one that held conviction only in terms of Fleming's prejudices.

FOR YOUR EYES ONLY: HIGH QUALITY TRAVEL WRITING?

The publication in 1960 of a collection of short stories, subtitled *Five Secret Occasions in the Life of James Bond*, provided Fleming with an opportunity to reveal his fine ability to create powerful impressions of different environments. This was especially true of the West Indies, which provided a setting in two of the stories, but also of New England, the Indian Ocean, Italy, and the more homely Forest of St. Germain near Paris. The five stories were very varied, but, precisely because they were short stories, in each of them the rendition of the environment was a major theme in the text. In "From A View To A Kill," there is, however, a jaundiced view of Paris, modernity, and the French that was not necessary to the story and that presumably reflected Fleming's ire, as well as the crises of the French Fourth Republic. Paris was a city that had sold its heart not only to tourists, but to Russians and Rumanians: "of course, pawned to the Germans. You could see it in the people's eyes—sullen, envious, ashamed." Should Bond bother to look for a girl, she would no doubt prove disappointing in the end despite outward appearances. "On closer examination she would . . . have the heavy, dank, wide-pored skin of the bourgeois French. The blond hair under the rakish velvet beret would be brown at the roots. . . . The peppermint on the breath would not conceal the midday garlic. The alluring figure would be intricately scaffolded with wire plus rubber."

The condescension of this physical disgust, with its attack on the deception of French beauty, reflected a fear of being deceived. There was also an implicit contrast with British women and female integrity that looked back to a long tradition of British adventure stories.

The story was set not in Paris, but in the nearby Forest of St. Germain. The Soviet killing of a British motorcycle courier leads Bond to uncover a deep-penetration unit. The presence of such a unit mechanically concealed underground in the forest echoed Fleming's concern in *Thrilling Cities* about the "subterranean redoubt," with "a mass of brilliant machinery" from which a German rocket of the future would be fired at England. This motif was to be taken up in the films.

"From A View To A Kill" was very much a Cold War story, published in the year (1960) in which the U-2, a high-flying American reconnaissance plane used to spy on Soviet rocket and other military programs flown by Gary Powers, was shot down. In the story, there were also important tensions within the Western alliance. A victory for Bond would allay M's fears that the independence of Britain's Secret Service might be lost. Indeed, Colonel Schreiber, the American chief of security, and Bond do not get on. They are different people with different methods. Schreiber is Bond's antithesis: greying hair; the air of a bank manager; his desk crowded with silver-framed photographs of his family and a single white rose in a vase. Color was employed to make the point about Schreiber's colorlessness. The clash between the two men prefigures that between Bond and a British agent, Captain Paul Sender, in "The Living Daylights," a short story first published two years later.

Fleming's interest in World War II was reflected in the role of Hammerstein, an evil Nazi killer, in the short story "For Your Eyes Only." He contrasts with Bond's Canadian contact in the Royal Canadian Mounted Police, the youngish Colonel "Johns," who is good because he served in General Bernard Montgomery's Eighth Army on the battlefield in World War II, a reference to British skill and success. "Johns" had a role in Canadian espionage, characteristically described in sporting terms: he had "been on one or two hunting trips" himself.

"For Your Eyes Only" also raised the question of revenge and the nature of justice, because Bond was sent to kill Hammerstein, not in order to fulfill some national goal, but because the killer had ordered the slaughter of two of M's friends, Colonel and Mrs. Havelock, an elderly retired couple at whose wedding in Malta, a center of British imperial power, M had been best man. M's use of Bond was a challenge to the legitimacy and role of Bond and the Secret Service. Partly as a result, the slaughter of the elderly couple was described in unusual detail. This provided Fleming with a fine opportunity to display his skills as a depicter of Jamaican landscape, but it also set the scene in a far more effective fashion than the briefings generally given to Bond at the outset of his missions. This was also necessary in order to explain why M was justified in ordering the death of the killers. There was no real threat to Britain. The killings were designed to force an acquisition of land from people who did not wish to sell. It became clear to Bond that M had known the couple, and that this personal connection made M question his partiality in the case. "M wanted someone else, Bond, to deliver judgment. There was no doubt in Bond's mind. . . . 'I wouldn't hesitate for a minute, sir. If foreign gangsters find they can get away with this kind of thing they'll decide the English are as soft as some other people seem to think we are. This is a case for rough justice—an eye for an eye.' "

The story probed revenge and justice through a number of perspectives. Aside from M and Bond, the couple's daughter, Judy Havelock, was also involved. She traveled to Vermont in order to dispatch the killers, and, in a totally implausible coincidence, attempted to do so at the same time as Bond. A similar device was employed in *Goldfinger*.

The question of the validity of killing, voiced in the very first novel, *Casino Royale*, was repeated. Then the deadly nature of SMERSH's activities had served to justify Bond's mission. Now, it was a wider sense of justice in a world that lacked it, a response to the anarchy of will. The killers were not megalomaniacs, like Blofeld or Dr. No, but, at their smaller level, their evil was just as pernicious.

Thus, on the small, as well as the large, scale, Bond emerged as the servant of justice and the enemy of arbitrariness. The degree of self-indulgence, displayed in his smoking and drinking, was controlled, and did not detract from his dedication and morality. The veneer of stylish insouciance, present on occasion in the novels and, more obviously, in the films, was subordinated to the sense of mission and its requirements. This was seen elsewhere in the novels, for example *Dr. No*, when Bond disciplined his consumption in rigorous, self-imposed training regimes.

The morality of killing also emerges as a theme in the short story "The Hildebrand Rarity," in which Krest, a villainous American collector of rare species, is killed, but not by Bond, who has only a secondary role in the story.

In "For Your Eyes Only," Fleming offers another side of Bond that emphasizes his personal response to his task, and both distances him from utilitarianism and stresses the romantic appeal of the past. Jetting across the Atlantic to Montreal, Bond becomes nostalgic for the days when the crossing took a leisurely ten hours. "Now it was all too quick. The stewards had to serve everything almost at the double, and then one had a bare two hours snooze before the hundred-mile-long-descent." This was very much a clubland approach, that of an older man disenchanted with change, Fleming not Bond. Jet travel across the Atlantic was to be very much associated with the latter on the screen.

"Quantum of Solace" is a short story about marital relations, about life, not death. It was set in the West Indies, but this is not an idyll. Instead, a sense of boredom is readily apparent, again a boredom that was presumably Fleming's. Bond complains about the people in Nassau—their wealth, their idle gossip, their petty problems.

The politics was provided by the explanation for Bond's presence. He had been sent to stop the shipment of arms from Jamaica and the Bahamas to the Castro rebels on Cuba. Bond had indeed blown up the two big cabin cruisers in question, but his position was revealed as more than ambivalent, while that of the British government was scarcely reputable. The British government had struck a deal with the Cubans—British goods for Cuban sugar—but any assistance or aid to the rebels could put the bargain in jeopardy. Bond's own sympathies lay more with the rebels. This subordination of policy to commercial gain left an uncomfortable feel.

Fleming's sympathies were underlined in "For Your Eyes Only." Hammerstein had been Batista's head of counterintelligence and he had made a lot of money out of extortion, blackmail and protection rackets. This linkage by a Conservative writer of ex-Nazis with right-wing Latin American regimes was designed to damn the latter. The reference to "big American gangster money" in Fulgencio Batista's Havana was not designed to help. When, in the same story, M tells Bond that it looks as though Castro may seize power and, earlier, Colonel Havelock tells his wife that Batista will be on the run soon, neither expresses anxiety. Indeed, the British find it easier to get information about Hammerstein from Castro's people than from Batista's.

This is a long way from the concern later voiced in the novel *The Man with the Golden Gun* (1965) or Bond's destruction of the latest Cuban fighter plane at the outset of the film *Octopussy* (1983), but, by then, the Cuban revolution was more clearly part of the Cold War. Earlier, the Batista regime had been badly hit by the loss of

American support. The Eisenhower administration put an embargo on arms shipments to Cuba in May 1958, and, on 10 December 1958, the State Department withdrew recognition of Batista's government, plainly showing support for the rebel forces. Batista fled on 1 January 1959, and there was early American goodwill toward Castro's rule. It was not until the summer of 1960 that relations between Castro and the United States began to deteriorate seriously.

In "Quantum of Solace," the tensions and struggle are all personal, with the exception of brief mention of Anglo-American economic competition on the Nassau–New York airplane route: the Bermuda Agreement of 1946 had opened up the British empire to American fliers on a bilateral basis. The story is a powerful tale of marital betrayal and revenge, the cruelty of sexual mores and the need for common humanity, a tale that rises to "bestial cruelty," but a cruelty that is not that of torture or killing, but rather of the strife at the end of marriage.

This is a powerful tale, and one in which Bond plays only a tangential role. Far from providing evidence of Fleming wearying of his own creation, "Quantum of Solace" suggests the range of his writing and his willingness to offer a complexity of emotion and moral judgment that is not present in the films. The story is even more interesting because, although one of the protagonists, Philip Masters, is well realized, far more attention is devoted to the other, Rhoda, his erring wife. Her personality is captured, as is her moral journey. Although Rhoda Masters was not presented from within, as Vivienne Michel was to be in the full-length novel *The Spy Who Loved Me* (1962), it is with Vivienne that comparison should be made. Both are unsettling challenges to any reader convinced that Bond equates with violent action and uncomplicated sex, which is, indeed, the general assumption. Furthermore, unlike in *Dr. No*, the colonial governor, the figure of authority, does not emerge in an unsympathetic light: initial appearances are, again, deceptive.

Adventure and a narrative set in the present tense returned in the next short story, "Risico." This finds Bond at war with drug smugglers, a theme that will be stronger in the films, but, at the height of the Cold War, one seen as outside his true role. Indeed M is revealed as opposed to the use of the Secret Service for such ends: their "duty was espionage, and when necessary sabotage and subversion." He tells Bond that he had opposed Special Branch pressure for his assignment and also the pressure from the home secretary and the minister of health. However, the prime minister (in 1960 Harold Macmillan) had overruled M, taking a line that M found very persuasive: heroin was being used to subvert the power of the nation as a means of psychological warfare.

This view of drug traffic was a comment straight out of Buchan and other interwar writers. Bond is instructed to make contact with Kristatos, the top American narcotics agent in Rome, and to use him to buy off the smugglers. Kristatos is willing to help, yet insists not only on payment but also on the killing of the head of the smugglers' network. Bond is not keen on becoming part of a private vendetta, one very different from that in "For Your Eyes Only," but Kristatos portrays the network as wide-ranging and powerful. This offered Fleming an opportunity to reveal his knowledge of crime, but also to present it, as he always liked to do, as international and sinister, a threat equal to that of many sovereign states. A core group of Italian-American thugs, exiled from the United States and distrusted even among their own, had put together a smuggling operation ranging from Beirut to Tangier to Macao and fronted by a Milanese pharmaceutical firm. After processing the drug "the couriers, using innocent motor cars of various makes, ran a delivery service to the middlemen in England."

This was very much Fleming's style: a wide-ranging conspiracy was given credence by particular details, and England was the target. Furthermore, as an example of the politics of threat (and response) in the Bond books, this was far more credible than SPECTRE, which was to be introduced the following year in *Thunderball*. It is also a very European account of smuggling, one in which the crucial routes ran from Asia to Europe. The West Indies and Latin America did not feature, unlike in the films *Live and Let Die* (1973) and *Licence To Kill* (1989).

Bond sets out to discover more about the head of the network, Enrico Colombo, only to be captured and told by Colombo that while indeed he was the best smuggler in the Mediterranean, he did not deal in drugs. Instead, it is Kristatos who is the drug smuggler, trying to throw police attention onto Colombo. Assisted by Bond, Colombo's men attack Kristatos's Albanian drug smugglers and Bond kills Kristatos. Albania, the entrepôt, was then a Communist state. Colombo reveals that there is indeed a political project behind the drug trade. Kristatos was importing opium to process it into heroin in Naples, but the opium cost him nothing. The Russians drew upon their sources in the Caucasus and provided it to Kristatos for free— as a weapon against England.

Thus, criminals within the West serve the cause of its enemies, a theme repeatedly found in Fleming's universe, a world that has to be without loose ends. The order Fleming advocated was challenged in his stories by opponents out to serve criminal schemes and ends, in which chaos or destruction on a massive scale were serious possibilities. Bond was the vital agent of preservation. The image of heroin as a massive "projectile" fired into England repeated the language employed to describe rockets. Drugs were seen in the same light, both metaphorically and literally with the hypodermic syringe.

Politics played a smaller role in the last of the stories, "The Hildebrand Rarity," but Bond's presence in the Seychelles had to be explained. He couldn't be on holiday: such an explanation might suffice for Fleming, who had an aversion to work, but not for Bond. Bond's presence was accounted for in terms of the Cold War and related both to Britain's imperial range and power and to a world of regional bases, prior to that of the stress on intercontinental missiles. Naval strength was still crucial to the projection of power, indeed more so after the loss of the Indian Empire, Britain's great Asian base, in 1947. M asks Bond to check out the security conditions in the Seychelles, because the admiralty may need a safe fall-back position for the Maldives. Having decided that the situation in the Seychelles is in fact acceptable, Bond joins a cruise organized by the obnoxious Milton Krest. Krest gives Fleming an opportunity to show his suspicion of Americans and Germans. He had a Prussian father and, according to his British wife, he had a German habit of dismissing Europeans as "decadent."

Krest is an arrogant sadist who uses money to get his way, pressuring people to sell what they treasure and what is rare and protected. He uses the American tax system to his benefit, setting up the Krest Foundation to collect specimens for the Smithsonian and having a tax-reducing holiday while doing so. His quest for a fish, the Hildebrand Rarity, is motivated by the tax authorities' threat to disallow five years' expenses. To capture the fish, Krest pours poison into the sea, bringing destruction to a beautiful community of fish, in a powerfully described and horrific passage. The helping Bond is appalled and compares himself to the airman who manned the bomb sight at Nagasaki. Krest's name was later used for the second-in-command to the drug baron Franz Sanchez in the film *Licence to Kill* (1989).

Krest's celebration leads him to a drunken desire to irritate Bond. He treats him to an account of English inconsequence similar to that which was to be expressed by Tiger Tanaka in the novel *You Only Live Twice* (1964):

Nowadays, said Mr. Krest, there were only three powers—America, Russia and China. That was the big poker game and no other country had either the chips or the cards to come into it. Occasionally some pleasant little country . . . like England would be lent some money so that they could take a hand with the grown-ups. But that was just being polite like one sometimes had to be—to a chum in one's club who'd gone broke.

Bond finds this argument oversimplified and naive and recalls an aphorism about America lacking "a period of maturity." The sadist, a wife-beater, is murdered that night, but his words reflect the growing perception of Britain as weak. This perception was unsettling to Fleming and also was to pose a problem of credibility about plots that centered on Britain and her empire. The Maldives themselves gained independence in 1965, the Seychelles following in 1976. Britain was soon no longer to be a power in the Indian Ocean.

The British had to adapt to America, a major theme in the politics of the novels and films, where intelligence services formed part of a global strategy in containing Soviet expansionism and the menace of third parties. Bond's style could barely conceal the diminished British political and military presence in Cold War confrontations. In "The Hildebrand Rarity" no such adaptation was necessary. There was no need to turn to American strength in eliminating Krest. However, in the person of Krest, wealth and power became insensitivity and sadism. This was an unsettling account of what British weakness could lead to.

2

At War with SPECTRE

THUNDERBALL: **SPECTRE'S ENTRANCE**

> Planes with atom bombs don't get stolen in real life. Except that
> they do.
>
> —Felix Leiter

Thunderball, published in 1961, represented a new departure, with
its introduction of SPECTRE and of Ernst Blofeld, a commanding
villain who was to reappear in *On Her Majesty's Secret Service* (1963)
and *You Only Live Twice* (1964). This gave a measure of continuity
to the later Bond novels. SMERSH took second place to a very different challenge, ironically so as these were years in which the Cold
War itself heated up again. Kennedy repeatedly, and inaccurately,
claimed in the 1960 presidential campaign that a missile gap in favor
of the Soviet Union was opening up. In April 1961 the Soviet Union
launched the first manned space flight and a CIA-sponsored invasion
of Cuba by anti-Castro exiles was defeated at the Bay of Pigs. That
August, the Berlin Wall was constructed. In October 1962 the Cuban

Missile Crisis took the world close to nuclear war. The Soviet attempt to establish ballistic missile bases in Cuba led to an American blockade that nearly escalated to war before the Soviets backed down.

Heightened confrontation also characterized the world of espionage. In November 1962 Macmillan told the House of Commons that "hostile intrigue and espionage are being relentlessly maintained on a very large scale." In 1960–63, the Americans discovered that their National Security Agency had a number of Soviet agents, including William Martin, Victor Hamilton, Cornelius Drummond and Jack Dunlap. Irrespective of its Cold War setting, the Cuban crisis emphasized the importance of accurate intelligence and the ease with which war could break out. The gap between decision, use and strike had been shown to be perilously small.

In a sense, SPECTRE represented evil unconstrained by ideology but centered on a quest for money. The shift from SMERSH to SPECTRE can be seen as a surrender to fantasy occasioned, in part, by the decline of the British Empire and Fleming's consequent lack of certainty. That is more credible than the idea that SPECTRE offers a means to criticize unbridled (or new money) capitalism.

The origins of *Thunderball* were complex and involved litigation. Fleming's novel was intended to be the book of a film to which he and several others, especially Ernest Cureo, Kevin McClory and Jack Whittingham, had contributed the theme and script. After the book appeared, McClory took legal action against Fleming.

Invented for Bond (unlike SMERSH), and unrelated, except tangentially, to the Cold War and its matrix of transnational acronyms such as NATO, SPECTRE required a long introduction. This was provided in chapter 5 of the novel, after the excitement and violence already offered by Bond's conflict with Count Lippe, a SPECTRE agent, at Shrublands, a British health-care center. An entire chapter was devoted to SPECTRE's founder and head, Ernst Stavro Blofeld, and this offered Fleming an opportunity to reflect on leadership:

he was one of those men—one meets perhaps only two or three in a lifetime—who seem almost to suck the eyes out of your head. These rare men are apt to possess three basic attributes—their physical appearance is extraordinary, they have a quality of relaxation, of inner certainty—and they exude a powerful animal magnetism. . . . Certain great men of history, perhaps Genghis Khan, Alexander the Great, Napoleon, among the politicians have had these qualities. Perhaps they even explain the hypnotic sway of an altogether more meagre individual, the otherwise inexplicable Adolf Hitler, over eighty million of the most gifted nation in Europe.

Born in 1908, Blofeld studied economics and political history at the University of Warsaw and engineering and radionics at the Warsaw Technical Institute before beginning employment with the Polish Ministry of Posts and Telegraphs; concluding quickly that communications would play a key role in securing world power—a modern and perceptive analysis. Blofeld used his position, first to profit from stock dealing and then to become a source of intelligence for the German Abwehr secret service, inventing an entire network, TARTAR (possibly a reference to Genghis Khan or to the Soviet occupiers of Eastern Europe), in order to justify the cost of the information he provided. He then widened the espionage market to include the Americans and the Swedes.

Having amassed a fortune, but fearing discovery, Blofeld closed down his system and destroyed details about his identity, cutting out his baptismal entry from the church records at Gdynia. Taking shelter in Istanbul when World War II began, the opportunistic Blofeld then created another network like TARTAR, only this time selling his information to the Allies after it became clear that they were likely to win.

Blofeld next established SPECTRE—the Special Executive for Counterintelligence, Terrorism, Revenge and Extortion, a somewhat improbable mix. The structure, purpose and activities of this body were fully described. Aside from Blofeld, there was a twenty-member council. All men in their thirties, they were divided into two groups. The first comprised two scientists, the second were the men of action who had "quick, hard predatory eyes, the eyes of the wolves and the hawks that prey upon the herd." These eighteen consisted of cells of three, each from one of the world's leading criminal or subversive organizations. Three were from the Mafia and another three from its French counterpart, the Union Corse. Three were former members of SMERSH and another three from the Gestapo, the last a reminder of Fleming's benchmark for evil. Three had left Tito's Secret Police and the last three were Turks who had been responsible for the Middle Eastern heroin pipeline that finished in Beirut. All of them had a solid cover and no known criminal record.

At the meeting of the council described in the novel, Blofeld recaps SPECTRE's activities in its first three years, which had yielded £1.5 million, a large sum at the time, but not one of world-threatening proportions. The activities provided a glimpse on the intersection of crime and espionage, the suggestive details of which helped to establish the credibility of Fleming's narrative. Himmler's jewels had been recovered from the Mondsee and disposed of in Beirut. The safe and contents from the headquarters of the Soviet Secret Service in East Berlin had been seized and sold to the CIA. Mafia heroin, captured in Naples, had been sold in Los Angeles, while the British Secret Service had paid for Czech germ warfare vials. A former SS commander living in Havana had been blackmailed, the French had paid for the assassination of a defector who possessed atomic secrets, and the daughter of an American gangster, Magnus Blomberg (a German Jewish name) of the Detroit Purple Gang, had been kidnapped and held for ransom.

The last provided the opportunity for Blofeld to display the nature of his organization, and, implicitly, for Fleming to contrast it with the British Secret Service, the institution described in greatest detail in the Bond novels and the crucial context of his moral world and purpose. As already indicated by the activities outlined, there was no justice among thieves: both Blomberg and a former SS officer had suffered from SPECTRE. Blofeld revealed to the council that the kidnapped girl had lost her virginity while a captive, despite the promise that "the girl would be returned undamaged." Blofeld makes clear that she might have been willing and that sexual experience might be beneficial, a view that might also have been expected from Fleming and Bond. He also underlines the rationale of SPECTRE, namely that it was not concerned with morals and ethics. However, precisely because of this, discipline and self-discipline were crucial to SPECTRE. As a result, the guilty party, Pierre Borraud of the Union Corse, SPECTRE No. 12, is electrocuted at the council meeting, just as two former members had earlier been killed at council meetings.

Plan Omega is SPECTRE's biggest project hitherto. Two airborne atomic bombs are to be seized from a British Villiers Vindicator experimental bomber when it is hijacked while on an Atlantic training flight. The bombs are then to be ransomed, the ransom parachuted onto the slopes of Mount Etna, moved with Mafia help to Catania, loaded onto a ship, and transhipped, at sea in the Arabian Gulf, onto a merchantman owned by the leading Bombay bullion brokers. The payment was to be transferred from Goa by chartered plane to Zurich for deposit. The details reflected Fleming's fascination with the mechanics of international crime, and his concern to rest his plots on practicalities. He did not know, however, that the secret of the Blue Diver and Red Steer radar jamming devices fitted into the V-bomber force had been betrayed to the Eastern bloc by Nicholas Prager, a RAF technician run by Czech intelligence.

SPECTRE demanded £100 million in gold bullion in return for the bombs, threatening, in the event of refusal, first to destroy a piece of property belonging to the western powers with a value of at least that sum, and second to devastate an unnamed major city. The demand was made in the form of a letter to the prime minister, with a copy to the American president (then Macmillan and Kennedy), a statement of British importance. It enabled Bond to play a major role, and was not, therefore, intended to suggest that Britain was a softer target than the United States. In concert, Britain and the United States decide not to pay but rather to try to defeat SPECTRE. The response was presented from the British perspective, with Britain playing a major role: "We've teamed up with the CIA to cover the world. Allen Dulles is putting every man he's got on to it and so am I," declares M, as if the two powers, or, at least, MI6 and the CIA, are equal. The irony of M's remark is not brought out. M thinks the targets likely to be in America, because the Americans are more bomb-conscious and have more installations worth more than £100 million.

Wrongly suspecting Soviet involvement and doubting the existence of SPECTRE, Bond is sent to the Bahamas, to see if the hijacked British bomber was taken there. This brings him into contact with Blofeld's second-in-command, Emilio Largo, a wealthy yacht owner whose start in life was as the head of the Neapolitan black market. While World War II may be crucial in the backgrounds of many of Fleming's characters, the socioeconomic chaos after 1945 is also vital, both in allowing his villains to prosper and in dislocating and unnerving the economies of the West.

Bond is given CIA support, and this provides an opportunity for probing the unsettled nature of the Anglo-American relationship. He fears he will be sent "a muscle-bound ex-college man with a crew-cut and a desire to show up the incompetence of the British, the backwardness of their little Colony, and the clumsy ineptitude of Bond in order to gain credit with his chief in Washington." Bond is, however, eager for the agent to bring the equipment that he had earlier requested, a radio transmitter and receiver that would free them from dependence on cable offices, and modern portable Geiger counters. Fleming is in no doubt that American equipment is superior, and Bond displays "no false pride" about borrowing it.

Fortunately for Bond, the CIA man turns out to be Felix Leiter, first introduced in *Casino Royale*, now recalled to the colors during the crisis, and as helpful as ever. Leiter readily cooperates, but there is a difference of emphasis between them. Leiter is less inclined to see the world in confrontational terms and tells Bond that he felt "like a damned fool" using the Geiger counter on Largo's yacht: "He looked keenly at Bond. 'You don't find you grow out of these things? I mean it's all right when there's a war on. But it seems kinda childish when peace is bustin' out all over.' " In response, Bond, presumably voicing Fleming's opinion, feels no such security and sees no such easy distinction between war and peace. For England, the war seems to continue in places as wide-ranging as Berlin, Kenya and Suez—not to mention SMERSH activities.

The popularity of the Bond books and films in the United States, fears about Communism and the vogue there during the 1950s for films with invading aliens, such as *Invasion of the Body Snatchers*, suggests that the sense of security in America was less solid than Fleming imagined it.

Leiter, anyway, has the backing of a superb military machine. He complains about the waste of fuel and manpower involved in keeping American forces in readiness, but has at his sole disposal a half squadron of Super Sabre fighter bombers from Pensacola in Florida and the *Manta* atomic submarine. Somewhat surprisingly, this revelation comes as part of a diatribe against expenditure on, and by, the "power-struck fatcats at the Pentagon" and against promotion jobs "to help along the Navy Estimates." Given that the *Manta* is to help against Largo, Leiter's error is a warning about the need for vigilance—as more generally is his entire mistaken attitude.

The abundance of American military resources makes the lone hero less credible, although no less popular, in the United States. This forces a writer to invent means to separate the hero from his possible backup, frequently by suggesting official complacency, if not worse. In the case of Bond, a lack of support, except, in the films, the initial provision of Q's latest devices, heightens the adventure.

Leiter and Bond also discuss possible targets for SPECTRE, providing an opportunity to offer readers an idea of what could be at stake. The SPECTRE letter had referred to "a piece of property belonging to the Western Powers." The sole local site of value that Bond can think of is the Anglo-American rocket base at North-West Cay on Grand Bahamas. Leiter adds the American rocket base at Cape Canaveral, the naval base at Pensacola and, for civilian targets, Miami and Tampa. He also comments that the SPECTRE phrase could well refer to an established operation, perhaps the Congolese uranium mines, a reminder to Fleming's readers about the nature and range of Western strategic interests. The granting of independence to the Congo (later Zaire) by Belgium in 1960 was followed by the outbreak of civil war there. Leiter's comment implies that the fate of the Congo is of continued importance to the West. Independence for colonies does not lessen the need for vigilance. Due to its use in atomic bombs, uranium was of great strategic importance.

Having identified Largo as the villain, there is still the problem, as in *Dr. No*, of deciding how best to deal with him within the law. Until the bombs are on board Largo's *Disco Volante*, there are no legal grounds for seizing him or it. What Fleming terms "democratic processes of the law" are the problem. Bond tells Commander Pedersen of the *Manta*, a sympathetic character, that their situation mirrored that of a detective tailing a suspected murderer: "there's nothing the detective can do but follow the man and wait until he actually pulls the gun out of his pocket."

This Largo does when he seeks to plant the first atom bomb on the seabed near the Bahamas rocket station. Shadowed by the *Manta*, Largo and his men are attacked while underwater. Largo is killed by his former girlfriend Domino Vitali, the sister of Giuseppe Petacchi, the NATO observer on the British Vindicator bomber who had killed the crew and delivered the plane to Largo only to be murdered. The NATO traitor had thus been an Italian, not a Briton, a choice that again was symptomatic of Fleming's national prejudices, which, to him, were based on ethnic considerations.

Thunderball worked well as an adventure story. The casino details—Bond yet again beating the villain at cards—were formulaic and of limited interest, but the theme of the theft of atom bombs seemed pertinent and modern. The vulnerability of society to such weapons gave credence to the tale. The science by which it was possible to explode atom bombs without delivering them by plane or rocket was twice explained. Pedersen told Bond, "These atomic weapons are just too damned dangerous. Why, any one of these little sandy cays around here could hold the whole of the United States to ransom—just with one of my missiles trained on Miami."

Indeed, this reflection pointed the way forward for the espionage/adventure novel. Aside from the Soviet atomic threat, which was to escalate into the Cuban missile crisis in October 1962, with the atom bomb it was possible to think of terrorists as staging the ultimate challenge. It thus became reasonable to suggest an alternative threat to that from the Soviet Union, a threat of great, even equal, magnitude, but one that came from a smaller unit. This prophetic warning about the danger of nuclear proliferation also looked toward the emphasis on drug barons and private armies in the later Bond films.

The device of dual villains, Blofeld and Largo, permitted the destruction of one but allowed the second to survive: Blofeld was able to escape from the debacle of the scheme and to flee the SPECTRE headquarters in Paris, because of the failure of Largo to send the expected radio signal; also the sign to the British Secret Service at the beginning of *Dr. No* that something was amiss. This escape was to provide a continuity with subsequent novels, a continuity that, like that of SMERSH, explained Bond's personal impetus, a point of great, indeed growing, importance to Fleming. Bond was not primarily an agent who responded to *ad hoc* challenges. His world was shaped and given moral direction by wider struggles. SMERSH came first, but the duel with Blofeld provided a major boost to Bond's dedication and energy.

ON HER MAJESTY'S SECRET SERVICE: BLOFELD ROUND TWO

Published in 1963, *On Her Majesty's Secret Service* returned to a European setting, dispensed with American assistance, let alone an American angle, and was based on a threat to Britain alone. In countering the threat, Bond had eventually to distance himself from the service, while he also allied with the Union Corse, a powerful criminal organization, as *Thunderball* had reminded Bond's followers. This cooperation, potentially the most ambivalent aspect of the book, was matched by Bond's romantic surrender, for this was the book in which he married, only for Tracy, his wife, to fall victim to Blofeld before her wedding day was finished.

Following Operation Thunderball, Bond had been instructed to concentrate all his efforts on the pursuit of Blofeld and any surviving members of SPECTRE. For nearly a year, he had had no success, and had come to doubt that SPECTRE had been revived or that Blofeld was still alive. Mentally drafting his letter of resignation, Bond loses a road race near Royale to a Lancia Flaminia Zagato Spyder driven by a dashing young woman. He later meets her at the casino, the scene of his triumph over Le Chiffre, and rescues her from the ignominy of failing to honor a gambling loss. They spend the night together, only for Tracy to reject him the following morning. Bond stops her attempt to commit suicide in the sea that afternoon, but they are both seized by gunmen and taken to meet Marc-Ange Draco, the head of the Union Corse, and, it turns out, Tracy's father.

Concerned about his depressed daughter, Marc-Ange offers Bond £1 million to marry her. Bond refuses, but agrees to see her again and, in return, obtains the information that Blofeld is still alive, indeed that he has recently bribed three men away from the Union Corse, and that he is in Switzerland. Initially, this proves a dead end. Swiss Sécurité deny any knowledge of Blofeld or SPECTRE and refuse to search the anonymous numbered bank accounts on the grounds that Blofeld had committed no crimes on Swiss soil, a response that moves Bond to anger.

The hunt for Blofeld is given new direction when the College of

Arms in London receives a letter on his behalf from a Zurich firm of solicitors detailing Blofeld's desire to obtain evidence to support his claim to be the Comte de Bleuville. Blofeld's desire for recognition is his fatal flaw, part of the process by which the villains are shown to demand not only acceptance in society, but also the ability to dominate and fleece it. Drax at Blades in *Moonraker* is another example.

Bond is sent to Switzerland as the college's emissary, under the pseudonym Sir Hilary Bray, and discovers Blofeld to preside over Piz Gloria, an alpine resort containing ten young women from various parts of Britain, and a male staff of Corsicans, Germans, Slavs and others with Balkan features. Bond also finds out that the young women are being cured of agricultural allergies and being taught by hypnosis to wish to improve British crops and breeds.

However, Blofeld's men capture Shaun Campbell, a British agent from Zurich, whose "control was shot to pieces" by a beating and who directs suspicion onto Bond by recognizing him. Fearing that Campbell will reveal all under torture, Bond decides to flee but first breaks into the laboratory at Piz Gloria and obtains the names and addresses of the girls.

Escaping, Bond excitingly outskis both his opponents and an avalanche, but he is then cornered, only to be spirited to safety by Tracy, whom he meets, by chance, at a Christmas party in the nearby village, Samaden. She had been searching for him. Returning to London from the Zurich airport, after Tracy accepts his offer of marriage, Bond has Christmas lunch with M, and the two then reveal Bond's report to 501, the head of the Scientific Research Section, and a Mr. Franklin from the Ministry of Agriculture. 501 suggests that the Soviet Union is linked to Blofeld's plans, that a Captain Boris who was at Piz Gloria "was the paymaster or supervisor of the scheme and Blofeld the independent operator."

The Soviet link is supported by 410, the head of the Zurich station, who reveals that his number two, Campbell, had been "tailing one of Redland's men. Chap's been buying some pretty odd stuff from the local rep of Badische Anilin . . . thought he'd better see where it was being delivered to." The reference to the German company echoed the theme of German-Soviet cooperation seen in *Moonraker* and also reflected current anxieties about the activities of Germans and German companies, for example in the Egyptian rocket program.

Franklin produces a map of the agricultural and livestock resources of the British Isles, relates the areas where the symbols were densest to the addresses of the girls, and reveals that, within the last month, 3 million turkeys had been slaughtered after an outbreak of fowl pest. Christmas lunch had been saved only by the import of 2 million turkeys, and Franklin warns that successful biological warfare could bankrupt Britain. He explains the potential of such warfare in a lecture intended for the readers, rather than M, Bond and 501. Franklin also links fowl pest to a girl who had already left Piz Gloria and explains that what Bond had seen in the laboratory were dangerous viruses.

In response, the British authorities detain the girls on entry, but M is convinced that the Swiss will provide no help in seizing Blofeld, and that, even if they were to agree to do so, Blofeld would have the opportunity to flee. Bond proposes an unorthodox approach which M approves, only warning that he would not be able to obtain prime ministerial backing. In a topical reference, designed to add verisimilitude, and complementing 501's suggestion that Gagarin had been hypnotized in order to achieve his maneuvers in space, and M and Bond's earlier lunchtime discussion of Gary Powers and the American U2 spy mission, M tells Bond "we don't want to get the Government mixed up in another U2 fiasco."

Bond obtains the support of Marc-Ange for a helicopter-borne assault on Piz Gloria, a scene almost designed for cinematic treatment and one that fed on interest in such operations. The British were using helicopters extensively in their current confrontation with Indonesia. The assault is successful, but Blofeld escapes down the bob run, evading Bond's pursuit. At the close, Blofeld returns to ambush the newly married Bond and Tracy as they approach Kufstein. Tracy is slaughtered and the book ends on a powerful tragic note, with a broken Bond repeating the haunting line "Don't worry. . . . We have all the time in the world."

Far from this being a formulaic work, there were some important novel features. The love interest both opens and closes the book and is more sustained than in the other novels. However, the implications had Bond stayed married are not explored. A married Bond was not compatible with the Fleming formula, and in *From Russia, With Love*, M would hate to see Bond "permanently tied to one woman's skirts." Although M's comment about women hanging "on your gun-arm" was intended to refer to "neurotic women," the earlier remark indicated that he regarded marriage as likely to compromise Bond's effectiveness. This would also have been true of his stylish image.

As Blofeld has already appeared in the previous book, it was not necessary to explain who he is or to account for his evil. Bond's two meetings with him in *On Her Majesty's Secret Service* are meetings as

Sir Hilary Bray, not Bond; and Blofeld talks about his ancestry, not world domination or a variant thereof. There is no disclosure scene to a captured Bond. As a result, the plot is not explained until near the close of the book. Prior to that, Bond is already hunting Blofeld as a result of *Thunderball*. The nature of Piz Gloria is not appreciated until the very end of the work, when, indeed, the biological warfare scheme is easily thwarted by the detention of the girls. Bond's escape from Piz Gloria is the exciting climax of the book, but it occurs three-fifths of the way through it. There is far less suspense in the final assault on Blofeld's base. The big, but empty, finish was cinematic. As with *Casino Royale*, excitement peaked before the last section of the book. In the film of *On Her Majesty's Secret Service* a disclosure scene is introduced. The formula required one and it gave Blofeld an opportunity to take a greater and more melodramatic role.

As far as the politics of the book are concerned, it is Marc-Ange who is the most interesting character. A good rogue, like Enrico Colombo in "Risico," he appeals to Bond and is presented as a thoroughly engaging individual, a description that necessarily leads to a questioning of the customary distinctions between criminality and legality. Marc-Ange himself draws attention to the manner in which war offers opportunities for a redrawing of the distinctions. The medals he wears to his daughter's wedding include the king's medal for foreign resistance fighters, an honor that Bond admires and that recalls World War II. Marc-Ange admits both to enjoying the war greatly and to taking advantage of the opportunity to seize the funds of a section of the Abwehr (German Intelligence). As so often, World War II is a way of distinguishing good from evil, and the world of Bond represents a continuation of war in the midst of peace.

Marc-Ange also indicates his preference for stability, rather than revolution: "I do not like revolutions. They make chaos everywhere. Today, I never know when an operation of my own is not going to be interfered with by some damned emergency concerning Algerian terrorists, the rounding up of some nest of these blasted OAS. And road blocks. House to house searches! They are the bane of my existence." His reference was to French instability arising from the Algerian independence struggle and the subsequent opposition by right-wing French military elements to De Gaulle's abandonment of Algeria.

This attitude contrasts with that of villains who preferred to exploit disorder, such as Blofeld. Indeed, Fleming allows Marc-Ange to offer a distinction between criminals: "I am a criminal, a great criminal. I run houses, chains of prostitutes, I smuggle, I sell protection, whenever I can, I steal from the very rich. I break many laws and I have often had to kill in the process. . . . But this Blofeld, he is too bad, too disgusting."

The counterpointing is related to that between the British and Swiss in the pursuit of Blofeld: "Your Chief is correct. You would get nowhere with the Swiss." In short, authority could not be trusted. This then leads to the switch: the likable rogues are willing to help. The good cause is served by their individualism, a development of the benefit derived from Enrico Colombo in "Risico." Marc-Ange and his men attack Piz Gloria, and that is an achievement possible only because of Bond's appeal to women and the nobility of his conduct toward Tracy. The help is Marc-Ange's wedding present. Bond's ability to win the love, and thus support, of women is even more crucial to the Secret Service than his skill with cards.

In *On Her Majesty's Secret Service*, a meeting with M contained a valedictory passage that encapsulated the world of Bond in print; part juvenile escape, part based in reality, and overall a sense of (ongoing) loss, especially of "nobility" of character and service. Over coffee after lunch, M continued with his stories about the Royal Navy, which Bond greatly appreciated. Fleming continued, "Perhaps it was all just the stuff of boy's adventure books, but it was all true and it was about a great Navy that was no more and a great breed of officers and seamen that would never be seen again".

YOU ONLY LIVE TWICE: BOND GOES EAST

The third in the Blofeld trilogy was set in Japan, a novelty for Bond, but one that reflected Fleming's visits in 1959 and 1962. In 1959 he had visited Tokyo for three days as part of a trip round the world for the *Sunday Times* that had already taken him to Hong Kong and Macao and subsequently on to the United States. In Tokyo, Fleming had not followed the customary improving tourist rituals, but had instead visited a judo academy, a Japanese soothsayer and a geisha house. In 1962 he spent longer in Japan, traveling around and meeting a number of Japanese. Fleming worked hard to discover details of Japanese culture and society. He had already planned the plot and found a role for two friends with whom he traveled in 1962: a Japanese journalist, Torao Saito, known as Tiger, whom he had met in 1959, and Richard Hughes, the Australian-born Far East correspondent of the *Sunday Times*.

The story was published in 1964. The same year, Fleming produced the fantastical children's adventure story *Chitty Chitty Bang Bang*, a successful work that indicated his range. Also in 1964,

Harold Wilson brought Labour to power, ending the long period of Conservative government since 1951 under which Fleming had produced the Bond novels. *You Only Live Twice* reflected Fleming's increasing melancholia, with Bond mirroring the author's moods. It opened with a Bond different from the character at the start of *Casino Royale*.

Tracy's death had had a very different impact from that of Vesper. It did not give Bond drive and purpose. Instead, her death had left him depressed and without purpose and with his efficiency as a secret agent ended. Bond then bungled two assignments, the details of neither of which are provided. Even as a failure, Bond must not be shown to fail.

In response, M sends Bond on a new and very different task. He is appointed to the Diplomatic Section and given a mission that should involve no violence. It enables Fleming to suggest his knowledge of the world of espionage. M tells Bond that the Japanese have made major advances in deciphering, enabling them to discover Soviet secrets. However, although the Japanese provided the information to the CIA, the latter was no longer passing this on, and Bond's mission is to persuade Tiger Tanaka, the head of the Japanese Secret Service, to provide the intelligence information to Britain as well.

The American refusal to pass on information was attributed to their treatment of the Pacific as a "private preserve," but also to their concern about Britain as a security risk, a comment on the impact of Burgess, Maclean, Blake and Philby. The last had defected to the Soviet Union in 1963, one of a series of intelligence scandals in the last years of the Macmillan government. Indeed, in September 1963, Sir Roger Hollis, the head of MI5, went to Washington to warn John McCone, head of the CIA, and J. Edgar Hoover, head of the FBI, about the Peters Affair, namely that Graham Mitchell, the deputy director-general of MI5, might have been a Soviet agent, and that, as a result, many American operations might have been compromised. The CIA's counterintelligence staff understandably had little confidence in British intelligence.

The meeting between Bond and M also provided Fleming with an opportunity to reflect on the decline of Britain. It no longer seemed credible, as in *Thunderball* (1961), to suggest that Britain was still great, and that she and the United States were partners. The empire was shrinking rapidly and the Profumo Affair had sapped confidence in British politics and society, suggesting that the traditional leadership of the country, as represented by John Profumo, the minister of war, was dishonest and incompetent, with possibly serious consequences for British security. Profumo was shown to have shared a lover with others, including a Soviet naval attaché, and then to have lied to the House of Commons about the scandal. The scandal helped to create an impression of a decadent and troubled government and society. In M's estimate, Tanaka probably does not hold the service in very high esteem, his only knowledge coming via the CIA.

M's comments follow his complaint about the treatment of the British Secret Service by the press in "this so-called democracy of ours." M contrasts this with the freedom of the KGB from public scrutiny and criticism. Bond reflects on the recent (fictional) Prenderghast case, in which "a Head of Station with homosexual tendencies" had been found guilty of treason, leading to an inquiry that had greatly held up the work of the service. This reflects Fleming's concern about the debilitating effects of what he saw as the excesses of democracy and liberty. In July 1963 a strong MI5 case against Giuseppe Martelli, a physicist with the Atomic Energy Authority who was indeed a Soviet agent, ended with an acquittal. Martelli subsequently agreed to be debriefed by MI5. Temperamentally, Fleming was an elitist, but one who was concerned about the caliber and integrity of the changing elite.

Britain is weakening. That is the message of *You Only Live Twice*. Poor relations with the United States are also a contrast with the cooperation with Felix Leiter in the earlier novels. The chief of staff of the Security Service, Bill Tanner, tells Bond that the British have already been prevented by the Americans from taking a role in the Pacific. The Secret Service had crossed paths with the Americans on numerous cases—often with dangerous results. In his 1959 tour, Fleming had noted Britain's greatly lessened influence in East Asia and the Pacific. This was indeed the case. In 1951 Australia and New Zealand had independently entered into a defense pact with the United States (ANZUS). In December 1962 the British position in Southeast Asia was challenged when the Indonesia confrontation erupted, committing Britain to conflict in defense of Malaysia and Brunei.

Most of *You Only Live Twice* contains no politics. It instead involves the last and final stage in the hunt for Blofeld and is a travelog-adventure story. In this adventure, Blofeld is involved in a totally improbable situation and scheme—a phrase that really has weight in a book about Bond. Nevertheless, Blofeld does not emerge in the book, and is not identified, until a far later stage than in *On Her Majesty's Secret Service*. Unlike that book, *You Only Live Twice* is not totally devoted to the hunt for Blofeld. Indeed, the book lacks a central focus. The first section can be seen as scene setting for the eventual confrontation with Blofeld and is indeed necessary in plot terms, but it is too long for this purpose. Instead, there is a "buddy tale," that of the developing relationship between Bond and Tiger, a one-act equivalent to the Bond-Leiter friendship, and one that is played out in response to the stages of Bond's engagement with Japanese culture and society, an engagement that occupies much of the text. Fleming had made scant effort to explain American, Turkish or Black Jamaican society, but in Japan he, again, revealed his ability as a travel writer.

Political reflections can also be found in this section. They are important, both to the plot of this part of the book and as evidence of Fleming's assessment of the Japanese and of much else. As Japan is a new environment for Bond, it has to be explained to him, and thus Fleming is able to convey ideas, opinions and information far more readily than in his other books: Paris does not need explaining to Bond. This is done in an interesting fashion by setting up two different sources of information: Tiger and the Tokyo representative of the Australian Secret Service, Richard "Dikko" Henderson, who is modeled on Fleming's journalist friend Richard Hughes. They are both convinced that Japan and the Japanese are different from the West. This sense of exceptionalism is important to the work and is established early in the book. Although occupation by U.S. troops has resulted in the surface appearance of a true alliance, "once a Jap, always a Jap . . . And time means nothing for them either. . . . These people . . . think in terms of centuries." The last was a point that was to be made about the North Vietnamese-backed Viet Cong during the Vietnam War; it gave them great resilience in their struggle.

The American occupation of Japan had ended in 1952, but an American military presence remained important. The ratification of the Mutual Security Agreement with America had led to demonstrations in May 1960. Henderson goes on to offer an affirmation of lasting ethnic characteristics, and a ranting summary of politics that may be seen as a mixture of Fleming's views and what he felt he could portray in the mouth of a drunken Australian:

The Japanese are a separate human species. They've only been operating as a civilized people, . . . for fifty, at the most a hundred years. . . . [T]he UN are going to reap the father and mother of a whirlwind by quote liberating unquote the colonial peoples. . . . I stand for government by an *élite*. . . . And voting graded by each individual's rating in that *élite*. . . . You give me any more of that liberal crap and I'll have your balls for a bow tie.

These were stark views, however distanced by the drunken persona of Henderson; the statements about the Japanese were also completely misguided. From Bond, these views would have been totally out of place. Bond changes the subject but admits that "there's a certain aboriginal common sense" in Henderson's words. Bond's remark might suggest that Fleming did indeed wish to be identified with Henderson's diatribe, but the use of the word *aboriginal* imparted an irony to Bond's comment. Henderson's lack of sympathy with democracy, contempt for liberalism and support for nobility or elitism all reflected themes found elsewhere in the Bond novels, although never expressed hitherto with this bitterness and bluntness. Indeed, the comment on the "colonial people" would not have been out of place on the lips of one of Fleming's villains, although their serpentine guile and viciousness lacked the bluntness and honesty of Henderson. In *From Russia, With Love*, Kerim had also been skeptical about democracy. Lunching with Bond, he berates the waiter and explains that such treatment is all "these damned people" understand. "All this pretence of democracy is killing them. They want some sultans and wars and rape and fun. Poor brutes, in their striped suits and bowler hats. They are miserable."

Such views were commonplace in the late 1950s and early 1960s. The racism of Henderson's diatribe was very much Fleming's. He believed in distinct races and particular ethnic characteristics, and this sense of the Japanese as different, an attitude supported by many Japanese commentators, provided much of the energy behind the Japanese travelog. Fleming's sense of inherent characteristics is revealed later in the book when Bond queries Tiger's criticism of Americans in Japan. Bond suggests that such men are likely "second generation" Americans of Irish, German, Czech or Polish blood who would be better suited to work in the fields and mines of their homelands rather than serving as occupying troops.

Taken to meet Tiger, Bond is at once put upon the defensive by the latter's knowledge that the CIA is no longer providing Britain with information as willingly as in the past. Bond counters that, thanks to Australia, Britain has legitimate interests in the Pacific. Tiger, however, emphasizes British weakness, telling Bond that had Japan struck at Australia, rather than Pearl Harbor, in 1941, Britain would have been unable to defend it or New Zealand, and that Japan would now own half the Commonwealth. This was a not unreasonable view. Without America's leading role in the conflict with Japan, Britain would not have been in a good condition to defend its South Asian empire and Dominion allies in 1942.

Tiger subsequently reveals that M's pride, an intelligence network in China known as the Macao Blue Route, has been penetrated by the Japanese. To demonstrate the value of Japan's MAGIC 44 decyphering system, Tiger provides Bond with an intercept from Khrushchev to Soviet envoys in which he spells out his plans. Britain is to be threatened with nuclear attack in order to obtain the removal of all American bases from Britain and its nuclear disarmament, a nuclear blackmail indeed comparable to that feared by the Americans in 1962 as likely to arise from the deployment of Soviet missiles in Cuba.

According to Tiger's intercept, Khrushchev doubts that the United States will risk a nuclear war to protect an ally with so little remaining value. If successful, the same strategy will be pursued in Europe and, then, the Pacific in order to end up with a secure USSR. As a prelude, all Soviet citizens will be withdrawn from Britain. Indeed Soviet planning did aim to exploit NATO divisions in order to encourage defections or neutrality. Furthermore, the British government feared nuclear blackmail. A paper of 1959 from the Department of Operational Research considered the possibility that the Soviets would destroy three or four British cities and then threaten "wholesale destruction" if British Polaris submarines were not recalled.

Warned by the leak from Tiger, the British in *You Only Live Twice* confined Soviet personnel in Britain, while Kennedy threatened nuclear war if the Soviets used a nuclear bomb anywhere outside the USSR. As a result, Khrushchev abandoned his scheme. Firmness in short succeeds. This success is related to one of Fleming's characteristic doubts about the public. He believes the man-in-the-street to be unable to understand and appreciate the role of brinkmanship in world politics.

In return for this help, Bond is asked to kill Dr. Guntram Shatterhand, a wealthy Swiss national recently settled in Japan, who had created a garden of poisonous plants in the grounds of the castle he had restored, and had recruited to his assistance former members of the Black Dragon Society, a more powerful version of the now disbanded Chinese tongs. This secret society had included Fascist politicians, thus enabling Fleming to distinguish between Japanese patriots who had fought Britain but were, in other respects, apparently acceptable, such as Tiger, and their more sinister compatriots. The toxic plants of the garden tempt suicides in large numbers and this causes embarrassment to the government, which, somewhat improbably, decides to ask Bond to kill Shatterhand, after an initial attempt to get a Japanese agent into the garden has failed. This is explained as an opportunity for Bond to redeem the reputation of his country, an opportunity outlined by Tiger in a speech that paints a dismal account of modern Britain. Not only has Britain lost her vast empire, but her attempts to flex her muscles at Suez in 1956 only succeeded in a "pitiful bungle." The "moral fibre" of Britain has been sapped by the excessive power of the trade unions, leaving behind "a vacuous, aimless horde . . . whining at the weather and the declining fortunes of the country, and wallowing nostalgically in gossip about the doings of the Royal Family." Bond replies defensively that England (for some reason not Britain) had been bled thin by the World Wars, welfare state politics made the people expect too much for free, decolonization had been overly speedy and the politicans were incompetent; however, "we still climb Everest and beat plenty of the world at plenty of sports and win Nobel Prizes."

This was very much the language of the League of Empire Loyalists, a movement founded in April 1954 by A. K. Chesterton, brother of the novelist G. K. Chesterton and formerly one of Sir Oswald Mosley's lieutenants in the British Union of Fascists. The league never had many members, and the four candidates it ran in parliamentary elections in 1957–64 all did very badly; but it put forward ideas that the bulk of the population had not quite sloughed off. The league merged with the National Front when the latter was formed in 1967, and Chesterton became president of the National Front.

More generally, the contrast made or implied between the "people" (essentially good, effective and efficient, but threatened by bad politics) and the polity (implicitly in decline, corrupt and incompetent) was a stock in trade of people with Fleming's attitudes. Furthermore, his comments offered a social politics: to gamble with the pools or at bingo was presented as vulgar, while the world of the casino was presented as offering an opportunity for "noble" conduct: acts of bravery and chivalry. Snobbery, however, was not restricted to those on the right. In 1947, the prominent historian G. M. Trevelyan complained of living in "an age that has no culture except American films and football pools."

Bond's defense is lamer than the criticism, but, since Tiger claims to agree, it may be taken to represent Fleming's views. The preference for one-liners and wisecracks in the films saved them from the problems and weaknesses of such passages in the novels. Such a honing was an important aspect of the shift from novels to films, and one that reflected the general conventions of adventure films. It also ensured that the politics became less clear, as well as primarily a matter of visual images and thus essentially dependent on the perception of the viewer.

Tiger says that he has taken the same line as Bond with the Japanese prime minister (in real life, Hayato Ikeda while Fleming was writing) only to receive the reply that if Bond can kill Shatterhand he will accept the idea that there is still an elite in Britain and that the valuable information from MAGIC 44 can be entrusted to this group. Bond is to redeem Britain's reputation. This was confused. The idea that the existence of an elite was to be demonstrated by assassination was curious.

For the sake of the mission, Bond is disguised as a Japanese and this leads to an extensive account of Japanese customs. Eventually shown a photograph of Shatterhand, Bond recognizes him as Blofeld, translating his task into a private quest for revenge, rather than anything to do with MAGIC 44. He does not reveal his identification because he fears massive police intervention and an end to any chance of gaining personal revenge. This lack of discipline is not probed but instead is vindicated by the contrasting characters of the two men. Having penetrated the garden of the "Castle of Death," Bond speculates that Blofeld's intention was to revive the Black Dragons and drive democracy from Japan, but he overhears Blofeld explain to Irme Bunt that he is motivated by a desire for fame, the creation of something new in history, a shrine to death, where he can see people die. This was the "politics" of Hitler in the Bunker, not of the expansionist interwar Hitler. Blofeld is presented as unhinged, his scream of anger compared to that of Hitler, while he speaks German, always an indicator of trouble. Thus, the captured Bond is called a *Britischer*.

Bond's capture, when he enters the castle by night, provides an opportunity for a meeting with Blofeld. Bond is treated to an apologia, an account that is very different from the commercial rationale of SPECTRE laid out by Blofeld in *Thunderball*. Instead, in *You Only Live Twice* SPECTRE has been dispensed with as no longer credible or useful. Blofeld has simply become an unhinged megalomaniac, devoured by his own evil. This was an aspect of Fleming running out of steam. His novels were becoming programatic, and their plots were coming to lose bite. This could be presented as a consequence of a limited, or at least static, political, social and moral vision, but it is more realistic to attribute the problem to the difficulty of maintaining drive and novelty and the growing mental exhaustion of the increasingly ill and demoralized Fleming.

In his apologia, Blofeld offers a powerful critique of power politics, but placing such sentiments in the mouth of someone already described as a madman possibly implies that they are dishonest and dangerous. He had used two atomic weapons to hold the Western world hostage in Operation Thunderball. He compares the scenario to that of a poor child holding for ransom the expensive toys of some rich boys. "If I had been successful, and the money had been handed over might not the threat of a recurrence of my attempt have led to serious disarmament talks, to an abandonment of these dangerous toys that might so easily get into the wrong hands?" Blofeld believes that England is sick and that "hastening the sickness to the brink of death" would inspire a renewed national effort.

The emphasis on the need for revival and national effort, the belief that war makes a people strong, accorded with the views of disaffected right-wing commentators. It had Social Darwinian, and even Fascistic, connotations but was by no means restricted to the right. No such explanation is offered for the evil castle. Blofeld confesses, as Mr. Big had done in *Live and Let Die*, to total boredom, a lassitude that required sharp stimulation. This had led him to devise his suicide garden, which he presents as a public service. Although earlier in the book it had been suggested that the poison plants could serve as a source for toxins, this theme, similar to that of *On Her Majesty's Secret Service*, is not developed. Instead, Blofeld is revealed to share Mr. Big and Dr. No's interest in cruel experiments.

Having fought off Blofeld's attempt to kill him and strangled the villain, Bond escapes by balloon, only to be hit by gunfire from the castle. The castle itself then explodes as a result of Bond having earlier altered the wheel controling the geyser underneath it after he had killed Blofeld. Falling into the sea, Bond is rescued by Kissy Suzuki, the Japanese pearl-fisher with whom he had been living when preparing for his mission. He has lost his memory and is cared for by Kissy, but he is puzzled by dreams of a different world and, having seen the word Vladivostok on some newspaper used as lavatory paper, determines to go there in the hope that he will be able to awaken his memories.

At the close of the novel, the outside world had meanwhile been treated in the *Times* to Bond's obituary. Penned by M, this included an example of the interplay with the real world that Fleming liked so well. In this case, the ironic and somewhat overlong joke was at his own expense, as the obituary noted that James Bond had inspired a number of popular fictional works, written by a colleague in the Secret Service.

If the quality of these books, or their degree of veracity, had been any higher, the author would certainly have been prosecuted under the Official Secrets Act. It is a measure of the disdain in which these fictions are held at the Ministry, that action has not yet—I emphasize the qualification—been taken against the author and publisher of these high-flown and romanticized caricatures of episodes in the career of an outstanding public servant.

3

The Later Fleming Stories

THE SPY WHO LOVED ME: A STORY OUT OF SEQUENCE

It's all out of date—Stone Age stuff.

—Vivienne Michel

The Spy Who Loved Me, published in 1962, is the joker in the pack of Bond novels; not that it is at all funny—indeed, far from it. Bond is not central to the story; instead he appears only toward the close. As a consequence, he is not a narrator, and the full panoply of a Bond novel, animated by his presence, is absent. The nearest equivalent is "Quantum of Solace," a tale of marital relations in the West Indies told to Bond in *For Your Eyes Only* (1960).

In *The Spy Who Loved Me*, rather than being introduced to the plot through the world of "Universal Export," the apparatus of the British Secret Service, the readers are treated to the life story of a young Canadian woman in Britain, Vivienne Michel. By Bond's standards, this is very much "kitchen sink" realism, as seen in John Braine's novel *Room at the Top*, the film of which appeared in 1959. Her growing up is presented in unflinching terms, especially the loss of her virginity to a selfish sixth-form Etonian in a Windsor cinema. This, as well as the eventual nature of Vivienne's union with Bond— "he had taken me as his reward"—aroused the ire of critics, and *The Spy Who Loved Me* received the worst reception of all the Bond books.

In a way this was ironic, because some aspects of the book ensured that it was the most realistic of the series. That, in large part, may have affected its popularity. Here, as in *You Only Live Twice*, was an attempt to capture the details of life, a world beyond that of the glitz of the Ritz. Yet in *You Only Live Twice* this could be presented as travelogue. The use of women in the novel, for example as geisha girls, was in many respects more reprehensible than anything involving Bond in *The Spy Who Loved Me*, but, somehow, the unfamiliarity and exoticism of the setting and Fleming's success in conveying, through Tiger, the sense of relative values blunted the critical edge. This deployment of a sense of relative values was more generally the case with the British Empire (and empires of other European powers), especially with the use or abuse of women and servants.

The Spy Who Loved Me offered social reality in familiar settings— Windsor and London—and this aspect of the novel was thus harder to ignore. Furthermore, the story was much the most ambitious of the series. The narrator was a woman, she was presented as a complex character and Bond was seen from her perspective. These were new challenges for Fleming and, in general, he met them successfully.

The plot itself was possibly the darkest of the series, although it was not affected by the grave pessimism about Britain reflected in *You Only Live Twice*, which was published two years later. Nor did it anticipate the absurdity of the latter story. Instead, *The Spy Who Loved Me* was an account of the vulnerable under challenge, of the manipulative nature of individuals and of the possibility of being trapped by evil. Whereas the intended victims of Blofeld in his trilogy with Bond had been respectively the British and American governments, turkeys and British government finances, and the reputation of Japan, in *The Spy Who Loved Me*, the victim is a person, one whose life and experiences have been presented in the round.

There are, of course, other victims in the Bond novels, women such as Honeychilde Rider in *Dr. No*, whom Bond helps and saves. They are presented through their voices or, in the case of the tragic Vesper Lynd in *Casino Royale*, a suicide's letter. Yet, however important these women are to the plot, none of them is the story. Vivienne is different. Much space is devoted to her exploitation by her two previous lovers. These accounts provide Fleming with opportunities for stereotyping. The second lover, Kurt, is a caricature, a proper and cruel German, a racialist romantic who does not understand love or care. Having got Vivienne pregnant, he discards her, as lover, person, employee and link, and makes her get an abortion, a course that exposes her to the avarice of the Swiss—never Fleming's favorite people, as is seen most clearly in *On Her Majesty's Secret Service*.

The first lover, Derek, is equally manipulative and, in a way, even nastier. A wealthy English public schoolboy, he treats Vivienne cruelly, both emotionally and sexually. Having taken her, he refuses to see her and writes to tell her that she is socially unacceptable as a match and that he is already engaged to a near neighbor who is acceptable. Given Fleming's time at Eton and his social milieu, this account can be seen as more realistic than that of the caricature German. Moreover, it is difficult to understand how the novel can be seen as advocating callousness to women, for, however Bond's night with Vivienne is presented, her first lover is presumably intended as a contrast and he is clearly shown as vile. Bond was also supposed to have been at Eton prior to being expelled for a relationship with a maid, but in this he was not shown as akin to Derek.

Other appalling specimens present themselves when Vivienne, returned from the corrupt old world, sets out as a free spirit to go by motorbike from Canada to Florida, working, as necessary, en route, in order to supplement her meager budget. Her independence makes her vulnerable, a characteristic of Bond girls that reflected the dominant ethos of the period. She is left to close down a remote motel near Lake George, where she has been working as a receptionist at the end of the season. Alone, she has the solace of the radio, but she is interrupted by two vicious hoodlums, the appropriately named Slugsby and Horror, who claim to be working for the motel's owner, Mr. Sanguinetti, a name that reflects Fleming's hostile view of Italian-Americans. They make vicious threats toward Vivienne and block her attempt to escape. Sanguinetti wants Vivienne killed as part of an insurance fraud in which she would be blamed for the burning down of the motel. The combination of ethnicity and corrosive commercialism reflects Fleming's concerns. Prior to World War II, such anxieties and attitudes had been particularly directed against Jews. Slugsby and Horror are just about to rape Vivienne when Bond arrives and demands a room for the night, forcing the crooks to reconsider their plans. It is a scene out of melodrama. Bond is the providential deliverer.

Vivienne explains her plight and Bond reveals what he is doing there. A leading Soviet naval constructor with a specialty in nuclear submarines had defected to Britain, been debriefed and been settled in Canada. The Soviets wanted him killed and SPECTRE agreed to do so for £100,000. SPECTRE's role is not crucial to the plot, and indeed the organization plays only a minor role in the story. However, mention of SPECTRE helps to link the plot to the rest of the Bond corpus.

When the Mounties report that Horst Uhlmann, an ex-Gestapo agent in Toronto, had been trying to recruit local gangland support to kill the defector, Bond is sent to stop Uhlmann. Thus, as so often with Fleming, the Nazis and the Soviets are brought together. Soviet use of ex-Nazis underlines the evils of Communism. Criminals are also a threat. They provide opportunities for foreign opponents. Crime has to be held at bay.

Bond is substituted for Boris and the attempted assault on his apartment by the Mechanics Gang blocked, Uhlmann being fatally wounded by Bond. Bond is then ordered to Washington to get support in winding up the American end of the gang. He has a puncture en route and thus ends up at the motel.

Slugsby and Horror, comic-book villains with comic-book names, who recall the Spangs in *Diamonds Are Forever*, try to kill Bond and Vivienne, but, in a night of shooting, they are both apparently killed. Bond and Vivienne then have what Vivienne terms "full love." Slugsby comes back, is definitively killed, and Bond drives off, having ensured that Vivienne will receive care and a reward. An American police captain, Stonor, then offers the younger Vivienne his views on people like Bond:

This underground war . . . this crime battle that's always going on—whether it's being fought between cops and robbers or between spies and counter-spies . . . in the higher ranks of these forces . . . there's a deadly quality in the persons involved which is common to both—to both friends and enemies. . . . [T]he top spies and the top counter-spies are cold-hearted, cold-blooded, ruthless, tough, killers . . . whether they're called James Bond or Slugsby Morant . . . belong to a private jungle.

Such a jungle was indeed what had been displayed in *The Spy Who Loved Me*, but Fleming shows clearly that Bond's behavior was very different from that of Slugsby: Vivienne's response, in heart, mind and body, makes this readily apparent. Indeed, Bond is, as he confesses, a somewhat incompetent killer at the motel, missing opportunities to kill the criminals.

Bond himself had anticipated Stonor's point, suggesting that there was little of value in his job. Explaining double and triple agents to Vivienne, he says

It's nothing but a complicated game, really. But then so's international politics, diplomacy—all the trappings of nationalism and the power complex that goes on between countries. Nobody will stop playing the game. It's like the hunting instinct.

Vivienne replies

It all seems idiotic to my generation. Like playing that old game "Attaque," really. We need some more Jack Kennedys. It's all these old people about. They ought to hand the world over to younger people who haven't got the idea of war stuck in their subconscious. As if it were the only solution. Like beating children. It's much the same thing. It's all out of date—Stone Age stuff.

Bond smiles and says, "As a matter of fact I agree, but don't spread your ideas too widely or I'll find myself out of a job."

This description of Bond as redundant might be regarded as, at once, both a sign of his charming attempt to put a vulnerable woman at her ease and a hard-headed introspective view reflecting Fleming's disillusionment. He is one of "these old people," certainly in comparison to people of Vivienne's generation, or indeed, Kennedy. Yet a somewhat different account is provided when Bond explains why he has to stop Slugsby and Horror from escaping. He emphasizes their continued threat to himself and Vivienne, adding: "And I can't let them get away with it. These are killers. They'll be off killing someone else tomorrow." Bond has a duty wider than that of his role in Vivienne's "idiotic" game.

THE MAN WITH THE GOLDEN GUN: A LAST SHOT

The first law for a secret agent is to get his geography right.

Posthumously published in 1965, *The Man with the Golden Gun* was written while Fleming was ill and was only able to work for one and a half hours a day: he died on 12 August 1964. It is not Fleming's best story and lacks depth. Fleming's publishers, Jonathan Cape, hired Kingsley Amis, a successful novelist and Bond fan, to try to improve it. The plot continued from *You Only Live Twice* but was far from seamless. That novel had left Bond setting out for Vladivostok, and the new one begins with his return to London. His arrival from the dead causes surprise and suspicion that he has in some way been influenced by the KGB, but M agrees to see him. Bond tells M that he had been well treated by the KGB and persuaded of the "need for East and West to work together for world peace. They made clear a lot of things that hadn't occurred to me before." Bond tells M that he has used him as a tool, and that the Soviets are ready to disarm and to disband the KGB if the West would reciprocate, a standard theme in Soviet propaganda. Bond adds that he has returned in order to "fight for peace" and eliminate the warmongers, starting with M.

Bond then tries to shoot M with a cyanide pistol, but M, fore-warned by Bond's diatribe, saves himself by pressing a button that releases a ceiling-mounted sheet of armorplate glass. M orders a reversal of Bond's brainwashing by the Soviets and proposes to expiate his action by sending him against Francisco "Pistols" Scaramanga, the Man with the Golden Gun. A freelance assassin, mainly under KGB control through the Cuban secret service, Scaramanga had caused many causalities among the Secret Service and CIA since 1959, the year Fidel Castro came to power. Prior to that, he had worked for the Mafia as a Las Vegas executioner.

The "politics" of the plot are thin. Mark Hazard (Bond) is hired by Scaramanga as "muscle" to help him deal with potentially trouble-some investors in a Jamacian casino-hotel project that is behind schedule. These investors turn out to be prominent in organized crime in the United States, and Bond discovers Leiter and another American agent, Nick Nicholson, under cover at the hotel. The casino-hotel scheme is serving as the nexus for KGB and Mafia interests. Their association is designed to underline the threat from the Mafia, and it also implies that they are un-American. It is a parallel to the remark about "second-generation Americans" in *You Only Live Twice* and suggests that Fleming did not understand, and certainly did not sympathize with, the dynamics of American society. It is ironic that he appears nevertheless to have been conned by John Kennedy's charm, for the Kennedy clan were from Irish immigrant stock and had Mafia links. Fleming's essentially static idealistic conception of America and the Americans did not match the democratizing thrust of American history, and, as a description of the United States, was anyway one that was being rapidly eroded by change.

The plans of the KGB are detailed at length in order to make the sinister nature of Soviet schemes both apparent and threatening. Bond overhears Hendricks, the KGB controller, discussing with Scaramanga sabotage against Reynolds Metal, Kaiser Bauxite and Alumina of Jamaica. The first two had already been mentioned by Fleming as Soviet targets in *Live and Let Die*, and the new reference reflects his concern with strategic metals. Scaramanga comments, "I sure snickered when I saw that the how-do-it labels on the drums were in some of these African languages as well as English. Ready for the big black uprising, huh?" This remark links Soviet interests, terrorism and Black Power, a standard theme in right-wing commentary of the period. Hendriks tells Scaramanga that his shares will be badly hit, a warning from Fleming to all shareholders, and then asks him if he can provide large quantities of marijuana for the American market. Scaramanga, in turn, tries to engage Hendriks's interest in supporting the casino scheme, portraying it both as a way to make money and as a possible source of political tension:

Coloured people'll be turned away from the doors for one reason or another. Then the Opposition party'll get hold of that and raise hell about colour bars and so on. With all the money flying about, the unions'll push wages through the roof. . . . This'll be a cheap way of raising plenty of hell. That's what your people want, isn't it?

The implication is clear: opponents of racial discrimination and trade unionists both serve Soviet interests. Scaramanga also presses Hendriks on the need to block the Maracaibo Bar in Venezuela in order to harm the oil industry, or to employ the threat of such action in order to extort money from the oil industry.

Aside from future plans, there were also present schemes, especially sabotage of the Jamaican and Trinidadian sugarcane crop, in order to improve the sales position for the Cuban competition, and thus support Castro. Scaramanga provides Rastifarians with marijuana in return for fires in the plantations. He also wants to use drugs in order to win Mafia support for Communist schemes. As in "Risico," one of the stories in For Your Eyes Only (1960), drugs serve as a link between organized crime and the Soviet threat. The rising threat of drugs had been neglected in the early Bond novels but became more prominent thereafter. Drugs were a source of SPECTRE's funds.

The Americans are presented as seeking to keep the price of sugar low in order to put pressure on Castro. A certain amount of skepticism is expressed about the likely success of American policy. Scaramanga tells Hendriks that "largely thanks to the Americans leaning on Cuba the way they do, he's [Castro's] kept the country together. If the Americans once let up on their propaganda and needling and so forth, perhaps even make a friendly gesture or two, all the steam'll go out of the little man."

It is likely that this expressed Fleming's view, but it was couched cautiously. The room for the robust independence of the United States displayed in the early Bond novels had been undercut by Suez, the dismantling of empire and domestic problems, as was noted by Tiger Tanaka. It was credible to see the British Secret Service as playing a role in Jamaica, a former colony, but the global scope last outlined in *Thunderball* (1961) had gone. The British had played only a marginal role in the Cuban Crisis of 1962.

In the violent climax to the book, Leiter sabotaged a train carrying him, Scaramanga, Hendriks, the Mafia men and a captive Bond. Bond kills Hendriks on the train, while he later shoots Scaramanga dead in a nearby swamp.

Britain is no longer the imperial power. Unlike at the close of *Dr. No*, the officials are no longer British and praise has now to be distributed at the behest of the independent government of Jamaica: independence had been granted in 1962. A judicial inquiry produces an account of Bond's operation that is misleading. The commissioner of police inaccurately reports that Bond, Nicholson and Leiter carried out their duties "under the closest liaison and direction of the Jamaican CID." The three men are awarded the Jamaican Police Medal for "Services to the Independent State of Jamaica." The empire had gone.

OCTOPUSSY: A FINAL BOOK FROM FLEMING

Fleming's three short stories, "Octopussy," "The Living Daylights" and "The Property of a Lady," were published together under the title *Octopussy* in 1966. The last had been written for Sotheby's yearbook, *The Ivory Hammer*, in 1963, while "The Living Daylights" appeared in the first *Sunday Times* color supplement in 1962, an issue entitled "A Sharp Look at the Mood of Britain" that depicted a new sense of national purpose and classlessness.

Written the same year, during a visit to Jamaica, "Octopussy" was a powerful work about guilt and punishment, but not one with a political agenda. Shorn of the large cast of other Bond stories, the story presented Major Dexter Smythe, a former British commando officer living a purposeless life on the north coast of Jamaica, his only real company the octopus Octopussy and the local fish. He is visited by Bond, who questions him about his conduct at the end of the war when he had been part of a unit tracking down Gestapo and Abwehr hideouts in the Tyrol. Having discovered the location of two bags of hidden Nazi gold, Smythe had arrested Oberhauser, an alpine guide, got him to lead him to the site and then killed him. His secret at last exposed, Smythe, the major character in the story, is told by

Bond that he will be arrested and tried, but he first dies when trying
to feed scorpion fish to Octopussy.

Oberhauser had taught the young Bond to ski, and had, for a time,
been a father figure. Thus, the story represented the working out
of a crime from the war, with a resolution that ended the ruin of
Smythe's life. As so often with Fleming, World War II was the defining moment or period, although, in this case, the temptations of
the conflict had led a Briton to show evil. When Bond arrived,
Smythe was already drinking himself to death, and both that and his
unwanted killing by Octopussy were apparently regarded as more
appropriate than "the indignity, the dreary formalities, the headlines,
the boredom and drabness of a life sentence that would inevitably
end with his third coronary." Fleming's juxtaposition of the world of
the coral reef with human justice did not suggest that the latter was
better. The eventual film of the title had nothing to do with the story
with the exception of the mention of a figure modeled on Smythe,
who is, however, the father of the heroine, the *Octopussy* of the
screen.

"The Property of a Lady" was an account of the identification of
the Soviet head of section in London at a Sotheby's auction. Part of
the plot centered on the idea that the British were feeding false information to a Soviet mole they knew to be in the Secret Service.
The mole has a Jewish, Central European name, Maria Freudenstein,
not obviously so as she was born in Paris, and, in what is intended
as a psychological insight, Bond describes her as plain, unloved, and
illegitimate.

Perhaps her only pleasure in life was . . . the knowledge that she was cleverer
than all those around her, that she was, every day, hitting back against the
world. . . . One day they'd be sorry! It was a common neurotic pattern—the
revenge of the ugly duckling on society.

The notion that treason might arise from ideology was not mentioned. The Emerald Sphere that is auctioned at Sotheby's had been
a gift received by Freudenstein, which the British suspected had
come from the KGB. They hoped correctly that the KGB would send
a senior agent to bid up the sphere at the auction. He is identified
as a consequence. The physical description—"squat neck . . . slight
hump," is again harsh.

In "The Living Daylights," originally published in 1962 as "The
Berlin Escape," Bond is sent to Berlin to kill "Trigger," a Soviet sniper
ordered to assassinate "272" when he tries to cross from East to West
Berlin. M gives Bond a background redolent of Cold War tension.
272 has information on a series of planned Soviet atomic tests in-

tended to put pressure on the West over Berlin that "makes nonsense of the Geneva Conference and all this blether about nuclear disarmament the Communist bloc are putting out," the last a view that Fleming endorses by giving it to M. The courier that 272 entrusted with news of his crossing point was a double, but the British have broken the KGB code, giving details of the double's information. Thus signals intelligence complements, rather than clashes with, the role of agents in the field.

Bond and Trigger separately cover the crossing point. Bond recognizes Trigger as a beautiful woman he had admired from afar and deliberately shoots not her, but her gun. Trigger has time to get off a burst, but it misses 272, who crosses safely. As the story closes, Bond is told by his escorting officer that he will be reported for defying his orders to "exterminate Trigger." This is a clash far greater than the humorous, but harmless, kicks against authority of the film Bond, with the important exception of *Licence To Kill* (1989). On the screen the issue of obedience is trivialized. In the books it is serious.

4

Pressing the Boundaries

These blithering women who thought they could do a man's work.
Why the hell couldn't they stay at home and mind their pots and
pans and stick to their frocks and gossip and leave men's work to
the men. . . . For Vesper to fall for an old trick like that and get
herself snatched and probably held to ransom like some bloody heroine in a strip cartoon. The silly bitch.
—Bond totally misjudging Vesper Lynd in *Casino Royale*

Fleming was criticized frequently for crossing, if not ignoring,
boundaries in the Bond novels, boundaries of judgment, taste and
sensitivity. Such criticisms focused on gender and cruelty, more particularly accusations that his work disparaged women and revealed
a sadistic interest in pain, especially torture. Today, his presentation
of alleged national characteristics and conduct, as in *Moonraker*,
would lead to criticism on the grounds, at the very least, of insensitivity, if not racism, while his belief in racial characteristics might
also lead to charges of naivety or worse. Last, Fleming's disparaging

comments about homosexuals, for example the "pansified Italian" in *Goldfinger*, would not accord with modern sensitivities.

An article by Yuri Zhukov in *Pravda* of 30 September 1965 presented Bond as being without political bounds:

James Bond lives in a nightmarish world where laws are written at the point of a gun, where coercion and rape are considered valour and murder is a funny trick. All this is designed to teach people to accept the antics of American marines somewhere in the Mekong Delta in Vietnam or Her Majesty's Intelligence agents in Hong Kong and Aden. Bond's job is to guard the interests of the property class, and he is no better than the youths Hitler boasted he would bring up like wild beasts to be able to kill without thinking.

His creator is Ian Fleming, who posed as *The Times* correspondent in Russia in 1939 but was in truth a spy for the capitalist nations. Although he is now dead, James Bond cannot be allowed to die because he teaches those sent to kill in Vietnam, the Congo, the Dominican Republic and many other places. It is no accident that sham agents of Soviet counter-intelligence, represented in caricature form, invariably figure in the role of Bond's opponents, because Bond kills right and left the men Fleming wanted to kill—Russians, Reds and Yellows. Bond is portrayed as a sort of white archangel, destroying the impure races.

The Bond cult started in 1963 when the American leader, President Kennedy, unsuspecting that some American hero with the right to kill would shoot him, too, declared that Fleming's books were his bedside reading. As if by a magic wand, everything changed. The mighty forces of reaction immediately gave the green light to Fleming. And in James Bond he has created a symbol of the civilization which has used bombs to drown the voice of conscience. The men and women who allow their talents to be used in the making of films about the exploits of this man are also guilty of furthering the shameful aims of the Western Capitalists.

To another critic, Umberto Eco, Fleming's use of stock figures, myths and fetishes was reactionary and fascistic.

Much criticism is misplaced, because the Bond persona, from start to finish, is all about limits, and Fleming clearly attempted to give his creation both depth and complexity, certainly more so than "Sapper" provided his hero Captain Hugh "Bull-Dog" Drummond with, although they shared a taste for Bentleys. An image of Bond as an automaton is presented, "fired by M, like a projectile" ("The Living Daylights") and "a supremely effective firing-piece" (*The Man With the Golden Gun*). It is dismissed, however, in the words used by Bond and in Fleming's descriptions of him. He does not kill without thinking. This is true both of the novels and of the short stories.

Indeed, "The Living Daylights" establishes this contrast clearly. Both Bond and M dislike the task, while Captain Paul Sender, number 2 at Berlin, has no compunction about criticizing Bond for not killing the Soviet sniper. The contrast is worth bringing out, because, at a time when film was removing the complexity of the Bond character, this story underlines the notion of a spy with a conscience, not an extension of a weapon. It is significant that this episode was not treated on film until *The Living Daylights* appeared as a film in 1987. It was then transposed to Bratislava, but the essence of the story was the same. Bond again deliberately avoided killing a sniper, leading to recriminations, although in the film the sniper was in fact an amateur who was not intended to kill the supposed target. *The Living Daylights* was possibly the darkest portrayal of Bond on screen, a Bond contemptuous of his orders and willing to defy instructions accordingly, rather than to ignore them out of fun or to fulfill the mission. Such an account had hitherto been confined to the printed page.

When, in the story "The Living Daylights" M summons Bond, he is gloomy and bitter, disliking the orders he had to give: "This was going to be dirty work. . . . bad news, dirty news. This was to be murder." M is also presented as having a conscience. Far from being a "cold-hearted bastard," M, as Bond knows, puts on a "fierce, cold act of command," to take some of the pressure and guilt off the killer's shoulders, because M does not like sending anyone to a killing. Bond, in turn, has the sense of responsibility that Sender lacks: "He didn't like the job, but on the whole he'd rather have it himself than have the responsibility of ordering someone else to go and do it." Bond himself justifies his orders, but he is shown as angry about the situation: "it was the life of this man Trigger against the life of 272. It wasn't *exactly* murder. Pretty near it, though." Indeed, Bond communicates his anger by driving in an aggressive and angry fashion, an association that throws light on some of Bond's habits. He has to control the potential tension of his missions.

The notion of conscience is dramatized in Bond's relationship with Sender, the psychological drama of the story, for Trigger never speaks and no other Soviet representative is presented. Bond dislikes Sender at once, seeing him as a repressed, arid individual. At the sight of his Wykehamist tie (signifying that Sender attended Winchester College, a leading private school), Bond is launched on thoughts that presumably reflect those of Fleming and capture tensions within the "Establishment" that commentators such as Zhukov ignored:

He knew the type: backbone of the Civil Service; over-crammed and under-loved at Winchester; a good second in PPE at Oxford; the war, staff jobs he would have done meticulously; perhaps an OBE; Allied Control Commission in

Germany where he had been recruited into the I Branch and thence . . . into the Secret Service.

Sender, indeed, was far more typical of the Secret Service than Bond, and Fleming knew that the wartime buccaneering of his own naval intelligence days had long been replaced by a utilitarian bureaucracy, a theme that was to be captured in the films when Edward Fox in *Never Say Never Again* (1983) and Judi Dench in *Golden Eye* (1995) took over as M. In the story, Sender ignores both Bond's tiredness when he arrives and the vibrant cellist Bond spots on his first night of duty, and he causes a fuss when Bond pours himself a strong whiskey on his third night, threatening to report him for breaking training. Bond's response is that of the man of action who has already in the story sneered at his profession when faced with the bureaucrat. It is not that of the carefree Bond of the films:

I've got to commit a murder tonight. Not you. Me. So be a good chap and stuff it, would you? . . . I'd be quite happy for you to get me sacked from the Double-O section. Then I could settle down and make a snug nest of papers as an ordinary staffer.

They clash more seriously after Bond fires in order to miss Trigger, now revealed as the beautiful cellist, but, instead, to hit the gun. Sender demands to know why Bond altered his aim and, instead of lying, as he could easily have done, Bond tells him simply "Trigger was a woman" and subsequently explains that she was the cellist. Sender is unmoved, points out that the KGB has plenty of female agents and emphasizes "clear orders" and Sender's duty to report him. Bond, however, sympathizes with Trigger, probably wounded by his shot, her nerve broken, and likely to be court-martialed for failure. Wearily he notes "With any luck it'll cost me my Double-O number."

This is not the voice of a callous killer, nor the authorial conclusion of a writer delighting in slaughter and pain. Indeed, the pain in the story is of Bond's sharp pang of longing when he first sees the cellist. The story, it is true, includes a different version of the male-female relationship. Having decided against a visit to a Berlin brothel, Bond instead buys a novel about the fall and degradation of Gräfin Liselotte Mutzenbacher, a choice prompted by the jacket which depicted a scantily clad woman strapped to a bed, that he subsequently greatly enjoys. Sender, in contrast, is able to identify the pieces from Borodin's *Prince Igor* played by the orchestra seeking to cover Trigger's mission. Sender is the aesthete, doubtless proper in his treatment of women, but he is cold, lifeless and unable to understand, let alone share, Bond's response to Trigger. Bond is thrilled by his novel, although not obviously as a sadist: "Now then, Liselotte, how in hell are you going to get out of this fix?" Furthermore, however much he can be presented as a voyeur, it is Bond who is sensitive to female appeal and who has both a sense of conscience and a concern about his task.

The limits displayed in "The Living Daylights" are also found elsewhere. Unlike "Red" Grant in *From Russia, With Love*, Bond does not like to kill in cold blood, although he owes his 00 status to one such mission against a Japanese cypher expert in New York. In *The Man With the Golden Gun*, Bond is also hesitant about such killing even when up against a deadly and sadistic assassin, but his reasons are shown to be complex in a fine account of mixed motives. Entering the car behind Scaramanga, Bond debated whether to kill the man with a quick shot to the back of his head—"the old Gestapo-KGB point of puncture."

A mixture of reasons prevented him. . . . an inbuilt dislike of cold murder, the feeling that this was not the predestined moment . . . these, combined with the softness of the night and the fact that the "Sound System" was now playing a good recording of one of his favorites, "After You've Gone", and that cicadas were singing . . . said "No".

The contrast with the Gestapo method is instructive. Bond can never be seen to operate like a Nazi, and any mention of Nazi methods establishes a frame of reference. In reality, while Anthony Eden was prime minister (1955–57), the Secret Service made plans for the assassination of President Gamal Abdel Nasser of Egypt. This, however, was not the tradition of the British adventure story. For the Bond stories to be effective as moral tales, Bond had to be a killer, but not a terrorizer. The novels were primarily tales of antiterrorism, in the sense of identifying a source of terror and then destroying the most visible element of the terror at that time, rather than novels about espionage in the sense of collecting or disseminating information. The ability of the stories to work as tales of antiterrorism rested both on a public sense of being under threat and also on Fleming's success in creating effective villains.

Goldfinger begins with a reflective passage in which Bond reviews an operation against the drug trade, in which, in self-defense, he had killed a Mexican thug. He is revealed as an agent who had never liked killing people and is shocked by the enormity of death. A tense introspection, not present in the films, is portrayed. Bond is "tired of

having to be tough" and has "seen too much death." To the novelist
Kingsley Amis, who made a study of the character, Bond was a "By-
ronic hero."

In salving his conscience and in angry reaction to the recent killing, Bond offers in *Goldfinger* a morbid and rather confused view of
the universality of violence, one that presents him not as the cleanser
of a potentially pure society, but as a product of a world of force and
of a diseased humanity in which people kill each other with cars,
communicable disease and carelessness. "How many people, for example, were involved in manufacturing H-bombs, from the miners
who mined the uranium to the shareholders who owned the mining
shares? Was there any person in the world who wasn't somehow,
perhaps only statistically, involved in killing his neighbour?"

This unsettling passage raises the point about what Bond is fighting
for. As England/Britain and the world are not what they were or
should be, it is not clear why Bond is fighting for them. This is a
point that the novels raise and the films ignore. Fleming's answer,
seen particularly in several of M's comments, is a sense of stoical
duty and an almost disillusioned love of country verging on a cynical
patriotism. This brings the novels closer to those of, for example,
John Le Carré (1931–   ) than is generally claimed—and than Le
Carré, who described the Bond novels as "candyfloss," allowed. They
are superficially more glamorous and less bleak, but, looked at
closer, the bleakness shows through. It is therefore the escape from
the ordinary, the sense of duty for its own sake and the disgust for
a corrupt world that drives Bond on. Fleming offered his readers a
world of barracudas. Without the likes of Bond (and in some stories
him alone), alarming though he was, the readers—the minnows—
would soon be devoured. They are not necessarily worth saving, but
he will risk his life anyway and doesn't expect thanks.

Bond's brief stay in Miami at the start of *Goldfinger* also provides an
insight into his approach to pleasure, again an insight that offers an account rather different from the film persona. In the novels and on
screen, Bond's appeal, in part, lies in being the man who knows what
to do. He is apparently at home in any social situation, knows what
drinks to order and what is regarded as inappropriate or stupid and
what is not, creating an image that appeals to many. Yet, in Miami,
Bond is presented as someone pulled in different directions. Treated
to a sumptuous meal by Junius Du Pont, and told that this was probably the best dinner eaten in the world that night, Bond reflects upon
Du Pont's wealth and the easy life, and he feels disgust but also shame
at this puritanical disgust.

Earlier that evening, self-disgust had led him to think he would drink until "stinking drunk" only to be returned to his bed by "whatever tart he had picked up." Far from being a self-indulgent libertine, Bond had not in fact been drunk for years. Thus, although Bond's womanizing was anathema to M's "Victorian soul," Bond, in turn, was presented as, at least in part, self-disciplined, and this was an important facet of his character. His interest in women was not self-indulgence, but rather the product of restlessness. *The Man With the Golden Gun* closes with a moment of self-recognition:

He said, and meant it, "Goodnight. You're an angel." At the same time, he knew, deep down, that love from Mary Goodnight, or from any other woman, was not enough for him. It would be like taking "a room with a view". For James Bond, the same view would always pall.

Throughout the stories, a moral sense is portrayed. Bond is a gentleman. This is a matter not only of background and conduct, but also of an understanding of self and others. Knowledge, rather than style, is the key to his strength. Bond's self-awareness, as a man with great power, thanks to his 00 status, but with a need to restrict that power in order to retain his self-regard, emerges throughout. To replace self-regard by sanity would be going too far—Bond's psyche is not continuously dramatized—but there is an awareness that his mind, as well as his body, have been placed under great pressure throughout, culminating in the breakdown at the start of *The Man With the Golden Gun*.

This mental battle is all about boundaries and the pressure of roles. Bond cannot be "The man who is only a silhouette" of *Moonraker*. Yet, despite thoughts of retirement and the desire for "easy, soft, high" life, Bond cannot accept a way of life without action. In *From Russia, With Love*, Bond is a man being strangled by "the blubbery arms of the soft life. . . . In his particular line of business, peace had reigned for nearly a year. And peace was killing him." This need for action was far more than psychological, an important point that Fleming drums home with his continual reiteration of danger and menace in the world. In "From A View To A Kill," Bond had warned of the danger that the English would be seen as "soft."

But action is not easy. When, in "For Your Eyes Only," Judy Havelock—who had earlier talked casually about killing—kills Hammerstein, she feels an unexpected sense of pain. Bond responds that "It had to be done. But I told you this sort of thing was man's work," the last a stereotypical comment of the age, but also one designed to emphasize the difficulty of the task. The need to be a man of action, his duty and his conscience create psychological tensions throughout Bond's career.

PART II

TO THE BIG SCREEN

5

The Transition to Film

Tiffany Case: My God. You've just killed James Bond.

Bond, pretending to be the smuggler Peter Franks: It just proves no one's indestructible.

—*Diamonds Are Forever* (1971)

The modern world knows James Bond through the films, not the novels. The intentions of the creator, Ian Fleming, are glimpsed at third hand, and even then only fitfully so after *Goldfinger* (1964). There are naturally many contrasts between the stories of individual books and films, and some will be discussed. Yet it is this very plasticity of the Bond persona that has permitted his adaptation to different contexts.

On the screen, the narrator ceases to be omnipotent. Instead, it is the camera that narrates. That both requires and permits a very different kind of observation. Bond is seen from outside, a process aided by the paucity of reflective passages offered by the screen character and the preference, instead, for one-liners, by the emphasis on

Bond as an action hero and by the somewhat wooden presentation by two of the actors.

If the characterization is different, so also are the politics. The films belong, in the main, to a different era. They largely followed the last flourish of self-assured Edwardian Conservatism under Harold Macmillan, who resigned as prime minister in 1963, the year of Kennedy's assassination. The difference in politics between the books and the films is true both of method and of content. The dossier approach to background materials, seen, for example, in the introduction of Le Chiffre in *Casino Royale*, is, perforce, abandoned, as is the use of other documents, for example, Nikita Khrushchev's decyphered instruction to Soviet envoys from *You Only Live Twice* (1967). Instead, villainy has to be suggested by visual images, for example, the black clothes and dark glasses of the helicopter pilots in *You Only Live Twice*, the black clothes of Largo's men in *Thunderball* (1965) and the black helmets and clothes of the motorcyclists in *For Your Eyes Only* (1981). Such images work best if they are clearly very sinister. When they are diluted, the formula fails to have the same effect. This was true of Elliot Carver, the villain in *Tomorrow Never Dies* (1997). The situation reflects that of a world in which hostile rulers, such as Saddam Hussein, Colonel Muammar Gadhafi or President Slobodan Milosevic, have to be demonized in order to persuade the public to treat them as enemies.

More generally, politics plays a smaller role in the films than in the novels, or, rather, a smaller explicit role. In part, this reflects the different nature of novel and film, but this point cannot be pushed too far. The film *Octopussy* (1983), a work very different from the short story of the title, has an important early plot-setting scene in which a project for a surprise Soviet invasion of Western Europe is outlined by General Orlov and then rejected by the Soviet planners, led by General Gogol, the KGB commander who appeared in numerous films. The idea of Soviet "hawks" and "doves" was indeed popular in Western discussion at this point. *Octopussy*'s plot was explicitly political. Concerned that a "handful of old men in Moscow" were bargaining away the Soviet advantage in disarmament talks, Orlov decides to destabilize the Western alliance by arranging the explosion of an atomic bomb within the main American air base in West Germany, in order to create pressure for unilateral nuclear disarmament: the bomb would not show up on radar as coming with a Soviet missile. This would suggest that it was an American bomb, and thus that the storage of bombs in West Germany and Britain was dangerous.

As a threat, this is a world away from the global destruction of, for example, the film *Moonraker* (1979). In such works, unhinged megalomaniacal plutocrats either sought to exploit global power politics to their own destructive ends, as in *The Spy Who Loved Me* (1977) and *Tomorrow Never Dies* (1997), or are happy to confront all, as in *Diamonds Are Forever* (1971) and *Moonraker*. Whichever approach is taken, the figure of the megalomaniac builds essentially on Fleming's portrayal of Blofeld, and his creation SPECTRE, rather than developing the Cold War theme of the novel *Casino Royale* and the threat from SMERSH.

Initial attempts to translate the Bond stories to the screen had been unsuccessful. It had proved impossible to obtain the necessary financial backing. In 1960 Canadian-born film producer Harry Saltzman bought an option. He was unable to obtain backing until in 1961 he teamed up with American producer Albert "Cubby" Broccoli. They set up Eon Productions and in June 1961 persuaded United Artists to provide the money needed for the production. A six-picture deal was agreed. *Thunderball* was to be the first film, but legal disputes arising from Kevin McClory and Jack Whittingham's work on the original *Thunderball* project in 1959–60 led to the substitution of *Dr. No* (1962).

The Cold War was not central to this film, although it played a role. Directed by Terence Young and produced by Broccoli and Saltzman, the film introduced much of the longstanding cast and devices of the Bond films, most obviously Sean Connery as Bond, but also Bernard Lee as M, Lois Maxwell as Miss Moneypenny, the theme tune by Monty Norman and orchestration, fusing rock and jazz, by John Barry. The film had a master villain and a striking girl, played by a dubbed Ursula Andress. Yet the very start, also, located *Dr. No* as a work of the early 1960s. Having worn a hat in the title sequence, Bond then turns up as one of the dinner-jacketed players in Le Cercle playing chemin-de-fer. Bond is both a timeless figure and one who reflects the circumstances of particular periods.

Dr. No begins with two views of empire—the club in Kingston that is the center of white, male society, and imperial Westminster, a night shot of Big Ben and the Thames, as a prelude to the casino scene. Big Ben and Whitehall were to be employed in many films, for example *Octopussy*. They were symbols not only of Englishness, but also of the timelessness and power of a strong Britain. They were also used in episodes of *The Saint*, a popular television program of the period based on Leslie Charteris's novels and starring Roger Moore as a stylish agent. In *Thunderball*, SPECTRE forces the government as a signal to order Big Ben to strike seven times at 6 P.M., a sign of a fundamental disjuncture.

After the preliminary scene setting, however, *Dr. No* is set in Jamaica. Nevertheless, the British scenes near the start of *Dr. No* have already provided a clear introduction to the political situation. Instead of the slow-paced development in the novel, with Bond sent to Jamaica to investigate Strangway's disappearance, M told Bond at the outset that the Americans have been complaining about massive interference with their Cape Canaveral rocket tests, specifically "topping" by radio waves. Bond's task is to pursue Strangeway's investigations of this subject, rather than the birdlife initially at stake in the novel. Thus, the mystery element of the latter is lacking. Support for the United States, central to British policy during the Cold War, is important to Bond's role. Relations between the two powers had improved since the Suez Crisis of 1956, and America's public image as an ally benefited from Kennedy's election and from his popularity.

In 1962, the year of the film's appearance, a Pentagon memorandum, released in November 1997 by the Assassination Records Review Board, suggested, as part of the campaign to discredit Castro, that if John Glenn failed to return from his first orbit of Earth, "various pieces of evidence could be manufactured which would prove electronic interference [by] the Cubans." The memorandum reflected contemporary confidence in the effectiveness of such interference, while its ruthlessness and mendacity contrasts with the general integrity attributed to Bond.

Furthermore, space was a crucial site of superpower rivalry in the late 1950s and 1960s, an arms race in which the United States, not Britain, represented the West. The importance of Cape Canaveral in strategic terms was enhanced in July 1960 when the submarine USS *George Washington* was responsible off the cape for the first successful underwater firing of a Polaris missile. Two years earlier, in November 1958, the Americans had launched the *Atlas*, their first intercontinental ballistic missile. The ethos and policy of brinkmanship and the threat of massive retaliation developed by John Foster Dulles, secretary of state in 1953–59, was extended from airpower to rockets. They were to provide powerful motifs for the Bond films. In *Dr. No* the Americans are about to send MA7 into a lunar orbit.

The American role in the film *Dr. No* is also made clear when Bond is given a new gun. His Beretta is discarded and M tells him to use a Walther PPK, mentioning that the CIA "swear by them." Bond flies to Kingston via New York, arriving by Pan Am, both signs of American influence, and Felix Leiter is at the airport: he plays no role in the novel. The American role recurs later in the film. Leiter says that the "Limeys" are touchy about his checking to see whether there is any radio interference from Jamaica, while Bond insists that it is up to him, not Leiter, to investigate Crab Key: "it's my beat," an assertion of imperial control. Policing is an expression of power.

As in the novel, Crab Key is the base of Dr. No, but, this time, a Chinese theme was pushed, with Chinese men in uniform in the doctor's entourage. The woman who tries to trap Bond on Jamaica offers him a "Chinese meal," while Bond is certain that Dr. No is from the East because of his callous disregard for human life, a theme repeated in Kingsley Amis's Bond novel *Colonel Sun* (1968).

The Chinese also played sinister roles in the films of *Goldfinger* (1964) and *You Only Live Twice*, although not in the books. In the *Goldfinger* film, Mr. Ling, a Chinaman in Mao uniform, is in league with Goldfinger. He is the agent who recognizes Bond when he is captured by Goldfinger and is a specialist in nuclear fission who arms the "dirty" nuclear bomb that is placed in the vaults of Fort Knox. China has provided Goldfinger with the device, in what 007 terms "an inspired deal . . . they get what they want. Economic chaos in the West." The theme of Oriental menace, which both recycled earlier treatments, such as the Fu Manchu stories, and drew on their continual impact, is underlined in the film *Goldfinger* by the large number of blue-uniformed Orientals who seek to capture Bond in and near Goldfinger's Swiss factory.

China was seen as a growing threat in this period. In 1957 the Soviet Union had signed an agreement with China to provide a prototype atom bomb and the technical data necessary to produce one. The Soviets, however, did not fulfill the agreement and, after the Sino-Soviet split of 1960 and the end of Soviet technical assistance, the Chinese began an independent nuclear program to produce their own bombs and missiles. In October 1964 the Chinese exploded their first atomic bomb, ending the monopoly of such weapons enjoyed by "European" peoples. Concern about China was far stronger in the United States than in Britain and can be seen as an aspect of the Americanization of Bond in the films. In *Thunderball*, SPECTRE distributes Chinese drugs in the United States.

However, the film *Dr. No* is not dominated by the East-West struggle. The meeting between No and Bond reveals the former to be a member of SPECTRE who wishes to look Bond over to see whether he can be recruited for the organization. Unlike in the novel, Dr. No is free of alignments: "East. West. Just points of the compass. Each as stupid as each other." The films were to follow through on this theme, increasingly emphasizing East-West shared interests and cooperation, so that, toward the close of *The Living Daylights* (1987), Bond could tell the villainous arms dealer Brad Whitaker, "If the Russians don't get you, the Americans will."

In *Dr. No*, the two men deride each other. Bond calls Dr. No a minnow pretending to be whale, refers to "world domination. Same old dream," and says the asylums are full of people like Dr. No. The latter, in turn, refers to Bond as "just a stupid policeman whose luck has run out." Of course, Bond escapes and rescues the situation, saving the American missile test and killing Dr. No in an overheating nuclear reactor, after a man-to-man struggle, a crucial feature in the films, but not indeed of the novel *Dr. No*.

Dr. No was based on many past screen villains, such as Fu-Manchu, and set a pattern for future ones, each determined to mold the world to their wishes. Bond's mission became perforce a personal quest to stop them, a theme that reached a high point in confrontations between the captive Bond and his megalomaniac adversary. To the latter, Bond is an irritant, a distraction from the doom of a decadent civilization, but, in fact, Bond becomes the villain's nemesis. Bond's boldness and the villain's hubris are instrumental in the outcome.

As a film, *Dr. No* established the Bond genre and persona on screen. It also made money, lots of money, the basis of Bond's continuing access to the screen. *Dr. No* cost $950,000 and made vast profits, both for the filmmakers and for the publishers, leading to the sale of 1.5 million copies of the book within seven months of the appearance of the film. Popularity led to satire, especially the British film *Carry On Spying* (1964), in which Dr. Crow controlled STENCH, the Society for the Total Extermination of Non-Conforming Humans, and, in place of Bond, the British could rely on agents such as Desmond Simpkins (played by Kenneth Williams), James Bind (Charles Hawtrey), and Crump (Bernard Cribbins) and Honeybutt (Barbara Windsor), the last a play on the Honeychilde of *Dr. No*. Williams and Hawtrey, both homosexuals, were an epicene contrast to everything Bond was supposed to represent, deliberately and hilariously so. Morecambe and Wise's *Intelligence Man* (1966) was another film parody by established British comics. A very different undercutting was provided by the portrayal of Boysie Oakes in the film *The Liquidator* (1965). Oakes was apparently a Bond, a sybaritic assassin for British Special Security, but, in fact, was a coward whose reputation rested on the contract killer he secretly hired.

The pattern of success of *Dr. No* was repeated over the following decade. Sean Connery's Bond films were extremely popular, first in Britain and then elsewhere. *From Russia With Love* (1963) was followed by *Goldfinger* (1964), for which a studio recreation of the Fort Knox vault was created, an expensive task that reflected the profitability of the films. Near the close, there was also an expensive fight sequence involving a large number of actors. In Britain, 200,000 viewers saw *From Russia With Love* in the first week of its release. It was far more stylish, exciting and international than the top television programs in Britain that year: The *Royal Variety Show*, *Coronation Street*, *Steptoe and Son*, *Dr. Finlay's Casebook* and *Drama 63*.

Goldfinger, in turn, grossed nearly $10.5 million in the first fourteen weeks of its North American release. The films spread the popularity of Bond to countries such as France, where the novels had made scant impact. In France a million viewers saw *From Russia With Love* within a month in 1964. Sales of the books, in Britain, the United States and elsewhere, also rose, and more translations appeared. Having sold just over 500,000 copies in Britain in 1961, the total was nearly 6 million in 1964, nearly 7 million in 1965 and 22,792,000 in total in 1962–67.

This popularity can be, and has been, variously explained, making Bond a crucial figure in cultural studies. No single explanation is appropriate for the vast success among a very varied following. Any explanation is unlikely to focus on the politics, understood in the narrow sense of the plots and their presentation of world politics. In a wider sense, however, political meanings can be found in the films, and their appeal, in part, rests on politics. At the most basic level, this is the politics of killing and the attendant mayhem. Politics and plot must provide a situation in which it is both legitimate and necessary to kill, a necessity in the plots of both novels and films. There can be no ambivalence about this, because any would threaten to cut approval of Bond's exploits. Ambivalence might also risk commercial appeal in a more specific fashion by making Bond's mission unacceptable in particular markets.

Thus, plot and appeal required a politics of conviction, specifically the notion of the British Secret Service as a benign force, a view that helps to explain Soviet criticism of the Bond works. M must be authoritative as well as authoritarian, his analysis of the situation fair as well as accurate, Bond's mission necessary as well as legitimate. This moral absolute conditions the bulk of the Bond works and differentiates them from those produced by Len Deighton and John Le Carré. With *The Ipcress File* and *The Spy Who Came In from the Cold*, respectively, their plots reached the screen in 1965 and the protagonists were played by major actors, Michael Caine and Richard Burton. Betrayal played a major role in these plots, as indeed in lesser films, such as *The Kremlin Letter* (1970). Deighton and Le Carré offered espionage stories, and betrayal was central to plot and atmosphere. In contrast, betrayal played far less of a role in the Bond tales, which were adventures masquerading as spy stories. Deighton helped write the script for *Warhead*, a Bond film that was due to be filmed in 1977 but that, for legal reasons, was never produced.

Unflappable competence, frequently underlined by wisecracks, was very important to the characterization of Bond in the films. It suggested an omnicompetence that was important both in specifics, helping Bond thwart villains at particular moments, and in general terms, as an aspect of his character and appeal. Style meant competence, competence ensured style. Competence was enhanced by presence, the presence reinforced by the accoutrements and accessories of the Bond persona. Unflappable competence offered protection against the schemes of villains and, more generally, served both to shore up traditional notions about Britain and to support notions of an effective new Britain. The spoof feature film *Casino Royale* (1967), in which Bond was played by David Niven and Woody Allen played his nephew Jimmy Bond, was a failure, in part due to the combination of a lackluster script and a character that was then difficult to spoof successfully in such a film.

In the Connery and Roger Moore films, there is no sense of moral confusion about either Bond or the Britain he represents. In place of confusion, there is a certain self-depreciation, but it is far from enervating or crippling. The films offered a moral universe in which reliance on Bond representing a reasonable order was total and did not need to be stated. As such, Bond matched the role of lawman in the moral westerns of the period. He is not false, but, instead, as Octopussy remarks, "a man of principle." Although she intends this as a critical remark, her story is, in the end, about the need for principle. In *Diamonds Are Forever*, Bond's integrity contrasts with the cringing insincerity (and consumerism) of Morton Slumber of Slumber, Inc., the crematorium on the diamond-smuggling trail, and also with the "devotion to larceny" of Tiffany Case, who is only too ready to betray the smugglers, and with the deceit of Bert Saxby, Willard Whyte's right-hand man. This element of deceit is captured by Blofeld's willingness to have himself replicated through plastic surgery, by his use of a voice box to disguise his voice and by his escape dressed as a woman. In *Octopussy*, General Orlov and Kamal Khan are happy to betray Octopussy, their partner in jewel smuggling. They trick her and she has to be rescued by Bond. Even a woman who controls a criminal network needs a male rescuer.

Bond expresses no doubts when challenged about his role or ethics. When, in the film of *The Man With the Golden Gun* (1974),

Scaramanga mocks his low rewards, Bond replies that he kills only killers and then only on the orders of the government. Similarly, he tells Octopussy that he is not for hire, only to meet the rejoinder "Naturally you'd do it for Queen and country . . . a paid assassin." Scaramanga derides Bond's sense of fair play, although he then proposes "an indisputable masterpiece . . . a duel between titans" as the "true test" for the two men. This duel reflects Scaramanga's sense of fair play, severely limited as it is. As he shows, he could have killed Bond on his arrival on his island, but he prefers the contest in his trick room. This contest contrasts with Scaramanga's usual killings in cold blood, and the last defined a difference between Bond and his opponents. Bond's willingness to serve was conditional. He did not wish to slaughter the defenseless or even the unwary. In the novel *From Russia, With Love*, Bond is unhappy at the shooting of the killer Krilencu by Kerim Bey: "Bond had never killed in cold blood, and he hadn't liked watching, and helping someone else to do it." This doubt, indeed resentment, is ignored in the film but surfaces in *The Living Daylights* (1987) and *Licence To Kill* (1989).

Although he both represented and safeguarded the Establishment, Bond also reaffirmed the power of the individual. He did so in two ways. First, Bond was presented as a somewhat anarchic figure, defying rules and conventions, having, for example, to be summoned to the office from assignations. He is the last agent to arrive at the meeting for 00s in the film *Thunderball*. Second, his ability to thwart the dastardly schemes of others emphasized the capacity of the individual to affect, indeed effect, a solution in the world of great power politics. This also involves the supremacy of the individual and his qualities over technology and mechanization, a frequent theme of the modern adventure story that reflects unease about modernity and concern about technology, as well as the desire to locate heroism and proficiency in one individual, rather than in the collective. In *Thunderball, You Only Live Twice* and *GoldenEye*, Bond finds camouflaged planes and bases in areas pronounced clear by aerial surveillance.

As an anarchic figure, Bond naturally finds other individualists sympathetic and readily allies with them. This is true both of those who work for his own side, most obviously Kerim Bey in both the book and the film of *From Russia, With Love*, and, more commonly, of independents, such as Pussy Galore, Drago, Colombo and Octopussy, whose commitment to wrongdoing is a matter of illegality, rather than villainy, and of crime, not devastation. The central axis in many of the films becomes that of Bond and these independents against the villains. "We're two of a kind," says Octopussy to Bond.

The Secret Service does not control this relationship, and the independents are the crucial adjunct, a substitute for national strength that is secured by Bond's ability and integrity.

This is analogous, and often linked, to his ability to win the backing of women. The widening circle of Bond's allies eventually extends to include the Soviets. Common threats may lead to political cooperation with the West, as in *The Spy Who Loved Me*, but it is Bond who secures respect, as at the close of *For Your Eyes Only* in which the Soviet KGB leader, General Gogol, a familiar figure, appears as a warmly smiling rival, not an automaton of a vicious bureaucratic state.

Bond's anarchic element included a defiance that, however, was always, prior to *Licence To Kill* (1989), short of rebellion. It served to secure Establishment interests and affirm Establishment views, certainly in the majority of films. The mutual contempt of Edward Fox's M and Connery's 007 in *Never Say Never Again* (1983), the independent remake of *Thunderball*, was not prefigured in the earlier films and was not possible while Bernard Lee was M. The relationship between successive Bonds and Lee's M was far closer to the mutual respect of the novels. The description of Bond as a "sexist, misogynist dinosaur, a relic of the Cold War," by Judi Dench's M in *GoldenEye* (1995) likewise suggested an inappropriate criticism of Bond from the British camp, and again, was a major departure from the novels.

In the plots, Bond's anarchic elements were supposed to be contained by M and his instructions, but, repeatedly, these failed to keep pace with the accelerating spiral of discovery and danger. "You're on your own," as M remarked to 007 before he crossed through the Berlin Wall into East Germany in *Octopussy*. As a consequence, Bond invariably had to improvise, and his ability to remain self-contained at this stage was important both to his persona and to his success.

In control of himself, Bond's anarchic elements were restrained by the values of the amateur gentlemanly tradition, a set of values that reflected the self-image of the British imperial elite, albeit one presented by Bond with few echoes of social exclusion and with the enhancement of new technology. In particular, this tradition was contrasted with the greater orthodoxy, professionalism (in the narrow sense of abiding by rules) and resources of American operations. Indeed, this contrast suggested that the British imperial mission and gentlemanly tradition were still valid, because, thanks to their character and temperament, the British still had something to teach. Bond not only lends style to American operations; he is also instrumental in their success.

Ironically, the first portrayal of Bond on screen was an American, "card-sense Jimmy Bond," in a 1954 CBS hour-long television version of *Casino Royale*. In contrast to the novel, it was the British agent, called Clarence Leiter, who assisted Bond. The Anglo-American power relationship of the book was reversed for American consumption. Le Chiffre was played by a menacing Peter Lorre. In the live broadcast, the audience allegedly saw him get up from the floor when supposedly dead and walk off to his dressing room, but this is not in the video versions available at present. This television *Casino Royale* did not set the pattern for the films. Their Americanization of the Bond character, ethos, context and plot was always partial, certainly did not extend to his nationality and was particularly limited in the early plots.

This is clear from the outset. In the film *Dr. No*, it is Bond, operating alone, not Leiter, who saves the American missile tests, and Bond makes it clear that the American marines should be sent for only if he fails. In the film *Goldfinger*, Leiter and M talk by telephone, offering contrasting images of their societies, neither of which is presented in a negative fashion. Leiter speaks from a light office with the White House in the background, while M's office is a dark, if not somber, wood-paneled room. In one respect, this is the future as opposed to the past, but this past is not presented in a hostile light, is open to new ideas, as with Bond's Aston Martin, and, in the person of Bond, plays a crucial role. When he flies, near the close, to have lunch with the president—then John F. Kennedy—Bond is seen off by a thankful group of American military and civilian officials. They, however, have failed to prevent Goldfinger from hijacking the plane.

In both novels and films, Bond does not require American resources, or what is presented as a slavish German attachment to rules. Instead, he exemplifies the classic Edwardian values of the adventure stories of the interwar years. Bond was established well before the biting anti-Establishment satire of Macmillan's last years and was, indeed, a target for the satire of the period, for example in the magazine *Private Eye*. In the novels and films, in contrast, Bond's moral fiber is never doubted and, in some respects, Bond is thus both the last gasp of Edwardian Britain and a modernizing figure who manages the transition from the 1950s to the 1960s. To that extent, at least initially, he managed to represent the pragmatic and adaptable continuity that the Conservative governments of Churchill, Eden and Macmillan and Home sought in 1951–64 and, in part, managed to secure and maintain until a serious loss of dynamic, purpose, reputation and confidence in 1963–64.

Bond as 1960s modernizer became more apparent in the films, especially from *Goldfinger* (1964) on, with the emphasis on technology and the sophisticated ironic comedy that Connery offered. This matched a shift in British, American and global culture. In Britain the 1960s, with growing individualism, social change, the Beatles, the decriminalization of homosexuality and many other shifts, were challenging the traditions, certainties and myths of Britishness. The notion of the "swinging sixties" was intended as a reinvention of Britishness, but it necessarily involved a criticism and rejection of what had gone before.

There were also important continuities between the content and impact of the novels and the films. An intelligent male hero who does not follow the rules of the Establishment but is an Establishment figure, Bond reflects the way in which many men liked and like to project themselves. He competes with sinister organizations and is a gent, with a taste for the high life.

This identification provided a formula for entertainment success. It did not imply that the films had no political meaning or that they cannot be read as political texts. However, precisely because the politics were not explicit, while the intention of the films might be less important than how the audiences could be expected to respond, it is possible to present different readings. For example, the view of Britain can be seen as characterized by self-confidence or anxiety, the latter reflected in a despairing agenda in which Bond alone can save the country. The ability of the films to contain different readings and to appeal to varied constituencies has been seen as a reason for their success. Certainly, they had to sell in very different markets in order to obtain their global status. The commercial success of Bond relied on high viewing figures in Britain, America, Continental Europe and, increasingly, the rest of the world.

The films are rarely as politically explicit as the novels. There are certainly no equivalents to Bond's comments on British or American society. In the novel *From Russia, With Love* Bond tells Kerim Bey "As for England, the trouble today is that carrots for all are the fashion. At home and abroad. We don't show teeth any more only gums." Such a statement, an echo of interwar themes, such as in the novels of "Sapper," is not the message of the films. The major exception, *Never Say Never Again* (1983), with, for example, the cash-strapped Q, who cannot obtain spare parts and, when he can, finds that strikes prevent deliveries, was a film outside the series, and, in some respects, a satire on it. It was also a comment, looking back from the years of Mrs. Thatcher's Conservative ascendancy (1979–90), upon the troubled Conservative and Labour governments of the 1970s.

The identity and intentions of the enemy in the films does not always really matter. Once the enemy is dissociated from a specific setting, not least by posing a global threat, then he becomes simply another in an inexorable line of megalomaniacs. As such, he can, like Karl Stromberg in *The Spy Who Loved Me* (1977), sit above geopolitics and try to manipulate global rivalries while launching a bid for world domination. It is far from clear that such megalomania can be read as a proxy for the real threat, whatever that is supposed to be. Indeed, the notion of an inevitable ideological conflict was not at the fore in the Bond films. They were curiously unrooted in any particular political situation and thus had more purchase on audiences and were rendered more effective as films.

Such, however, is a very static view. The Bond films have been appearing since 1962 and have been far from constant in tone. Excluding the parody *Casino Royale*, but including Connery's return as Bond in *Never Say Never Again*, there have been twenty Bond films. All, except *Never Say Never Again*, were the work of the same production company, Eon Productions, established by Albert Broccoli and Harry Saltzman. Saltzman would be bought out but, until his death, Broccoli was the producer or coproducer of the series. Broccoli and Saltzman were both based in Britain, but neither was British. Broccoli was American, Saltzman Canadian.

Some of the variety in tone is due to the march of time and the changing expectations and opportunities of cinema. Much is also due to the different actors chosen to play Bond, each of whom had to match or transform the expectations of existing viewers, while inventing him for a new generation. A common line in discussion of the films is the expression of preference for one or other of the actors and the assertion that he is truest to the character. They certainly offer different accounts of the power plays with women and guns that are so central to plot, characterization and atmosphere. The choice was seen as important from the outset. There were six million replies to the campaign in the *Daily Express* in 1960 about who should play Bond. Different Bonds make for different films, most obviously with Roger Moore, whose unsubtle humor came to subvert the character and the genre, and who was possibly the most politically incorrect of the actors in his attitude to women. Yet the Moore films (1973–85) were probably in line with the audience expectations of the time and were very popular. The importance of his relationship with women to Bond's reputation and critical response suggests that, before approaching the films in order of appearance and then reexamining the politics, it is worth considering the sexual politics of Bond.

6

Sexual Politics in the Movies: Heterosexuality and Bond

In the Bond films, there can be no qualms about killing or about admiring killing, although it is sanitized, at least until *Licence To Kill* (1989). In part, such an approach depends on the presentation of the Secret Service's opponents as villains, malevolent, dangerous and sadistic. There is also an inherent rectitude in the British Secret Service. It is a mixture of gentlemen and harder-edged characters, the latter still, however, motivated by a sense of "fair play" as defined in traditional British terms.

Such an analysis was less credible in the 1960s, and even the late 1950s, than in the clubland world of the 1920s. Indeed, a series of scandals, such as the arrest of George Blake in 1961 and the defection of Kim Philby in 1963, compromised the public reputation of the Secret Service in the very period of Bond's greatest popularity. These were scandals of incompetence and dishonesty, of traitors within and failures without. These scandals leave few direct echoes in either the novels or the films, although they may have contributed to the ostentatious masculinity that is such an obvious feature of both. This must of course be traced to Fleming's sense of heroism and his view of the likely readership, but the repeatedly affirmed heterosexuality of Bond is a rejection of the ambiguity that Fleming saw in homosexuality, an ambiguity that was political as much as sexual. The homosexual traitor Guy Burgess was thus the antithesis of Bond.

This issue does not play a major explicit role in the novels. In the Prenderghast case, mentioned in the novel *You Only Live Twice*, homosexuality is linked to treason. In the novel *From Russia, With Love*, Bond disagrees with Captain Troop over the employment of "intellectuals" in the Secret Service. Bond suggests that intellectuals are necessary to counter the "intellectual spy." Troop replies: "I thought we were all agreed that homosexuals were about the worst security risk there is. I can't see the Americans handing over many atom secrets to a lot of pansies soaked in scent."

Bond's reply, "All intellectuals aren't" homosexual, is unacceptable by modern standards (and evades the question of whether "intellectuals" are ambivalent about the purposes and methods of a secret service), but it was enough to cast him as an isolated liberal on the Committee of Inquiry. Indeed, his emphasis on the need for agents who could frequent the Burgess and Maclean cliques, rather than on men "with a trench-coat and a cavalry moustache and a beta minus mind," was indicative of Bond as a forward-thinking individual and modernizer, part of Fleming's portrayal that is sometimes lost, but that helped to make Bond an attractive figure in the early 1960s. Style was not achieved at the expense of thought.

Both in print and on screen, however, Bond finds himself up against homosexuals. In the film *Diamonds Are Forever*, Willard Whyte is guarded for Blofeld by two lesbians, Bambi and Thumper. They are tough, but the two together are beaten by Bond, a symbolic mastering as much as a plot device, while he kills both of Blofeld's homosexual assassins, Wint and Kidd, at the close of the film.

More significant for the plot is the fact that lesbianism in the novel *Goldfinger* is linked to a willingness to serve the villain. Thus, Bond wins over and changes the lesbian Pussy Galore with his sexuality and concludes that her sexual confusion is attributable to women's suffrage and the push for sex equality. "Pansies of both sexes were everywhere, not yet completely homosexual, but confused, not knowing what they were . . . He was sorry for them, but he had no time for them!"

Quite, and indeed he need have no time for them. The passage just quoted indicates how far the attitudes expressed in the novels are seriously dated. In both novels and films, there was no fundamental ambivalence on the British side: neither treason nor homosexuality within the Secret Service. Bond tries to kill M at the outset of the novel *The Man With the Golden Gun* only because he has been brainwashed by the KGB. There might be questionable individuals within the British establishment, most obviously Drax in the novel *Moonraker*, but he was an interloper and there was a bedrock of white knights. Alec Trevelyan, the sole traitor in the Secret Service in the film series, leaves both country and service, and is anyway revealed as having Cossack background and loyalties. For the bulk of *GoldenEye* he operates as head of a Russian crime syndicate, not as a British traitor: the latter would have been far more disturbing.

The films made the point about integrity even more clearly than the novels, providing a visual fleshing out of the British Secret Service and, indeed, of much of the establishment. This is not a world full of what Fleming had termed "pansies," of either sex. Indeed, the scene of British intelligence experts in *From Russia With Love*, listening in London to Bond's radio report about the Spektor decoder, is a scene of ostentatious conventional masculinity: uniforms and cigarettes. No beards, baldness or long hair are in sight. The same is true of the RAF officers in *Thunderball*. In *The Spy Who Loved Me*, there is a scene of "safe" masculinity when Bond, in naval uniform, visits the British submarine base: everyone is male, all save the minister of defence are in uniform, Bond establishes a personal link from past service on the aircraft carrier *Ark Royal*, and he also addresses the minister as Freddie. In Fleming's short story "Risico," M is revealed as not employing men with beards and as distrusting men or women who are too "dressy."

Bond, himself, in the films is a visual guarantee of the maleness of the Secret Service, a role he carries forward from the novels without equivocation. His sexuality is central to this, because, in both novels and films, a notion of deviant sexuality fits in with menace. Thus, in the novels, Le Chiffre, like Krest, Slugsby, Horror and Scaramanga, is a heterosexual sadist, while Blofeld is impotent. In the films, Blofeld dresses up as a woman to flee Las Vegas in *Diamonds Are Forever*, while Dr. No has no time for women, and the self-obsessed Zorin does not consummate his relationship with May-Day. In *For Your Eyes Only*, the traitorous Kristatos fancies his young ice-skating protégé Bibi but does nothing to seduce her. She, in contrast, wants Bond. Kristatos's rival, Colombo, who helps the British, has a personable mistress. In *Diamonds Are Forever*, a distinctly camp Blofeld employs Wint and Kidd, a pair of homosexual lovers, who are presented in a very unsympathetic and unsubtle light, as deadly, effete and ugly, although none of the more recent films have employed such a negative characterization of homosexuals. Blofeld, throughout, prefers caressing a white cat to being with a woman, sufficiently so for the cat to be a visual signature.

There is no contrast between libidinous villains and an asexual or repressed hero, as in much earlier literature. In *The Mystery of Dr. Fu-Manchu* (1913), the narrator, Dr. Petrie, is attracted to Kâramanèh, the "seductive vision" who is held in thrall by the evil Fu-Manchu, but he resists her approaches. The heroes in Buchan's novels were asexual, as were their female "interests."

Instead, Bond's open sexuality is a counterpoint to the classlessness of his film image, both proclaiming him in 1960s terms as an emancipated figure who can act as a symbol for a new Britain; to employ a phrase from 1999, part of "cool Britannia." Bond's sexuality can be given a wider role. Aside from providing a guarantee that he is not a traitor for those who share Captain Troop's values, it also serves as an answer to questions about masculinity that surfaced in the 1960s, a decade in which sexual identities were under tension. The Bond films do not answer these questions simply by ignoring them. They also offer a model, derived from the novels, of the male hero as rescuer, in short of the male as hero. Bond has no sense of anxiety about his masculinity and no hint of sexual concern, a point captured very well on screen, albeit in very different ways, by Connery, Moore and Brosnan, and less so by Lazenby and Dalton. A variety of encounters are depicted, but with "goodies" there is a conservative, romantic conception of sexual relations, or a witty and painless view. Bond takes the initiative, and there is no disease in Eden.

The sexual politics of both books and films have aroused much attention and debate, but, in part, this is a problem of the place and placing of a very old-fashioned mode of male sexuality, as seducer, now located in a period of greater female sexual independence. Bond is a successful seducer, attractive to women "good" and "bad," and to both major and minor characters. They want him—"Any time James. Any place"—to quote the honey-blond physiotherapist in the film *Thunderball*. The first woman he meets on screen, Sylvia Trench in *Dr. No*, falls for him at once and goes to his flat. She returns in *From Russia With Love*, complaining that work keeps him from her, but she is still amenable. Played by Eunich Gayson, as knowing and not an ingenue, Sylvia is a "Bond girl," free from family and domesticity and able to follow her own fancy. In *Goldfinger*, Pussy Galore tells Bond she is immune to charm and, later, that he hasn't got what it would take to make her see things his way, and, indeed, informs Goldfinger that she wants no trespassers on the island of herself.

This is possibly a reference to the lesbianism of the character in the novel. However, she is seduced by Bond's appeal and betrays Goldfinger. The relationship between Pussy and Bond is presented as based on sex, not romance.

Goodnight, a British agent in *The Man With the Golden Gun*, turns Bond down, "killing a few hours as one of your passing fancies isn't quite my scene," only to reappear later in a revealing nightie: "My hard to get act didn't last very long did it," a transformation that subscribes to a male fantasy that women don't mean it when they say no. In return, Bond saves her from Scaramanga and, at the close, treats her in a romantic fashion, although one defined by his apparent superiority. In the fight scene on Scaramanga's island, Goodnight had been presented as foolish. In *Never Say Never Again*, Bond is hooked in the sea off Nassau by a woman whose hotel bed he quickly repairs to, thus saving himself from the bomb planted under his own bed by the villainous Fatima Blush.

Bond's appeal to women is an aspect of his character that can be irrelevant to the plot, other than contributing to a sense of charming virility and successful manliness, as with the seduction of Caroline, the Secret Service psychologist in the driving scene near the start of *GoldenEye*, and the scene with Professor of Danish, Inga Bergstrom, near the start of *Tomorrow Never Dies*. Bond's sexual appeal is also frequently important in terms of plot, where it is often instrumental in ensuring the "tipping point" from failure to success, as in the films *Goldfinger* and *Thunderball*. More generally, his successful sexuality is also a release from other aspects of the story, offering a variety of pace, scene and characterization, as well as an important source of humor, and sometimes pathos, and a crucial support to the notion of his competence. It is not compromised by marriage and fatherhood, as is that of Arnold Schwarzenegger in *True Lies* (1994), an adventure story that employed some of the Bond signatures. Instead, Tracy Bond is dead within a day of her marriage.

Nevertheless, several women are not seduced by Bond's charm and, despite having sex with him, still try to have him killed. This was true of Connery's Bond as well as Moore's. In *Thunderball*, Fiona Volpe, a SPECTRE killer, has sex with Bond and then holds him up at revolver point mocking the idea that she would have repented and been converted thanks to the sex. Like Fatima Blush in *Never Say Never Again*, Fiona is an assertive lover. She bites Bond and is very different from the more passive Domino, the good girl in the same film who kills the villain Largo, her former lover; while Fiona is unsuccessful in disposing of Bond. Fiona's sexuality leads Bond to tells her "You are wild. You should be locked up in a cage." In *You*

Only Live Twice, the captured Bond suggests to Helga Brandt that, instead of torturing him, they run off together. She releases him, they embrace, have sex—"Ah the things I do for England"—and, next day, she traps him in a plane plummeting toward the earth. In *The Spy Who Loved Me*, Bond is first revealed having sex with a woman:

> "Oh James I can't find the words."
> "Let me try and enlarge your vocabulary."

Bond is then ordered to report immediately to M by a message through his watch. The woman says "But James I need you"; Bond replies "So does England," and, as soon as he has gone, she tips off the waiting Soviet assassination team by radio. In *Never Say Never Again*, Fatima, SPECTRE's dramatic and attractive killer, has sex with Bond—"going down you should always be relaxed" in his words, before planting a homing device to attract sharks to attack him. This was both instrumental to the plot and symbolic, reflecting the idea that a man is weakest immediately after sex. Bond kills Fatima thanks to a pen-gun with a Union Jack design, whereas earlier Fiona (by accident) and Helga (deliberately) had been killed by SPECTRE, and in *Live and Let Die* the black Rosie Carver who works for the villainous Dr. Kananga and has sex with Bond is killed by Kananga's system. Bond's killing of Fatima is a shift that reflects the difficulty in the early films of Bond killing a woman, especially if he had had sex with her. Fatima is killed only to save his life. At the outset of *Moonraker*, Bond is kissing a girl and has his hand on her thigh, only for her to pull a gun on him and leave him in a plane that is out of control. Later in the film, Bond is tripped into a pond where a python is waiting for him. A bevy of beautiful women, Drax's trainees, watch with interest, eagerly anticipating his death.

In such episodes, female sexuality appeared as threat rather than simply challenge, but one which Bond is able, at least eventually, to overcome, although the cruelty of the villains also helps Bond greatly. In *A View To A Kill*, Zorin's assistant May Day is not overcome (or "repositioned") by Bond's sexuality but, instead, wrecks Zorin's plan when he is responsible for the death of her female assistants.

Bond's avoidance of fatherhood and emotional ties can be seen as analogous, but this would be misleading. Fatherhood is not presented on screen as an issue. Emotional ties and sexual attraction, however, were both limiting, in that they made Bond vulnerable, and yet they were also crucial to Bond's appeal. They distinguished him from the villains and were also instrumental in securing success in particular films. He manages to elicit love and to respond, yet without being trapped.

The stereotyping of women conforms to Hollywood norms. In films, dark-haired, darker, older and more sophisticated women tend to be villains, younger blonds good. Fatima Blush in *Never Say Never Again* and Xenia Onatopp in *GoldenEye* are dark, Fiona older and sophisticated, Goodnight and Stacey Sutton in *A View To A Kill* young, slight and blond. There are of course exceptions. Drax's trainees include blonds, but they are presented as unreal and devoid of feeling, an equivalent to the Aryan blond heavies, Eric and Stamper, in *For Your Eyes Only* and *Tomorrow Never Dies*.

Bond shared an overt sexuality with a number of other secret agents of the 1960s, especially Matt Helm, who was realized on screen by Dean Martin in *The Silencers, Murderer's Row, The Ambushers* and *The Wrecking Crew* (1966–69). However, Bond was far more stylish than Helm, and Martin was physically less suited for the role of adventure hero than Connery. Unlike Connery, he also brought with him an established stage persona, and perhaps the different expectations and problems of an American as opposed to a British hero. James Coburn, the protagonist Derek Flint in *Our Man Flint* (1965), was another aggressively heterosexual agent, and in *In Like Flint* (1967), he rescued the president from a militant feminist spy ring that was as implausible as Pussy Galore's female gang. Female self-assurance and competence was increasingly an element in film and television spy and adventure stories. It was demonstrated by Cathy Gale and Emma Peel in the popular television series *The Avengers*, which ran in Britain from 1961 to 1969 and in the United States from 1966 to 1969. Honor Blackman and Diana Rigg played the roles and both also appeared in the Bond films. Bond had to be able to surpass such women—whether good or villains—if his omnicompetence was to be assured.

7

The Connery Years

Ten will get you one, it's a drink or a dame.
                    —Felix Leiter on Bond's likely destination, *Goldfinger*

It won't be the nicotine that kills you Mr. Bond.
                    —Blofeld to the captured Bond in *You Only Live Twice*

Sean Connery was not Fleming's choice for Bond. His preference, David Niven, reflected Fleming's view of the character. Niven was a stylish, public-school educated gent, used to playing such roles. No youngster, Niven did not seem a killer, and certainly did not have the disconcerting edge that Connery could offer, as was to be shown when Niven starred as the retired Sir James Bond in the spoof *Casino Royale* (1967).

The producer, Albert "Cubby" Broccoli, did not want an actor or character like Niven. Instead, as he later explained, he wanted Bond to have a tougher, less British, persona. Britishness was to be diluted and transformed. Bond was to have a "mid-Atlantic" image, able to appeal to American filmgoers as a man of action without putting them off with jarring British mannerisms. Bond had to be self-contained, not self-satisfied. Indeed, the opening scene in the London casino in *Dr. No* was of Bond as a tough, certainly far tougher than the upper-class agent sent to summon him to action. Connery's Scottish accent lacked the connotations and social location of English accents, for example the rich near-drawl of Charles Gray's Blofeld in *Diamonds Are Forever*. However, the Edinburgh-born actor, a former male model and body-builder, born in 1930, who had been gaining major television and film roles from 1957, was not so far from an image of classic British style as to be implausible.

Connery made the role his own and created the Bond audience for the cinema. Bond's character was well realized by Connery. He revealed the spare, pared-down character of Bond, and the inner bleakness alongside the style. Introduced to the audience at the chemin-de-fer table, Bond speaks through his cigarette, a man in charge of himself and unconcerned by the reactions of others. Connery's Bond was not an automatic smiler.

Connery offered Broccoli what he wanted, a "man of the people," and one for a mass audience. This was a period in which "Angry Young Men" were playing a prominent role in British film characterization. In *Dr. No* Bond seemed less establishment, certainly less polished, than the aloof Julius No. Bond was also very different from Strangeways, the British agent killed at the outset. Strangeways's accent was more refined and his bearing more military. Both Bond and Dr. No are intruders on the colonial ease of Jamaica. Bond saves a society that has gone soft and cannot appreciate the threat posed by Dr. No, although this counterpointing is far less pronounced than in the novel, in large part because the unsympathetic portrayal of the acting governor is discarded. Instead, the counterpointing is provided by Bond as the man of action.

The Bond-Connery association was developed in *From Russia With Love* (1963), a film with the same director, Terence Young, again using a Richard Maibaum screenplay. The film began with the apparent stalking and killing of Bond, only for it to be revealed that the victim is wearing a Bond mask and taking part in an exercise. Far from the novel's Soviet attempt to lure Bond to Istanbul, the film centers on a SPECTRE plot. Indeed, the Fleming corpus on film is annexed to the struggle between SPECTRE and the Secret Service; it is in this film that Blofeld is introduced on screen. He states that Dr. No had been a SPECTRE agent and that one of the objectives of the plot is to revenge his death on Bond, thus linking the early films in the order in which they appeared. A similar function was performed in the novel *From Russia, With Love* when the Soviets decide to target Bond. Their planning meeting reviews his earlier successes against Le Chiffre, Mr. Big, Drax and the Spangs, although they note that the last case "did not concern" them. The order of their review is that of the novels.

In the SPECTRE plot in the film *From Russia With Love*, Bond is to steal a Lektor (not Spektor as in the novel) decoder from the Soviets and then is to be attacked on his return journey on the Orient Express. He is to be lured to Istanbul by the promise of defection by a Soviet consular official, Natalya, the "velvet woman" of the film's trailer. The Lektor is then to be sold back to the Soviets. SPECTRE entrust the mission to Rosa Klebb, formerly head of operations for the KGB, who seeks to exploit the rivalry between Britain and the USSR by stirring up their animosity. Klebb is intent that "the cold war in Istanbul will not remain cold very much longer," and, by a well-timed murder, gets the Bulgarians in Soviet service to attack the Turks and Gypsies who work for the British. As if to indicate the complexity of SPECTRE's role, their killer, Donald "Red" Grant, saves Bond in the Gypsy encampment when it is attacked by the Bulgarians, an intervention not present in the novel. SPECTRE's ability to benefit from all is suggested at the outset when Blofeld shows his subordinates some fighting fish. SPECTRE waits to see which will win and will then turn on the exhausted victor. Survival of the fittest is the theme.

The Lektor is seized by Bond when the Soviet consulate is raided, another scene missing from the less violent novel, but Bond's attempted escape is thwarted, forcing him to stay on the Orient Express. There he is captured by Grant, only to strangle him in the carriage at the close of one of the most gripping fights in the film series. In a dramatic sequence of adventures, Bond escapes overland and then across the Adriatic to Venice. Once there, Natalya kills Klebb when she tries to kick Bond with the poisoned knife in her shoe. This attack in a luxury hotel shows that nowhere is safe from SPECTRE.

The difficulty Natalya has in aiming and firing suggests that women are weak and is a world away from such powerful female leads as Pam Bouvier in *Licence To Kill* (1989). Klebb is a killer, but, as in the novel, she is presented as an ugly sadist with lesbian tendencies. A view of women as less effective was characteristic of the Bond films of the period, and of other similar films at this time. At the outset of *Goldfinger*, a treacherous attack on Bond is launched by a man; the girl is only a decoy. Later, in Miami, Leiter and Bond get rid of a girl with Bond by telling her they want "Man talk."

From Russia With Love is a film without America or the Americans, although M mentions that both the CIA and the French Secret Service were keen to get a Lektor. The British were thus at the cutting edge of the Cold War. The exotic setting is provided by Istanbul, where much of the film is set. At that stage few British travelers had visited the city. The trailer mentions wider horizons "From Zagreb to Sofia. From Venice to Istanbul. From London to Paris"; the last was the setting of the final scene in the novel but did not play a role in the film. Indeed the story both opens and closes in Venice. The plot itself is rather tenuous, and the story serves as the basis for a series of adventure scenes, especially the battle at the Gypsy encampment, the fight on the train, the confrontation between Bond and a pursuing helicopter, and the boat fight off the Dalmatian coast. The plot is even more incidental than in *Dr. No*.

In part, this difference stems from the absence of a villain to compare with Julius No or Auric Goldfinger. Grant is a psychopath, described by his superior as a homicidal maniac, but he is an assassin, a tool, not a megalomaniac with a vision of himself or a plan for the world. Grant is a fraud, not Captain Nash, the British agent he claims to be, and whom he has in fact murdered at Zagreb station. Grant repeatedly "old mans" Bond in an attempt to establish himself in the role, offering a caricature portrayal of a class-ridden Briton. However, he orders the wrong wine—red chianti—with his fish, leading to a social clash between the two men that is uncomfortable to modern tastes. Grant is revealed as a fake. There is something very dated about this and other aspects of the film. Bond's "taste" seems rather pretentious, making him appear less "real." However, the episode is also symptomatic of the social politics of the Bond world. Social conformity and positioning are involved in the choice of wine. More generally, whereas the "other ranks" usually got their fair share of roles in British war films, their presence in the Bond works was minimal.

Suspicious, thanks to the wine order, Bond still does not realize what is up when he is held at gunpoint. He thinks that Grant is a SMERSH agent, and, when Bond realizes that in fact SPECTRE has been playing off SMERSH and the British, Grant is justified in telling him that he has been fooled. Only through violence can 007 rescue the situation.

Although SPECTRE aimed to make gains from both the Soviet Union (cash) and Britain (Bond's life and reputation), there was no suggestion that, therefore, the two powers should work together, as later with *The Spy Who Loved Me* (1977). When Bond arrives in Istanbul, he finds, as in the novel, a relaxed approach to the Cold War.

One of Kerim Bey's numerous sons tells Bond that it is normal for British and Soviet agents to follow each other. Kerim Bey observes, "You're in the Balkans. We don't make life too difficult for each other . . . in day to day matters we don't make it too difficult to keep eyes on each other," and, later, he refers to a "sudden breach in the truce." This breach was due to SPECTRE, but this did not lead the two powers to cooperate. Indeed, with the exception of the psychopathic "Red" Grant, all the SPECTRE agents have Continental accents and appearances, suggesting a foreignness that helps to align them with the Soviets.

In contrast, in *The Man From U.N.C.L.E.*, a popular television series that first appeared in 1964 and that was intended as a rival to Bond, David McCallum and Robert Vaughn played Soviet and American agents, fellow members of the United Network Command for Law and Enforcement. The SPECTRE equivalent was THRUSH. *The Man From U.N.C.L.E.* and the resulting films shared with Bond implausible plots and preposterous villains, technology and gadgetry, but the sexual dimension was less prominent, and there was little attempt to locate the plots in the real world. Unlike U.N.C.L.E., the British Secret Service existed, while Vaughn's Napoleon Solo lacked the intensity and dangerous edge of Connery's Bond.

Goldfinger, released in 1964, was a very different work from *From Russia With Love*, one that set a new tone for Bond. This was a compound of style, setting and technology. There was a new director: Guy Hamilton. Refused a share of *Goldfinger*'s profits, Young preferred to direct *The Amorous Adventures of Moll Flanders* (1965). Like Young, Hamilton had served in the forces in World War II. They were very much part of a generation that had, if not shared assumptions, at least shared experiences.

The style of *Goldfinger* was more humorous than that of the first two films, more outlandish, closer to fantasy and with scant attempt to sketch realities of place or job. The precredits adventure set a light tone, with the frogsuited Bond using a dummy duck and wearing a white tuxedo under his frogsuit. The film's villain was more fantastic than Rosa Klebb, and this was certainly true of his muscle. In place of "Red" Grant, an escaped British murderer, Oddjob was a Korean killer who was Goldfinger's manservant. Played by the wrestler Harold Sakata, Oddjob was able to crush a golf ball with one hand, and his preferred killing technique was a razor-brimmed bowler hat thrown like a frisbee. His demise—electrocuted inside Fort Knox—was as fantastic as his killings and was not in the novel.

The girls were also the stuff of fantasy, and they were more central to the action than in either of the two previous films. Jill Masterson, played by Shirley Eaton, provided the most vivid image. Having been distracted by Bond, she had let Goldfinger down in his card-cheating and was killed by being sprayed with gold and left to die, her skin unable to breathe. This provided the most powerful visual image of the film, and one that lent itself to publicity stills. Her character-sister, Tilly Masterson, carried the female interest forward, before being dispatched by Oddjob's flying hat, and then a third character, Goldfinger's pilot, Pussy Galore, provided even stronger female interest toward the close. Galore was played by Honor Blackman, herself a glamorous star from the television series *The Avengers*, and this star appeal complemented that of Connery. The female role was therefore stronger than in the earlier films, establishing a pattern that was to be maintained.

The settings were glamorous. Although most of the film was in fact shot in Pinewood Studios in England, the settings included Miami, Kentucky and Switzerland. They provided an opportunity to maintain the pace of the plot by offering a series of new vistas. After the precredits adventure and the credits, the film opened with aerial shots of the Miami shoreline, a setting of luxury hotels, especially the Fountainbleau, presented without the criticism offered in the novel.

The technology also made a great impact. This was the first film in which Bond visited Q's laboratory, offering a different view of the Secret Service from that provided by M's office. In *Dr. No*, the armorer had been called Major Boothroyd, but in *Goldfinger* he was first billed as Q, a more modern-sounding title. Despite Q's crustiness, which possibly, in part, helped for some viewers to soften the potential conflict between traditional Britishness and high technology, the technology associated the Secret Service with the "white heat" of change that the new Labour prime minister, Harold Wilson, had advocated and sought to embrace. It was also necessary in order to combat Bond's opponents. Aside from Oddjob's hat, the villain was able to deploy an industrial laser beam with which to question Bond as he was strapped to a table. This led to one of the most memorable exchanges in the film. As the beam cut its way toward Bond's genitals, the victim asks whether he was expected to talk. Goldfinger replies, "No, Mr. Bond. I expect you to die." The laser beam was later used to open up the seemingly impregnable Fort Knox. This was the first display of a laser on film.

Bond in turn has his car, an Aston Martin DB-5, whose armament included machine guns, a rear bullet-proof shield, revolving number plates, an extendable tire shredder, a smoke screen, radar, an oil slick, and a passenger ejector seat, the last faithfully reproduced in popular toy models. This was not the supercharged Bentley of the Fleming novels, the car shown with Bond in *From Russia With Love*, a film in which he was also collected from Istanbul airport in an old-fashioned Rolls Royce, a very traditional image of British quality and elegance. Instead, in *Goldfinger*, Bond is told by Q that M has decided the Bentley has had its day. The Aston Martin symbolized the style and speed that the 1960s were held to represent. It was fast, stylish, British and deadly, an enabler for Bond's potency.

The car became the symbol of a filmic Bond style, not least because it was not mass produced. Instead, the Aston Martin was handmade, rather than machine-assembled, offering another aspect of Britishness. Extraordinary weaponry and vehicles and the effectiveness of the special effects became a crucial aspect of the appeal of the Bond films, helping, in particular, to attract male and younger viewers. The films appeared at a time when special effects were greatly improving. *Thunderball* followed, with Bond using a jet pack at the outset, a scene featured in the trailer, and with a rocket-firing motorbike, an underwater camera and a waterproof Geiger counter. The expense of gadgetry and special effects helped to drive up the cost of making the films. The gadgets had to be novel in order to have a major impact.

The car in *Goldfinger* was an adventure image of the present, a world away from the dinner at the Bank of England in which the elderly, crusty Colonel Smithers explained gold smuggling to M and Bond. The three men were dinner-jacketed and their meal a ritual, involving cigars, recondite knowledge of brandy, and a servant in tails. This was as dated as breast-pocket handkerchiefs, or the hat Bond still wore when he launched the shot that blooded the camera's eye in the opening credits.

All was not well with traditional Britain. It was not losing only gold. When Bond played Goldfinger at golf at a luxurious, traditional-style club, and his opponent demonstrated his menace by having Oddjob decapitate a statue with his flying hat, Bond asked what the club secretary would say. Goldfinger confidently replied that he owned the club. Britain was being taken over, prefiguring 1970s concerns about Arab prestige purchases, and those in the 1980s that focused on the Japanese.

The film itself was about technology overcome. Goldfinger's plan was not, as in the novel, to steal the gold, but, instead, to set off an atom bomb inside the American gold reserves at Fort Knox and thus irradiate the gold, in order to increase the value of his own gold. This required not only the bomb, but also the air-spraying of gas over the nearby American army base. Bond defeats the scheme by bravery, determination, luck and sex appeal. He, however, was only able to save Fort Knox because of Goldfinger's hubris. Bond had been handcuffed to the atomic bomb placed in the vaults in order to ensure that he would be the first to know of Goldfinger's success. Bond is thus able to kill Oddjob and so prepare the way for the American expert to defuse the bomb at the last moment. Bond significantly lacks that expertise. He is not the technician of power.

Premiered at the Leicester Square Odeon on 17 September 1964, *Goldfinger* broke the box-office records. It recouped its $3.5 million budget in a fortnight, becoming the fastest-grossing film hitherto. This owed much to the publicity campaign, although it also reflected another aspect of the Bond films. They were launched as a mass, not a trickle-down, product. A large number of prints of each film were speedily released. This eased cash flow and enabled the burst of initial publicity to have maximum impact. The profitability of *Goldfinger* greatly benefited from this technique. The film also benefited from having the first title vocal, a song, composed by John Barry and powerfully sung by Shirley Bassey, that went to eighth on the American charts. The musical style of the film greatly contributed to its popularity and impact.

The cult of the cinematographic Bond was well established, with fetishistic objects, such as the Aston Martin, and a form of devotion in which Bond became a real person. Future films were assured of a large initial audience, and, indeed, a rerelease of *Dr. No* when *Goldfinger* appeared was very successful. Furthermore, the profitability of the early films encouraged bigger budgets for those that came after. In part, this was necessary in order to differentiate the Bond films from imitators. The bigger budgets led to films of a greater scale. There were expensive underwater sequences in *Thunderball*, which was both the first of the Bond films that ran for more than two hours and the first to be made in Panavision, a widescreen process.

Goldfinger was followed by two other Connery Bonds, in succession, *Thunderball* (1965) and *You Only Live Twice* (1967), by *On Her Majesty's Secret Service* (1969), with George Lazenby as Bond, and by Connery, again, in *Diamonds Are Forever* (1971).

In each, the principal villain was Blofeld, although in *Thunderball*, as in the novel, the key enemy is Emilio Largo, played by Adolfo Celi, a cosmopolitan villain whose charm acts as a counterpoint to that of Bond. Unlike Julius No and Auric Goldfinger, Largo is attractive to women and has a mistress. Furthermore, he is fit and brave, although disabled, both physically and morally. The novels *Thunderball, On Her Majesty's Secret Service* and *You Only Live Twice* had been Fleming's SPECTRE trilogy. The reversal of the order in the films was part of the process by which the conflict with SPEC-TRE was extended into an apparently never-ending struggle.

As in the novel, the setting for *Thunderball* (1965) was the West Indies. As in the first two films, the director was Terence Young. Most of the film was shot in the Bahamas. Largo lived in Palmyra, a villa complete with a shark-infested pool, permitting the Bond films to begin their use of a character, the shark, that was to recur in *Never Say Never Again* and *The Spy Who Loved Me*. The British were able to play a leading role in the plot because it was their Vulcan bomber and atom bombs that were stolen, and the discussion of how £100 million worth of uncut diamonds was to be delivered to SPECTRE— by planes refueling in the British base of Aden—permits reference to the range of British power, an image further suggested by the portentous conference room and by the world situation chart. The scene at the airbase, with the planes lined up and the Vulcan taking off, indicated British strength, and the RAF characters had the assured mannerisms of countless war films: "What's the flap Dawson" says one bemedaled uniform to another.

Britain was still a world power at the time of the film and it was credible to think of her forces ranging widely, even if imperial territories were being surrendered. The V-bomber force was in fact obsolescent, far more vulnerable than relatively inaccessible submarines; but, on 15 February 1968, the first British Polaris test missile was fired from a submarine and, that July, *Resolution*, the Royal Navy's first ballistic missile submarine, arrived in its patrol area.

Nevertheless, the nuclear force was dependent on the Americans, and there was never any chance that Britain would use nuclear weapons or take major international action without the approval of the Americans. It had been intended to upgrade the British V-bomber force with Skybolt, an American air-to-surface nuclear missile, but after that was canceled by Kennedy's defense secretary, Robert Mc-Namara, Macmillan and Kennedy decided in December 1962, in what became known as the Nassau Agreement, that the Americans would provide the Polaris ballistic missile weapon system. This was to be fitted to a newly built class of four large nuclear-powered submarines, but American agreement was dependent on the British force being primarily allocated for NATO duties. Indeed, Blofeld refers to the SPECTRE plan as being directed against NATO, which is a way to link Britain and the United States.

With its setting in Nassau, *Thunderball* made reference to the agreement. A location in the Bahamas, which did not become independent until 1973, also helps support the British role. In the 1983 remake of the plot, *Never Say Never Again*, it was American cruise missiles, not British bombs, that were stolen. Even in the film *Thunderball*, it is American power that is crucial at the climax. Having been rescued by a U.S. Coast Guard helicopter, Bond joins an underwater battle off Miami in which, aside from himself, the forces of good are all American: frogmen parachute into the sea; American warships destroy the armed cocoon of Largo's ship, the *Disco Volante*, the section left when the front detaches and becomes a hydrofoil; and Bond and Domino are rescued from the Atlantic by an American plane using the Skyhook rescue system. For the first time, the world premier (on 21 December 1965) was in New York. London followed eight days later. The film was a great success in Britain, America, Western Europe and Japan.

Directed by the talented Lewis Gilbert, *You Only Live Twice* (1967) was faithful to the novel in its Japanese setting, but Blofeld and his schemes were more central to the film than the book. In place of Blofeld as a recluse with a perverse poison garden, a threat only to those who seek death, in the film the character, played by Donald Pleasence, controls a rocket base concealed beneath the apparent lake surface of a volcanic crater. He stands for future threat, not the bizarre past of the novel, with its sinister castle and his traditional Japanese armor and sword. *You Only Live Twice* was an example of the process by which the films used plots that were just as ludicrous as some of Fleming's but were also obviously more cinematic, not least in providing opportunities for explosions.

The plot, written by the successful writer of children's stories, Roald Dahl, who had known Fleming but never previously written a screenplay, revolved around Blofeld's attempt to cause a nuclear war between the United States and the USSR by intercepting space missions with a rocket from his secret Japanese base. The American spaceship, Jupiter 16, was swallowed up by Blofeld's rocket and the Americans left to think that the cause was Soviet interference. In retaliation, the Americans threatened war if their next space mission was interfered with.

The British were more prudent and cautious, pressing the Americans to explain what motive the Soviets might have and unconvinced that the Soviets had seized Jupiter 16. Indeed, in a lingering of imperial glory, it is Britain, the United States and the USSR who are depicted at the outset as debating the crisis at a meeting in a futuristic conference building. No other powers are present. The British mention that their tracking station in Singapore had reported a touchdown in the Sea of Japan. Their delegates appear as the most intelligent.

The scene then switches to British-ruled Hong Kong, where, in order to mislead his opponents, Bond is supposedly shot, his "body" discovered by two white British policemen, and then buried in the harbor from one British warship, before being collected by divers from a British submarine. The message is clear. This is still a power that counts, and the prime minister instructs M to have every effort made to prevent war. M himself briefs Bond in Hong Kong. The excess of the Hong Kong scenes suggests that the films no longer saw themselves as set in the world of "intelligence," used in both senses of the word, but, instead, in the realm of spectacle.

Bond follows a trail that leads first to Osato Chemical and Engineering Co. Ltd. and then to an island where an Osato ship had secretly unloaded rocket fuel. Osato's corporate headquarters acknowledged Japan's own hi-tech, as did the in-car monitor. Osato is controlled by SPECTRE, and Blofeld has agreed with China to cause war between the United States and the USSR in return for payment. The Chinese have provided him with the rocket equipment, for China, like Japan, is now a modern power, not the site of Oriental decadence and evil as in British novels earlier in the century. The Osato company might be taken to represent the threat from Japanese industry. After seizing a Soviet rocket in space, Blofeld then attempts to capture a second American rocket, thus precipitating military action by the United States against the USSR.

Indeed the film drew on the real proximity of both powers to war. In February 1965, McNamara felt able to state that the United States could rely on the threat of "assured destruction" to deter a Soviet assault. However, with fewer nuclear weapons, the USSR had adopted a nuclear strategy of a massive, simultaneous strike (rather than a graduated buildup), and this was intended to preempt NATO attack. The interest that both sides displayed in a counterforce strategy—destroying the nuclear strength of its opponents before they could act—thus encouraged first-strike plans, producing the tension captured in *You Only Live Twice*. The film suggests that such plans are open to secret exploitation by third parties and that this can be prevented only by vigilance.

Furthermore, the notion of Chinese action against the United States and the USSR in part reflected the idea that these two superpowers had lessened their animosity with the "hot-line" agreement of April 1963 and the Partial Test Ban Treaty signed in August 1963 that banned nuclear testing in the atmosphere, outer space, and underwater. A Non-Proliferation Treaty followed in July 1968. Thus, to be more credible the notion of all-out atomic war drew on the idea that a third power would cause it. The plot also reflected the view that apparent understandings between the superpowers were fallible and thus that there was a need to defend these understandings.

Bond, in what Connery had announced would be his last film, saves the world by thwarting Blofeld. The latter played a larger role than hitherto in the Bond films and this was the first in which his face was shown. The plot reflected the intense competition between the United States and the USSR in space but did so in a way that still gave Britain a role. It might not have any spaceships, but it was able, thanks to Bond, to determine the fate of the world. Interest in space was increased by the race to land on the Moon, including the first space walk in June 1965, the soft landings by unmanned Soviet and American spaceships in 1966 and by the explosion of an American Apollo spacecraft in January 1967.

Aside from the novelty of the Japanese setting, the film also featured some new technology, including the "Little Nellie," a miniature helicopter or autogiro. Blofeld's base with its sliding roof disguised as the lake surface was an impressive working set that cost £400,000, more than the whole of *Dr. No*. It helped set a trend for effective futuristic sets in the Bond films. *Dr. No*'s base within a mountain had been prefigured in the novel, and *From Russia With Love* had lacked such a set. *Goldfinger* had offered the vaults at Fort Knox, but *You Only Live Twice* created a fantasy set and one that was not prefigured in the novel. The film was a true spectacular, and a financial success, grossing $111.6 million, but it was not as successful as *Thunderball*. The established character of the Bond films was indicated on 12 June 1967 when, at the world premier at the Leicester Square Odeon in London, the queen was introduced to Connery. An atomic threat also played a role in *Operation Kid Brother* (1967), a very weak Italian production in which Sean Connery's brother Neil played 007's brother.

As well as Connery, there was Diana Rigg. An accomplished and well-established action heroine from *The Avengers*, she had a more attractive presence than George Lazenby, her male counterpart in *On Her Majesty's Secret Service* (1969), an actor who failed to match, let alone supplant, Connery. The trailer promised "The different Bond from the same stable," but the difference was not flattering. Lazenby got the role because of his appearance and because in his screen test he appeared effective as a fighter, but he lacked acting experience other than in television commercials. The wooden Lazenby lacked Connery's style, and some of his actions, such as goosing Moneypenny and admiring the *Playboy* foldout, were tacky. The casting of Rigg, the strongest of the Bond "girls," was a necessary response to the weakness of the new Bond.

Directed by Peter Hunt from Richard Maibaum's screenplay, the film stayed fairly close to the novel: it was a love story as well as an adventure, and, due to a deliberate decision on Hunt's part, gadgetry played a small role. This helped ensure that the film cost less than *Thunderball*, as did the cut in the salary of the male lead. Blofeld, played by Telly Savalas, was the villain, the Union Corse played a major role, and Bond fell for the brave and intelligent Contessa Teresa de Vincenzo or Tracy, described in the trailer as "The different Bond woman. This one's got class and style." Previous "girls" had class and style, but little in the way of self-determination. In the adventure, Tracy repeatedly showed resolution, driving in a high-speed car chase, dodging bullets while skiing, surviving an avalanche and using a broken champagne bottle to fight an attacker. Furthermore, these achievements were important: Tracy rescues Bond.

Whereas in the novel Blofeld threatened British agriculture, in the film it is the world, itself, that is at risk. Blofeld's "virus omega" can produce total infertility in plants and animals, and it is the United Nations, not the British government, that has to decide how best to respond. M waits to hear the decision. Such a role for the United Nations appeared credible. Possibly, the American government, then embroiled in Vietnam, did not seem a safe and acceptable defender of Western values. However, given the ongoing suspicion of the United Nations, this aspect of the plot may have added to the film's lack of impact.

The willingness of the United Nations to consider granting Blofeld amnesty is evidence that it cannot protect Western values or, indeed, morality. It is Bond who decides to break the impasse by attacking Piz Gloria, but he does so in clear breach of instructions. M tells Bond that he, M, has been informed that it is too risky to mount such an attack. Bond is primarily motivated by his desire to rescue Tracy, then held by Blofeld. M is not impressed: "This department is not concerned with your personal problems." The issue is not pressed, but Bond defies orders and turns to the Union Corse, who again provide help. Draco describes the helicopter assault force as "crusaders," and they wear white, in stark contrast to the villains.

The film portrayal is more romantic, because in the novel Tracy is not held by Blofeld and therefore does not need to be rescued. Furthermore, in the novel M supports Bond: "All right, 007. Go ahead. I can't go to the PM about it. He'd refuse. But for God's sake bring it off. I don't mind being sacked, but we don't want to get the Government mixed up in another U2 fiasco."

The film therefore stressed Bond's independence, his choice of a duty formed by love and morality rather than obedience to instructions. However, this clash was softened: there were no recriminations after the attack, and, instead, M and Draco were shown at Bond's wedding, happily chatting about a past clash.

As in the novel, Bond married Tracy, only for her to be shot by Blofeld's partner Irma Bunt at the start of their honeymoon. Like the novel, the close of the film has Bond holding Tracy's dead body. "We have all the time in the world," he says, in a touching echo of a future snatched away. This unhappy ending helped ensure that the film, the longest hitherto of the Bond movies, was less successful at the box office than its predecessor or successor.

In *Diamonds Are Forever* (1971), Connery returned in response to a vast fee: $1,250,000 and 12.5% of the gross profits. As in *You Only Live Twice*, the threat came from space. Space seemed increasingly closer to the audiences of the period. In 1962 the first transatlantic pictures were beamed to Britain from the Telstar satellite. Only seven years later, people were watching pictures beamed live from the Moon.

In the film, there was no echo of the Vietnam War, of the Soviet invasion of Czechoslovakia in 1968 or of Cold War tension and confrontation elsewhere. A series of trials in this period had suggested a continued high level of Soviet espionage against Britain. Josef Frolik, who defected from the Czech Intelligence Service in 1969, named two Labour MPs and three leading trade unionists as agents.

There was no echo of this in the escapism of *Diamonds Are Forever*, which was directed by Guy Hamilton from a final screenplay by the young Tom Mankiewicz. The plot of the novel was largely abandoned, although the theme of diamond smuggling and the spectacular setting of Las Vegas were both retained and used to effect. It was the villains and their villainy that had changed totally. In place of the Spangs and their devotion to illicit profit, the title was annexed to SPECTRE. The villain became Blofeld, played by Charles Gray, his scheme the creation of a space-mounted laser that he could use for world blackmail. The world is tracked as a moving target on the map recording the spaceship's movements. The diamonds were designed for the solar panels of the spaceship.

The attempts of the nuclear powers to enhance their nuclear attack and defense capabilities made a plot that centered on a space-mounted threat seem credible, and this replaced the original idea of a laser located on a supertanker. In June 1970 the Americans had deployed Minuteman III missiles equipped with MIRVs (multiple independently targeted reentry vehicles), thus ensuring that the strike capacity of an individual rocket was greatly enhanced. In August the USS *James Madison* made the first successful underwater launch of a Poseidon missile.

Prefiguring the subsequent theme of the danger of big business, or rather big businessmen, to be seen in *The Spy Who Loved Me, Moonraker, A View To A Kill* and *Tomorrow Never Dies*, Blofeld has gained his wealth by kidnapping Willard Whyte, a reclusive Las Vegas-based American billionaire, modeled on Howard Hughes, and taking over his wealth. The range of the plot, with episodes in Japan, Cairo, South Africa, Amsterdam, London, Dover, Los Angeles, Las Vegas and off the California coast, testified to the global extent of Blofeld's power, although most of the film engages with the United States, more so than any previous Bond film. This was significant both in terms of holding a soft audience (Americans seeing America) and because it offered a view of a crisis and threat within the United States, a theme replayed in *Live and Let Die*. Most of the supporting cast was American.

Britain plays only a peripheral role in the plot and is brought in solely to explain Bond's presence. A rise in diamond smuggling threatens the market, as the diamonds are apparently being stockpiled, in order either to dump them, and thus cut the price, or to expose the market to blackmail. Bond, who does not feel that his section should be brought in to deal with smuggling, is instructed to investigate. There is no hint of anything more sinister.

Bond sets off from Britain on a Seaspeed hovercraft, a testimony to British technology sporting British flags. The first hovercraft had flown in 1959 and regular services across the English Channel started in 1966. Thereafter, Bond has left the protective cocoon of British power. Instead, he is dependent on the backup of the CIA, but repeatedly this is insufficient. Thirty CIA agents can't keep track of Tiffany Case after she collects the diamonds in Las Vegas.

This suggestion of relative competence is matched by one of style, captured when Bond is the only individual at the Las Vegas gambling tables in a white dinner jacket, and, later, when, atop an elevator, he coolly goes up the outside of the Whyte House, dressed in a black dinner jacket and with a red carnation in his buttonhole. The American agents in contrast wear ordinary clothes. The hotel used in this scene was the Las Vegas International Hotel, then owned by Hughes, who was a Bond fan. The only competitor in terms of style is the deliberately British character actor Charles Gray's Blofeld, but his is a camp portrayal and, under pressure at the close, Blofeld loses his cool and humor, as Bond never does. Furthermore, to evade capture, Bond does not have to don female wig and lipstick as Blofeld does. The Bond image could not have taken such treatment, an indication of the nature and limits of Bond's heroic image.

As more generally with SPECTRE, Blofeld's scheme in *Diamonds*

Are Forever reveals a willingness to attack, and thus profit from, all and sundry. The demonstration of the laser's power involves the destruction of American, Soviet and Chinese weaponry: an American rocket belonging to the Strategic Air Command in North Dakota is followed by a Soviet submarine and a line of Chinese missiles. Blofeld plans to use his early version of a Star Wars missile, not to pursue the disarmament he mentions to Dr. Metz, the expert in laser refraction he has deceived into his service, but in order to stage "an international auction with nuclear superiority going to the winner."

The state system has been overturned by technology and when the Americans assemble forces to challenge Blofeld's base, he contemptuously refers to the "great powers" flexing their muscles like "impotent beach boys," a powerful image of change. In order to drive home his point and to underline his coercive power, Blofeld then searches for another target. Having rejected Kansas—"the world might not notice"—and New York—"it would provide an opportunity to start again"—as targets, both with remarks that play to American prejudices, Blofeld settles on Washington. He is thwarted, with less than ten seconds to go, not by the attacking force of American helicopter gunships, a military arm much used in Vietnam, but by Bond. The *Goldfinger* scenario again, successfully so, with the Americans, again, left to clear up the mess.

Blofeld had earlier mocked Bond: "Surely you haven't come to negotiate, Mr. Bond. Your pitiful little island hasn't even been threatened." This remark did not seem out of place when the film appeared in 1971. Far from being a superpower, Britain had lost its empire and discovered nothing to replace it, bar a leadership in "style": music, clothes and certain films, such as those about Bond. Although in 1964 the new Labour prime minister, Harold Wilson, declared "We are a world power and a world influence or we are nothing," by 1969 none of Africa remained under British rule, and the east of Suez defense policy, supported by both Labour and the Conservatives, had fallen victim to the consequences of the enforced devaluation of sterling in 1967. In 1968 Wilson had announced that Britain would withdraw from east of Suez.

The loss of imperial and relative power was a background to the Bond films. Independence was granted to Sierra Leone, Tanganyika and southern Cameroons in 1961; Jamaica, Trinidad and Uganda in 1962; Sabah, Sarawak, Singapore, Zanzibar and Kenya in 1963; Nyasaland, northern Rhodesia and the major naval base of Malta in 1964; Gambia and the Maldives in 1965; Bechuanaland, Basutoland and Barbados in 1966; Aden in 1967; Nauru, Mauritius and Swaziland in 1969; and Tonga and Fiji in 1970. The loss of Sierra Leone and Jamaica was especially important, because British forces based there had featured in Fleming's novels. Fleming's location of Bond as a servant of empire was increasingly dated.

Labour had continued a process of retreat from Africa begun by the Conservatives, and the Conservative opposition in 1964–70 did not criticize this imperial withdrawal. The unilateral declaration of independence in Southern Rhodesia (now Zimbabwe) in 1965 was supported in some right-wing circles, but not by the official opposition. It is unclear how far a major nationalist rising in, or foreign invasion of, a British colony would have led to a substantial response that might have proved bitterly divisive within Britain, but there was none in the 1960s. Decolonization did not prove traumatic. In part, this was because the empire was seen as being transformed into the Commonwealth, rather than lost. The contraction of empire was also relatively painless, because interest in much of it was limited. Fleming was increasingly an atypical figure in this respect.

British forces had played a major and successful role in the Malayan Emergency of 1948–60 and in the resistance to Indonesian attempts to intimidate Malaysia in 1963–65. They were sent to Jordan in 1958 and Kuwait in 1961, in order to prevent possible attacks by hostile Arab regimes, and resisted insurrection in Aden. However, there was thereafter a process of rapid retreat. Forces withdrew from Aden in 1967 and from the Persian Gulf and Singapore in 1971. There were serious defense cuts, including the cancelation of the TSR2 supersonic interceptor and a super aircraft carrier, and the British refused to support the Americans in Vietnam. British defenses were now clearly dependent on American weaponry, not only the Polaris missile that had been bought after the cancelation of the land-based Blue Streak intercontinental missile system, but also the Phantom jet that had filled the gap after the cancelation of plans for British jets.

The style of the 1960s had not translated into power, and Britain was seeking a role as a member of the EEC, the European Economic Community, now the European Union. Hugh Gaitskell, then leader of the Labour opposition, warned in a television interview on 21 September 1962 that entry into the EEC "means the end of Britain as an independent nation; we become no more than Texas or California in the United States of Europe. It means the end of a thousand years of history." In January 1963, the French president, Charles De Gaulle, had vetoed the first British application, a major humiliation for Harold Macmillan. After Labour, under Gaitskell's successor Wilson, came to power in 1964, a new entry bid was launched. De Gaulle, however, blocked this second attempt, emphasizing the underlying weaknesses of the British economy. The Wilson government responded by saying that it would not take *non* for an answer: Britain would leave the application "on the table." British options seemed no longer to be those of independence or alliance from a position of strength, but, instead, to be those of joining the American or European systems or only that of being a member of the latter because that was what the American government wanted. The "special relationship" with the United States was in difficulties. President Lyndon B. Johnson was angered by the failure to send troops to Vietnam, by the rundown of the British role east of Suez at a time when the United States was poorly placed to replace it, by British defense cuts and by British attempts to mediate in the Vietnam War. Edward Heath, Conservative prime minister in 1970–74, was determined not to be branded as the American spokesman in Europe. Instead, he pushed hard for British membership in the EEC, seeing this as crucial to his vision for the modernization of Britain, and as a way for it to play a convincing role on the world stage. De Gaulle's resignation in 1969 was a necessary prelude. A treaty of accession was signed in Brussels on 22 January 1972. Britain formally became a member of the EEC on 1 January 1973.

This was scarcely the stuff of heroism. Bond's role in *Diamonds Are Forever* reflected the insignificance of Britain. He might save the world from Blofeld, but he had gained his chance only by following the diamond smuggling lead to the United States. Blofeld scarcely needed to threaten Britain or to challenge the British Secret Service in order to demonstrate his power. The idea that an enemy would go to great lengths to remove Bond, the theme of the novel *From Russia, With Love*, was also anachronistic by 1971.

Indeed, the role of fantasy in the film *Diamonds Are Forever* was amply justified. Without it, the plot would have had nothing. Fantasy also played a major part in the setting of the film, a point highlighted by the contrast both with the more gritty 1965–67 films of three of Len Deighton's espionage stories, beginning with *The Ipcress Files*, and with the British expulsion of over 100 Soviet agents after the 1971 defection of Oleg Lyalin had revealed KGB plans for covert action in the event of war. Place, plot and personality were all very different in the Bond films.

Diamonds Are Forever cost $7.2 million, in contrast to the just over $1 million spent on *From Russia With Love*. Inflation was a factor, but far less than the proven profitability of the Bond films. *Thunderball* was the most successful film at the American box office in 1966.

Diamonds Are Forever made a handsome profit, earning $15.6 million in the first twelve days of its release. With such returns, the Bond films appeared set for a secure financial future, while the very familiarity of an ever-growing audience with the films made it easier for them to obtain responses, to strike echoes and to establish a self-referential world within which rituals were established.

8

Over to Moore

I'm not interested in extortion. I intend to change the face of history.
—the villain Stromberg in *The Spy Who Loved Me* (1977)

Although shown visiting Tracy's grave at the outset of *Live and Let Die*, Roger Moore was not an actor for pathos, such as that at the close of *On Her Majesty's Secret Service*, not for anger and violence comparable to that suggested by Connery. He took over the role in 1973, with *Live and Let Die*, and continued until *A View To A Kill* (1985), a sequence of seven films. With Moore, who had been considered for the role when the films began, Bond became formulaic, as the novels had never been, although it was difficult to avoid a measure of predictability. More seriously, the films lost an edge, largely thanks to the protagonist's difference from Connery, but also, in part, because the threats seemed distant, remote and far-fetched. It was easier to see the films simply as entertainment, in large part light entertainment, although that had been the trend at least since *Goldfinger* and was encouraged by the relative lack of success of the straighter *On Her Majesty's Secret Service*.

For a new generation of viewers, however, Moore was Bond and therefore had a more positive impact than on those comparing him to Connery. Moore's background in *The Saint* and *The Persuaders* fitted him ideally for a series centered on action over drama and style over substance, and the box-office returns suggested that this was exactly what happened. Moore looked the role but lacked Connery's sense of danger and sardonic poise.

In the first Moore film, *Live and Let Die* (1973), directed by Hamilton and written by Tom Mankiewicz, the Mr. Big of New York African American crime was really Dr. Kananga, the president of San Monique, an imaginary Caribbean state. Yaphet Kotto, who played Kananga, was shown in the film using a rubber face mask to adopt Mr. Big's persona. As in the novel, he relied on voodoo and was a threat to the United States—rather than Britain, no longer the ruler of Jamaica, let alone fictional states such as San Monique. This really was a job for the Americans, but they had to rely on Bond.

Mr. Big, however, was no Blofeld, no megalomaniac planning to blackmail the world. Instead, he aimed to take over the lucrative American drug trade by distributing two tons of free heroin through his Fillet of Soul restaurant chain. Drugs offer a new internationalism, one to match Communism and SPECTRE. Kananga tells Bond that he doesn't discriminate: "Man or woman, Black or White," are all his putative victims. He aims through free distribution to wreck the Mafia's hold on the trade and to double the number of addicts. Once Kananga has a monopoly, he plans to increase prices.

This was a presentation of the United States as vulnerable. The film linked black power in the cities with crime and implied that a failure to control both black neighborhoods and small Caribbean islands could undermine America. Dr. Kananga is a harsh depiction of Caribbean independence. The United Nations, which he uses as a sounding board, is also implicitly criticized. This was an attitude that drew on the same currents that had encouraged American military intervention in the Dominican Republic in 1965. More risibly, in 1969 the British government sent two frigates, a detachment of parachutists and a group of London policemen to invade the Caribbean island of Anguilla, which had rejected membership in the St. Kitts-Nevis-Anguilla federation. There was much concern that the island would become a base for drug smugglers. The invasion was in fact bloodless and, in part, the entire episode was ridiculous, but it testified to fears about the West Indies.

The menacing image of Harlem where Bond is easily captured was that of the novel, but it can also be traced to violence in American cities in the 1960s, especially the Watts riots of 1965 and those in

Detroit in 1967. The former had led to 34 deaths and the deployment of 14,000 National Guard troops, the latter to 43 deaths and the intervention of 4,700 state troopers. When Martin Luther King was assassinated in 1968, there were riots in over 100 cities and 350,000 troops and National Guard troops were placed on alert. This was the last outbreak of major rioting until the 1992 Los Angeles riots, but that was unclear at the time. Furthermore, black militancy and the drug trade were linked by some hostile commentators. Bond was able to overthrow Mr. Big, thanks to his seduction of his tarot reader, the virginal and virgin Solitaire. This was a world away from such gritty stories as Deighton's *Spy Story* (1974), the plot of which related to British attitudes to German reunification and the theme of betrayal.

In *The Man With the Golden Gun*, which quickly followed in 1974, Bond went not west to Jamaica, as in the novel, but east. His target was Scaramanga, played by a stepcousin of Fleming's, Christopher Lee. Scaramanga, the world's most expensive assassin, who charged £1 million a shot, was a free lance, who works for, among others, the Chinese, not, as in the book, the Soviets. Scaramanga was tracked down by Bond on his nearby island and killed in a shooting competition. This was, for most British viewers, an exotic world, certainly compared to the West Indies, which had now become through the Bond films familiar on screen. Having used the West Indies for *Live and Let Die*, a change of scene was essential. Much of the action was set in Macao, Hong Kong, Bangkok and on the Chinese (in fact Thai) coast. Directed again by Guy Hamilton, from a Maibaum and Mankiewicz screenplay, the film, in part, acted as travelogue, showing unfamiliar, indeed exotic, scenes, more so than the two previous films. The appearance of the wreck of the liner *Queen Elizabeth* early in the film was a reminder of British vulnerability.

The film also struck a contemporary note; in Macao, Scaramanga killed Gibson, the expert on solar cells whom the British were trying to persuade to come home. "The energy crisis is still with us," M told Bond, a year after the 1973 oil crisis. He later explained that the depletion of coal and oil and the dangers of uranium ensured that Britain had to think of solar energy. The theme of a crisis in energy supply was one that a global audience would have understood. Britain as yet did not have North Sea oil and gas flowing through the pipelines, while OPEC—the Organization of Petroleum Exporting Countries—had shown an ability to hold the rest of the world to ransom. Having acquired the secret of how to use solar energy, Scaramanga proposed an auction of the Solex technology. The highest bidder would be able to construct hundreds of solar energy power stations and, thus, use its monopoly to alter the balance of power, although, as Bond noted, one option was for the Middle Eastern oil producers to buy, and suppress, the technology. Solex could also be used as a weapon, rather like the laser gun in *Diamonds Are Forever*, and, indeed, Scaramanga destroyed Bond's plane in this way.

Oil rights had played a role in *The Girl Machine*, a comic strip involving Bond and written by James Lawrence, which appeared in *The Daily Express* in 1973. Hotshot, a weapon that magnified the sun's rays, is prepared in *Hot Shot* (1976), another comic strip story, and again there is a Middle Eastern dimension.

The Spy Who Loved Me (1977) began with two hostile acts: first, the mysterious disappearances of HMS *Ranger* and the *Potemkin*, British and Soviet nuclear submarines, and second, a Cold War Soviet attempt to kill Bond while skiing in Austria. This led to a dramatic show of national pride. Rick Sylvester, the stunt man playing Bond, ski-jumped off a 3,000-foot cliff and was saved by his parachute. The parachute opened to reveal the Union Jack, the Bond theme played and the film's song, "Nobody Does It Better," followed.

This national self-sufficiency was challenged by Karl Stromberg, a wealthy shipping magnate who had seized the submarines and held them captive in a supertanker with opening bows, in order to further his plan to destroy the world and build a new civilization under the sea. This civilization was to be controlled from his submersible Mediterranean base, Atlantis, a typically portentous name. Stromberg programmed his two stolen submarines to fire missiles at New York and Moscow, intending to bring on a nuclear holocaust: as in *Diamonds Are Forever* and *Live and Let Die*, it is significant that London is not one of the targets. He claimed that modern civilization was corrupt and decadent, that it would inevitably destroy itself and that he was merely accelerating the process, remarks echoing aspects of anarchism and global terrorism of the period, but also ones that paid tribute to concerns about the dangers of nuclear war. As the two submarines set off on their mission from his supertanker, *Liparus*, Stromberg turns to his captive: "Observe, Mr. Bond. The instruments of Armageddon." In 1976 Kevin McClory began work on a *Thunderball* reworking to be entitled first *James Bond of the Secret Service* and then *Warhead*. In this film, Blofeld was to sink a Soviet submarine and seize its atomic warheads. They were to be used to intimidate the United Nations into giving SPECTRE control of the oceans, which were being polluted by humanity. In the plot, Bond thwarts Blofeld's attempt to detonate a nuclear warhead that he had smuggled into Manhattan inside a robot shark. Legal disputes between

Eon and McClory prevented the filming of *Warhead*, but some of the themes in the plot are of interest. The concern with pollution was to strike an echo in the next Bond film.

In *The Spy Who Loved Me*, Bond has to save the world and, in doing so, he shows that Britain has a major role. The search for the heat-signature tracking device that enabled Stromberg to follow and intercept the submarines leads Bond to Egypt. There he competes for the device with the leading Soviet spy, Agent XXX, Anya Amasova, the first Bond girl who was a high-powered spy. This can be seen as a reaction to claims that the early Bond films were sexist and also to the growing feminist current from the 1960s; but, as part of the world of fantasy, Anya is a beauty who does not look or sound anything like Rosa Klebb, the more convincing spy in *From Russia With Love*. Furthermore, Anya is professionally outclassed by Bond.

Anya and Bond are both forced to thwart another fantasy figure, Stromberg's gargantuan killer Jaws, with his steel teeth. Bond and Anya are instructed to cooperate and, eventually, Stromberg is killed by Bond, who rescues the captured Anya. Jaws, played by Richard Kiel, was left to bite a shark to death, in order to survive and be available for a return engagement.

"A new era of Anglo-Soviet co-operation" was celebrated at the end of the film. It overcomes the animosity that had come from Anya's discovery that Bond had killed her lover in the alpine scene at the outset. She had vowed to kill him once the mission against Stromberg has been completed, but is overcome by Bond's appeal. They go to bed in an escape capsule at the close. In reply to "Bond, what do you think you're doing?" from the minister of defence, comes the reply "Keeping the British end up, Sir!"—a joke that plumbed new depths in banality and also directly linked Britain's strength to Bond's virility. The film also presented glamorous and improbable British technology, with a Lotus Esprit sports car adapted by Q branch so as also to be ready to travel underwater and to be capable of firing a sea-to-air missile.

Directed by Lewis Gilbert from a final shooting script by Christopher Wood, *The Spy Who Loved Me* was one of the most polished and effective of the Bond films. It combined an arresting pretitle sequence, a strong story line, well-paced and varied action sequences, a convincing villain and his intimidating henchman, tension as Bond struggled to send the rockets off course, gadgets, technology—rockets, the Lotus car, and the supertanker, a threatening lair—Atlantis, attractive women, Bond's one-liners and a set that was destroyed in the final battle. The filming took advantage of the creation at Pinewood Studios in 1976 of what was then the largest silent stage in the world in order to provide for the gigantic sets needed for the film. The title song, "Nobody Does It Better," sung by Carly Simon, captured both the implausibility and the vanity of the Bond persona, at this point, and the excitement and appeal of the film. The song itself rose to second in the American and seventh in the UK charts. At $13 million, the film was expensive to make but it was also far more commercially successful than *The Man With the Golden Gun*.

In 1977, the year in which *The Spy Who Loved Me* was released, the Americans tested a neutron bomb, an "Enhanced Radiation Weapon," while the first Soviet SS-20 missiles, mobile and more accurate nuclear weapons designed to be used in conjunction with conventional forces in an invasion of Western Europe, became operational. Both sides in the Cold War had for many years devoted much effort to submarine detection. Indeed Alistair Watson, head of the British secret submarine detection research section at the Admiralty Research Laboratory, had been dismissed as a suspected Soviet agent. The film made reference to the Cold War. Anya mentioned that she had been on a survival course in Siberia, leading Bond to reply "I believe a great number of your countrymen do it," an allusion to the Soviet persecution of dissidents. She also refers to Stromberg as "one of the principal capitalist oppressors."

This is badinage. The real enemy is elsewhere. Indeed, the presence of a true hidden enemy subverts the Cold War antagonism and suggests that it simply serves the pernicious ends of a third party, a recurrent theme in the Bond genre from the introduction of SPECTRE. The real enemy is not the USSR but SPECTRE with its complete absence of any political principle, although Richard Maibaum's original screenplay, which presented SPECTRE as now controlled by nihilistic radical terrorists, was rejected, in part because of legal disputes over the right to the idea of SPECTRE.

The notion of a sinister third party, however, was to help the Bond films outlive the fall of the USSR; 1977 was also the year in which Leonid Brezhnev, the general secretary of the Soviet Communist party, publicly proposed joint American and Soviet pledges to a no-first-use nuclear strategy. Such propaganda gestures made it harder to locate adventure films designed for a mass audience in a Cold War context. Jimmy Carter, who became the American president in 1977, sought to give new energy to détente.

The next film was first to be *Octopussy*, then *For Your Eyes Only*, but in the event was to be *Moonraker* (1979), a title and topic that enabled the Bond series to draw on interest in space developments and on the popularity of space epics suggested by *Star Wars* (1977).

In *Moonraker*, an American space shuttle on loan to the British for unexplained reasons disappears. There are no remains amongst the wreckage of the RAF jumbo jet that was bringing it to Britain: such a jet of course would have had to have been purchased from the Americans. Bond is ordered to investigate the manufacturers, Drax Industries, the creation of Hugo Drax. Whereas in the novel Drax and his company had been based in England, in the film, it was California that was the focus, albeit a California that was enhanced by Vaux-le-Vicomte, a seventeenth-century French palace, now the headquarters of Drax. As in the novel, Drax was a foreigner, but in the film there was no attempt at deception: Drax was played as a foreigner, not an American. The film was not a critique of American mega-capitalists, but, like *Diamonds Are Forever* and, later, *A View To A Kill*, suggested that such capitalism could be taken over by sinister foreigners.

In a globetrotting adventure, Bond went on to Venice, where he discovered that Drax was manufacturing nerve gas, and Brazil, whence Drax launches his space shuttles into orbit. He planned to create a master race in space based on his space station and to destroy the rest of the species by firing nerve gas back at the earth.

Bond cooperated with the Americans, but, in a reversal of an established format, on this occasion the CIA agent was not a man, but, instead, Dr. Holly Goodhead, a beautiful and talented NASA astronaut and astrophysicist. The two competed and then cooperated, secretly getting aboard a shuttle. Bond was able to overcome the stealth radar blocking device on the space station, another aspect of new technology, to kill Drax, and to destroy the nerve gas en route to the earth. The film complemented the Anglo-Soviet cooperation of *The Spy Who Loved Me*, down to Bond's antiseptic sex with his colleague in the closing sequel. More substantially, the assault on the space station was mounted by an American shuttle.

Bond had less expensive weapons, including armor-piercing and cyanide-coated darts activated by nerve impulses from his wrist muscles. The darts twice save him. Drax clearly thinks Britain insignificant. His cosmopolitan establishment includes a French helicopter pilot, a Japanese killer, an American scientist and Cavendish, an English butler complete with tails. Drax tells Bond "your country's one indisputable contribution to world civilization [is] afternoon tea." The idea of Britain having a major espionage base in the Brazilian interior, as the film suggested, was a fantasy. Instead, Latin America was very much a sphere of American activity, and Britain's political and economic role there had greatly diminished.

Moonraker, written by Christopher Wood and directed by Lewis

Gilbert, was a hugely successful film, breaking box-office records for
a Bond film, although the critical response was more hostile than for
most of the series. The success of the Bond films, hitherto, not only
in the cinema but also with the sale of television rights, encouraged
a major investment. The film cost $34 million to make, as much as
the first eight Bond films together. Its popularity reflected, in part,
the appeal of space at the time of the Star Wars films. The Bond
genre could be adapted to respond to shifts in public interest and the
rise of particular icons. The return of Jaws in this film, as the only
subsidiary villain to bridge stories, reflected a public letter-writing
campaign, and perhaps paid tribute to the success of the shark film
of that name. The British trailer proclaimed, "Guess who's dropped
in for a bite. Jaws is back."

Politics played scant role in *Moonraker*. When Drax's space station
appeared on radar, the American Colonel Scott telephones the KGB's
General Gogol from NASA headquarters. Each confirms that it was
not their station. Scott informs Gogol that the Americans were sending up a shuttle to intercept. Gogol grimly replies that the USSR will
act unless the Americans settle the matter, but the element of menace is greatly lessened when, having told Scott on the phone that he
had "nothing but problems," he turns to reveal a woman in his bed.

Instead, the menace is very much that of Drax, a threat to the
entire world. In the space station, he addresses his followers from
on high in a Fascistic fashion, offering a millenarian future in which
his germ-laden globes will create "a necklace of death round the
earth," which will be followed by "a rebirth, a new world," with "a
new super race, a race of perfect physical specimens."

This was fantasy, but a fantasy that drew on anxiety about change
and technology. No private individual could mount such a challenge.
Paradoxically, the threat of biological attack did, indeed, exist in the
1980s. As an interview with Kanatjan Alibekov (formerly an official
in the program) in the *New York Times* of 25 February 1998 revealed,
the Soviet Union prepared anthrax and smallpox and plague virus
cultures that would have been delivered by intercontinental ballistic
missile warheads at several days' notice in the 1980s. Such a film
plot would have been disconcerting and regarded as alarmist. The
extensive role of shuttles in *Moonraker* reflected a responsiveness to
recent developments. They had first landed successfully two years
earlier and were to enter service in April 1981. Drax's space station
drew on the American Skylab, which went into operation in 1973,
and, in their quest for realism, the producers used NASA advisers.
They claimed that the film was "science fact, not science fiction."

The film testified not only to the commercial importance of the

Anglo-American markets, but also, at least indirectly, to the reassertion of Atlanticism in British overseas policy after Heath was replaced in 1974 by the Labour governments of first Harold Wilson, again, and then James Callaghan. In contrast to Heath's exploration of Anglo-French nuclear collaboration, the Labour government renewed the nuclear alliance with the United States through the Chevaline program. In 1979, the government was the only one of the then nine EEC states to decide not to join the Exchange Rater Mechanism, a measure designed to stabilize and unify the financial systems of the EEC countries. Britain had voted in a referendum held in 1975 to stay in the EEC, but there was only limited interest in a European identity.

Directed by John Glen, the next film, *For Your Eyes Only* (1981), was far less melodramatic and cataclysmic. Given the unprecedented commercial success of *Moonraker*, this shift was surprising. In part, it offered a new realism for the Bond films. The space theme of *Moonraker* and the global span of the earth scenes, captured in the varied landscapes from which Moonrakers 1–6 took off, was replaced by a more limited story, one less given to parody. More generally, the space theme in the films declined, reflecting in part a decline in the public's general interest in an apparently stalled American-Soviet space confrontation. Christopher Wood, who had penned the screenplay of *The Spy Who Loved Me* and *Moonraker*, was replaced by Richard Maibaum, who had written many of the early films. Technology played a smaller and less dramatic role than in the space epic.

Thanks to the theme of betrayal, the plot of *For Your Eyes Only* was more complex than that of earlier films. The film drew heavily on the twist of the plot of Fleming's short story "Risico." A British electronic surveillance ship, with a quintessential patriotic name, *St. George*, then decoding Soviet satellite data on British and American ship positions, is blown up off Albania by a mine without there being any opportunity to destroy its ATAC (Automatic Targeting Attack Communicator) transmitter. As the ATAC is employed to instruct British submarines to fire ballistic missiles, its capture would render the British Polaris submarine fleet useless and would give the Soviets the opportunity to order the fleet to attack British cities, an improbable scenario. As the *St. George* went down too close to the then hostile Communist state of Albania for overt salvage operations, the British turn to the marine archaeologist Sir Timothy Havelock, only for him and his wife to be machine-gunned by a Cuban hit man, Hector Gonzales, a swarthy individual with a moustache and dark hair.

Bond is ordered to find out who hired him, but Gonzales is shot with a crossbow by Havelock's daughter, Melina, as he dives into his pool, a scene based on the short story "For Your Eyes Only." Gonzales was the name of Hammerstein's principal assistant in that story. Bond, nevertheless, identifies the paymaster as Émile Locque and this leads him to the world of top Greek smugglers—Kristatos and Colombo. As in "Risico," Kristatos is discovered to be a villain, while Colombo, who smuggles gold, diamonds and pistachio nuts, not heroin, helps to defeat Kristatos. The visual clues are clear: Colombo smiles and is exuberant. Kristatos is prim. However, the villain, played well by Julian Glover, was not disfigured, as Joseph Wiseman's Dr. No and Donald Pleasence's Blofeld had been.

Kristatos had arranged to sell the ATAC transmitter to the Soviets: he was their "usual friend in Greece," according to Gogol. However, in the climax of the film there is a successful assault on Kristatos's mountaintop eyrie, Kristatos is killed and, before the Soviets can get the ATAC transmitter, Bond throws it off the mountaintop, telling Gogol "That's detente, comrade. You don't have it. I don't have it." Gogol is presented sympathetically. Having told his escort not to shoot Bond, he laughs at his remark. At the outset, Gogol had kissed the hand of his beautiful secretary. He was very different from Eric Kriegler, the East German ski champion, a killer who helps Locque and is a KGB agent. Eric is the antithesis of Bond, a tall blond who dresses in black, doesn't smoke, won't talk to women and eats only health foods. Gonzales and Eric represent visual examples of two physical and psychological profiles (self-indulgence and fanaticism) compared to whom Bond is a happy medium.

At the close of the film, Bond was congratulated by Margaret Thatcher (Conservative prime minister, 1970–90)—"Your courage and resourcefulness are a credit to the nation"—in a call taken by Melina's parrot in a comic ending in which the parrot pretend-Bond gets away with asking Mrs. Thatcher for a kiss—"Really Mr. Bond!" says a delighted Margaret Thatcher, who is clearly not immune to the right approach. Her quest for vengeance complete, Melina more fully yields to Bond, but until the close of the film it was this quest that had taken precedence for her. The film itself lacked the possibility of a megalomaniacal villain and global holocaust offered by The Spy Who Loved Me and Moonraker and was more realistic as a consequence. The settings, while still far from the grittiness of conventional spy stories, were less otherworldly than those of the two previous films. They were also all in Europe.

There were a number of independent forces in the next film, Octopussy (1983), including good Russians, bad Russians and the Octopussy Organization, an improbable criminal sisterhood based on an island in an Indian river that is inhabited only by beautiful women and dedicated to jewel smuggling under the cover of a traveling circus. Octopussy, however, was used by Kamal Khan, an exiled Afghan prince, well played by Louis Jourdan, working for Orlov, the Soviet general planning to explode an atom bomb on an American airbase in Germany. Especially in its last stages, the film, again directed by John Glen, offered a series of fast-paced chases and action sequences.

Afghanistan had indeed been the site and cause of a marked raising of the temperature in the Cold War. The Soviet invasion of December 1979 had been followed by a civil war in Afghanistan, and by an increase in tension with America. The United States imposed a grain embargo on the USSR in December 1979 and followed this up with a boycott of the Moscow Olympics in 1980. Once Jimmy Carter was succeeded by Ronald Reagan after the 1980 presidential election, the Americans took a more assertive line in the buildup of nuclear strength and in attacking Soviet allies, including support for opponents of the left-wing government in Nicaragua and, in October 1983, the invasion of the Caribbean island of Grenada, which had been violently taken over by a hard-line left-wing group. In March 1983 Reagan publicly condemned the Soviet Union as an "evil empire . . . the focus of evil in the modern world," and he followed this up in June 1983 by pressing the case for the Strategic Defense Initiative (SDI), better known as Star Wars—the use of lasers and satellites to protect the United States from missile attack.

This assertive line was strongly backed by the British under Thatcher. She supported the United States over Afghanistan, Star Wars and the deployment of cruise missiles in Britain, although not over intervention in Grenada. Thatcher told a dinner held in Washington in 1985 to celebrate 200 years of Anglo-American diplomatic relations: "There is a union of mind and purpose between our peoples which is remarkable and which makes our relationship truly a remarkable one. It is special. It just is, and that's that." Reagan was willing to let Thatcher take a role that was disproportionate to the respective strength of the two countries. Although she did not always take the lead, the relationship was indeed special to Thatcher, for it gave her great influence on the world stage.

Thatcher felt that Britain was under threat. In 1987 Britain spent 5.2 percent of her gross national product on defense, compared with 4 percent for France, 3.1 percent for West Germany and 6.7 percent for the United States. Soviet espionage in Britain remained a source of concern. In 1982 Geoffrey Prime, formerly a Soviet agent at the Government Communications Headquarters (GCHQ) at Cheltenham, was convicted of espionage. Two years later, Michael Bettaney was arrested for espionage and the KGB resident expelled, and, in 1985, the defection of Oleg Gordievsky, the KGB resident-designate, led to the expulsion of twenty-five Soviet intelligence officers. There was also suspicion that left-wing trade unionists were willing to help Soviet interests.

A View To A Kill (1985) was the last Moore film and was again directed by John Glen. The villain, Max Zorin, was yet another billionaire industrialist, and, yet again, both California and a French palace featured in the action. This was a world away from Britain's recent conflict with Argentina over the Falklands in 1982 and from contemporary Cold War confrontation. The latter had become acute again, with the Soviet fear of attack during the NATO command and control exercise Able Archer 83, the Soviets shooting down a Korean civilian airplane in 1983 and the deployment of American Pershing II rockets in West Germany from 1983. *A View To A Kill* was also a long way from the theme of "the enemy within." Thatcher was convinced that on the left individuals and organizations, such as certain prominent trade unionists, especially within the National Union of Miners, and also the Campaign for Nuclear Disarmament, were fronts, often willingly so, for Communist propaganda and Soviet subversion. This theme led to an emphasis on countersubversion, rather than counterterrorism, especially in 1981–85 while Sir John Jones was director-general of MI5, the sister service to Bond's MI6. There was no echo of such themes in *A View To A Kill*, possibly because they were controversial. The Thatcher/Reagan approach was strongly criticized and, in Britain, the Labour Party abandoned any idea of a consensus on defense and foreign-policy issues: NATO's policies were seen as contributing to a situation of nuclear menace.

Zorin was a microchip manufacturer, with a portrait of Napoleon in his study, who, rather like Auric Goldfinger, sought to enhance the value of his product by wrecking the competition, thus ending the world surplus of microchips. His plan was for the devastation of Silicon Valley by a massive flood caused by an earthquake on the San Andreas Fault that was to be triggered by an explosion. Initially, the plot had Zorin alter the course of Halley's Comet in order to achieve his goal.

Although the main section of the film began in imperial London with a shot of Horseguards and then of a trooper of the guards, and some of the initial action took place in France, both in Paris and at Zorin's estate (the palace of Chantilly), this was a film about California. Most of the action took place there, and it is the target. Zorin himself was both unhinged—a sadist without conscience—and at the cross of troubling associations. In a variant of *The Boys from Brazil*, he was a product of Nazi eugenics, born in Germany as part of an attempt to create a race of superhumans. This, at once, links him with Drax, another manipulator of genetics. Zorin worked for the Soviets, only to break with them near the outset of the story. He was thus a free lance, pitched against another, for Bond operated with the minimum of control in this story.

By this film, Moore was a world away from the Bond of *Live and Let Die*, let alone Connery. In *A View To A Kill*, he was fifty-seven years old, recognizably aging, overweight, unfit and with thinning hair. This caused hostile criticism, but, aside from the protagonist's physique in this film, there was a sense that both Moore and the Bond industry had lost direction. Moore was increasingly improbable, his jokes directed at the Bond icon. There was a campness in his portrayal that contrasted with the darker intensity of Connery. The latter's films were not without their humor, especially in the last, *Diamonds Are Forever*, but Connery had retained control and continued to suggest danger. Moore had lost these elements. To many, he seemed a tailor's dummy come to life, his wisecracking not able to cover his fragile "man of the world" style and his lack of toughness. He became an appendage to the stunts and the machines.

The genre itself was mocked in the precredits adventure in *A View To A Kill*, when the Siberian ski chase scene was trivialized with the use of the Beach Boys' song "California Girls." Bond escaped in a submarine, disguised as an iceberg, navigated by a ductile blond (and no one else) and equipped with champagne, a fantasy ludicrous even by the standards of the films of the period. Furthermore, Jaws' improbable survivals in *The Spy Who Loved Me* and *Moonraker* and the gondola chase in the latter were spoofs, as was Jaws' conversion to love to the accompaniment of romantic Tchaikovsky strains.

The weakness of Moore was highlighted by Sean Connery's reappearance as Bond in *Never Say Never Again* (1983), Kevin McClory's effective and witty reworking of *Thunderball*, directed by Irvin Kershner, with a credible villain and a plot brought up to date with cruise missiles, retinal-scan recognition devices and cost-cutting in the Secret Service. American cruise missiles based in Britain, rather than British atomic bombs, are hijacked by SPECTRE, and the NATO states are then held to ransom.

Bond was a figure from the past, literally so, as he was played by Connery repeating the plot of *Thunderball*. The porter at Shrublands greeted him with the remark that they no longer made cars like his, the new M had little use for the 00 section, which he sees as redundant, and instead was intent on purging toxins from the body, and

Q complains of slashed budgets, dullness and rule by bureaucrats and computers. Bond, in contrast, offers the "gratuitous sex and violence" that Q, and, presumably, the viewers, want. They can envy openly his mission to the Bahamas—"Lucky bloody you" is Q's response. There Bond meets his antithesis, Nigel Small-Fawcett, a British diplomat, a role brilliantly realized by Rowan Atkinson. He is a far from manly prat who is worried that Bond will cause trouble, jeopardizing the tourist trade. This safety-first attitude, in fact, threatens the national interest. Bond is necessarily robust in ignoring it.

Bond also depends upon American resources in the film. Although *Never Say Never Again* lacks a Cold War plot, it again finds Britain and America as joint targets and allies. The Soviet role is minimal, although Bond's reference to reading a Russian translation of an American service manual indicates the two-way espionage of the Cold War, and the cruise missile were of course designed to protect Western Europe from Soviet attack. Connery's revived Bond was widely praised in the press.

Bond as a character increasingly appeared out of place to many commentators in the 1980s. His easy sexuality seemed misplaced for a world, first, of women's emancipation and, then, of AIDS. Suggestive lines—such as "I love an early morning ride" or "Are you buying or selling?" in *A View To A Kill*, or "She's just coming" at the close of *The Man With the Golden Gun*, or "Bollinger. If it's 69 you were expecting me" to Holly Goodhead in *Moonraker*—lacked style. "The face is familiar. As is the manner," Holly's rejoinder to Bond in Rio, was a response to the tackiness of his approach.

Bond as a sexual liberator, as in Solitaire's "For the first time in my life I feel a complete woman," seemed increasingly inappropriate and unconvincing. Barbara Bach, who played Anya Amasova, publicly described Bond as "a male chauvinist pig." The Englishness of Bond, not least as the pretend racehorse owner St. John Smythe in *A View To A Kill*, no longer appeared to amount to much. In that role, he was paired with Patrick Macnee's Sir Godfrey Tibbett. The two were far more similar than Bond and Strangeways had been in *Dr. No*. Moore represented an American view of Britain, at once stylish and quaint, not lean and mean, the values of the Thatcherite mid-1980s. Moore's Bond was an outdated caricature even in British terms. His patronizing of Sir Godfrey is uncomfortable, not humorous. Furthermore, in *A View To A Kill*, Sir Godfrey is easily killed by May Day: the former John Steed from *The Avengers* now seemed charming but harmless.

The settings also appeared out of date, or at least out of keeping with the bulk of the viewers. Dinner-jacketed heroes were out, as was the world of casinos. Moreover, the *Whicker's World* feel of the Moore films—the search for eccentric billionaires in exotic locales, as in the travelogues of Alan Whicker, one of the leading British television interviewers of the period—became stale and formulaic and invited satire. The point at which a formula tips into staleness is to some degree subjective, but it had been reached with the latest Moore films. *For Your Eyes Only, Octopussy* and *A View To A Kill* were poorly received, and the takings for each successively fell. It was time for a change.

9

The Dalton Interlude

Timothy Dalton appeared in two films, *The Living Daylights* (1987) and *Licence To Kill* (1989), both directed by John Glen and written by Maibaum and Wilson. They were grittier in plot and tone than the later Moore films. This was a conscious reaction that was, in part, related to the more critical and sardonic, if not sarcastic, attitude toward heroism that could be widely seen on television and film in the period; the popular British television comedy series *Blackadder*, for example, closed in 1989 with programs presenting World War I as futile, cruel and unheroic.

Both Dalton films involved drugs and exotic locales. The first, released on the silver (25th) anniversary of the Bond films, linked themes from a number of films, including *Octopussy*. The Soviets were divided, seeking to embroil the West in their struggles, and personal profit, specifically drugs, played a role. The KGB still had a role in 1987, and the film employed notions of penetration and betrayal with more skill than the Moore films. This was a spy story in which there was a complex plot to unravel, as much as it was an adventure film.

After the French and American settings of *A View To A Kill*, *Living*

Daylights was set in Gibraltar, Czechoslovakia, Afghanistan and Tangier. Gibraltar offered the opportunity of a setting for an adventure in which Britain could still act as an imperial power: the 00 section is chosen to test the radar defenses of Gibraltar, defended for this exercise by the SAS (Special Air Service). Viewers were expected to know that the SAS represented British bravery and martial proficiency. The mission was penetrated by the Soviets, apparent proof of the need for vigilance. Czechoslovakia and Afghanistan provided the Cold War staple of the film, and Tangier permitted the inclusion of a mad American pseudo-general, Brad Whitaker, the arms dealer, yet another figure with a Napoleon complex.

However, as in *Octopussy*, there were good and bad Soviets; whereas, in contrast, in John Gardner's novel of that year, *No Deals, Mr. Bond*, both the KGB and its military rival, GRU, were presented as sinister threats. In *Octopussy*, Gogol had opposed the bellicose General Orlov. In *The Living Daylights*, Gogol, now with the Soviet Foreign Service, appears as a benign presence at the close, and his replacement, General Pushkin, is not the opponent of détente that he initially appears. Indeed, although the Soviet presence in Afghanistan is regarded as pernicious and the resistance are heroes, the film offers a warning against Cold War paranoia. Georgi Koskov, the KGB general who apparently defects to the British, warns M and the minister of defense that Pushkin is opposed to détente and intent on resuming the "Death to Spies" policy outlined in the novel *From Russia, With Love*.

In fact, Koskov wants the British to kill Pushkin, because the latter is blocking his corrupt and aggressive schemes to use the KGB to enhance his own wealth and that of his partner Brad Whitaker. These schemes center on the purchase of raw opium in Afghanistan from the Snow Leopard Brotherhood, worth $500 million on the streets of New York, and the sale by Whitaker of smart infantry weaponry to the USSR. Bond unravels and thwarts the plot. Pushkin emerges in a positive light. He despises Whitaker's "personal pantheon of military heroes," calling them butchers, and dismisses Whitaker's defense of them as "surgeons. They collect away society's dead flesh." Pushkin cooperates with Bond in misleading Koskov and, at the close, saves Bond from Whitaker's assistant. Far from a figure of menace, he is a fleshy smiler, a voluptuary with a mistress, closest in character to Kerim Bey. Bond's willingness to follow instincts, not orders, prevents him from obeying orders and killing Pushkin. *The Living Daylights* was more of a puzzle film than most of the Bond genre. Appearances were deceptive, and loyalties and betrayals complex. The positive view of Pushkin accorded with Mrs.

Thatcher's identification of Gorbachev as a Soviet leader with whom she could do business.

None of the action is set in the United States, and the CIA plays only a very small role in the film, principally in assisting Bond against Whitaker at the close. A misleading impression was therefore created. In Afghanistan, for example, it was the CIA, rather than MI6, that provided the Afghan resistance with money, armaments, communications equipment and satellite reconnaissance data. *The Living Daylights* offered a somewhat primitivizing account of the Afghans, presenting them as a mounted horde. In reality, by the summer of 1986, the CIA was distributing advanced Stinger surface-to-air missiles. They had already provided surface-to-air missiles, wire-guided antitank missiles, grenade launchers, mortars, recoilless rifles, bazookas, antiaircraft guns, long-range sniper rifles, communications equipment and targeting devices for mortars. The Soviet Union withdrew from Afghanistan in 1989.

In *Licence To Kill* (1989) the setting was Latin America, although the setting had originally been intended to be China. Instead, however, of an Asian drug king, the film offered a Latin American version, Franz Sanchez, a sadistic and ruthless drug king, sought to make his drug empire a global force, specifically to extend it to the Orient. He was based in Isthmus City, where he dominated the government through corruption and force. This was clearly designed to suggest Panama, especially to American viewers. General Manuel Antonio Noriega, who had dominated Panama since 1983, was accused of corruption and murder in 1987, and the American government unsuccessfully pressed him to resign. The following year, Noriega was indicted, in absentia, in Miami on drug trafficking and racketeering charges, and in December 1989 American forces invaded Panama and overthrew the regime. Noriega was seized and taken for trial in America. Sanchez, like Noriega, had a sinisterly marked face. As far as British viewers were concerned, the Falklands War of 1982 had led to an upsurge in critical coverage of South American military juntas. There was also growing concern that drug dealers were smuggling more South American drugs into Britain.

Bond's part in *Licence To Kill* could not, however, be explained in terms of any plausible account of Britain's role, and Britain played little part in the film's politics. Instead, this became very much a personal mission. At the beginning, Bond was in Florida to act as Leiter's best man. The wedding was temporarily postponed when Sanchez was tracked by an AWACS plane to the Bahamas, where he had gone to chase his fleeing lover. The use of the plane was fresh testimony of the concern of the films to stay up with technology.

Sanchez has to be captured before he can return to the shelter of Cuban airspace, a situation that focuses two central features of American demonology: drugs and Cuba. Bond was invited by Leiter to go on the surprise mission, "strictly as an observer," but he was instrumental in Sanchez's capture. However, Sanchez then escaped thanks to the treachery of an American lawman, the latter played by a tall, clean-shaven white in contrast to the non-WASPS used in the novels when Fleming wished to present bad Americans.

The escaped Sanchez captures Leiter and has him dropped into a shark tank, from which, although badly injured, he improbably survives. His new wife, Della, is raped and killed. Bond finds them and is then frustrated by the inability of the authorities to act against Sanchez, now, again, outside American jurisdiction. Told that many countries would be willing to shelter Sanchez and would refuse to extradict him, Bond argued that he should be pursued "by other ways" (i.e., by covert operations), and he criticized the agents of the American Drug Enforcement Agency (DEA) for wanting to let go and not press the issue.

Acting alone, Bond breaks into the marine-research laboratory run by Sanchez's deputy, Milton Krest, a Key West establishment based on that described in the novel *Live and Let Die*. Bond discovers that the laboratory is being used as a base for drug smuggling, the drugs significantly hidden under live maggots. Interrupted, Bond kills both the security guards and the treacherous lawman, the last devoured in the shark tank in a brutal scene of harsh, but just, retribution.

Subsequently reprimanded, Bond mocks the judicial system—"Do you have a law against what they did to Leiter?"—establishing a powerful contrast that is to be felt throughout the film. Authority is not benign, and Bond has a personality able to confront issues of duty and responsibility.

This is driven home when Bond clashes with M in Miami. Bond is criticized for failing to go to Istanbul, a Cold War cockpit, as ordered, and M tells him to leave Sanchez to the Americans, a remark that captures the circumspection of Britain's role and the absence of any universal quest against disorder. Told by Bond that Leiter had risked his life for him, M cruelly retorts "Spare me this sentimental rubbish" and, when Bond resigns, M replies "We're not a country club," revokes his license to kill, tells him he is still bound by the Official Secrets Act and demands that he hand over his weapon.

Bond violently escapes, although significantly without killing anyone. Whereas in previous adventures he had often been on his own under cover, that had been as part of an officially sanctioned mission and, generally, in accordance with his instructions. He had been

Britain's secret weapon, his skills and emotions subordinated to that task. In *Licence To Kill*, however, an important barrier was crossed, although the consequences were not fully probed. This is also true, although to a far lesser extent, of *A View To A Kill* when Zorin tells Bond that the Secret Service will seek to cover up his disappearance, not to investigate it. The theme of revenge had been applied in *Goldfinger*. After the killing of Jill Masterson, M had warned Bond that keeping an eye on Goldfinger "isn't a personal vendetta" and that, if he couldn't treat the mission "coldly and objectively," M would turn to 008. The potential difference was not, however, pressed, as it was to be in *Licence To Kill*. The same is true of Bond's resignation at the start of the film *On Her Majesty's Secret Service*—it becomes a fortnight's leave, not a cause for dispute—and of Bond's readiness to face dismissal for deliberately missing the pretend Soviet sniper in *The Living Daylights*. *Licence To Kill* was at first to have been called *Licence Revoked*.

In going it alone, Bond becomes a loose cannon on deck and wrecks both an attempt by the Americans to regain four Stinger missiles Sanchez had bought and one by the Hong Kong narcotics agency to infiltrate Sanchez's network, leading to the death of three agents. Yet he receives backing from Q, then on leave, thus lessening any rift arising from Bond's individual quest, as far as the expectations of the audience are concerned.

Bond is helped by one of the best-realized of his female leads, Pam Bouvier, played by Carey Lowell. She is an ex-flier who is an effective fighter, with a bigger gun than Bond's (a pump-action shotgun compared to his Walther PPK); she also saves his life. The two tussle over professionalism, the mission and the roles they should play. She asks Bond "Why can't you be my executive secretary?" and his reply—"We're south of the border. It's a man's world"—does not suggest that their role-playing as boss and secretary is desirable. Bouvier is presented as a capable, independent and mature person, a different woman from the girls who had dominated the portrayal of women in the early films.

Sanchez's system is striking deep roots in the United States. Producing a substantial cash surplus daily, he has "the world's largest investment fund," much of his money deposited in the United States, and thus serving to finance the American trade deficit. In short, consumerism and a lack of self-control weakens the United States, providing opportunities for Sanchez.

Technology is also an American weakness, for Sanchez takes American orders for drugs and sets the price under the cover of his employee, Professor Joe Butcher, who operates as a television evangelist seeking pledges over the television. Running an empire from Chile to Alaska, Sanchez is an entrepreneur who picks up many of the themes of the 1980s. His investment banker, Truman Lodge, is a yuppie fund manager, ironically killed at the end by Sanchez, who parrots Lodge's language by saying that he is cutting overheads. Like many fund managers and investors of the period, Sanchez sees huge potential demand in the Pacific basin. He offers the visiting East Asian drug dealers exclusive franchises, seeking $100 million in negotiable bearer bonds from each in return for deliveries of guaranteed quality and price for five years. His "East meets West. Drug dealers of the world unite" is an ironic echo of Communist propaganda and recalls Dr. No's indifference to the Cold War. As more generally with the Bond series, crime has transcended barriers.

Sanchez still, however, has to face the problem of disloyalty. Paradoxically, Bond is the most disloyal individual portrayed, other than the American lawman. Bond not only wins the trust of, and then betrays, the villain, as the secret agent is supposed to do; he is also responsible for killings in the Sanchez network by falsely suggesting that the number two, Krest, is defrauding Sanchez, and by throwing doubt on the loyalty of Heller, the head of security. Yet Bond is also defying M's orders. The difference is Bond's sense of mission. That has replaced the assigned mission. He is motivated by revenge, but a justified revenge, rather like that portrayed in the short story "For Your Eyes Only." Bond's goal is not financial, for example the $2 million that had been paid by Sanchez near the start of the film to spring him from jail, but satisfaction of a deadlier type that is at once personal and seen as cleansing society.

This is a troubling idea, made more so in the film by the detrimental effect of Bond on other operations. The entire mood is darker, far less subverted by Bond's mannerisms and wisecracks than in the Moore films. Dalton's Bond emerges as a certain moral presence against the ambiguities of others, for example the attempt to offer Heller immunity in return for the Stingers. Sanchez's plan to threaten to use them against an American aircraft unless the DEA agrees to back off from him is credible, but so also is a suspicion that the DEA might agree.

Bond's ambivalence is different, and less sinister. He is attracted to both the female leads and arouses Bouvier's suspicions by his links with Sanchez's lover, Lupe Lamora. Q urges Bouvier not to be harsh—"Field operatives must often use every means at their disposal to achieve their objectives"—and, in the end, Bouvier and Bond pair. The difficulties in their relationship have provided an acceptable level of uncertainty in the story. Their "Why don't you wait until you're asked?" "So why don't you ask me?" exchange captures the independence of both and, more generally, changes in the characterization of female roles. Bouvier is not the pliable victim that so many of the early Bond women had been.

Sanchez sees money as the universal solvent. The visiting drug barons are provided with face masks at the drug plant to prevent "our best customers developing a drug habit." Drugs are simply a device to obtain money, a new "view to a kill," and the sums are vast. Each of the road tankers containing petrol in which cocaine is dissolved is worth $80 million. This money is designed not to serve some other purpose, but solely for its own ends.

There had indeed been a "death of history," in the sense of competing grand ideologies, to employ a concept advanced after the end of the Cold War. Sacred space—Butcher's Meditation Institute—is a religious experience designed solely to act as a cover for the drug trade. This not only offers an ironic uniting of religion and drugs; in addition, there is an amusing satire on television evangelism and on alternative religion. Butcher's Meditation Institute even makes a profit from the latter. His "own private meditation chamber," constructed from the "sacred rocks" of the original temple, is for seduction. This is a less contentious target than an explicit attack on Christian evangelism.

Whereas at the outset of *Goldfinger* Bond had destroyed a store of heroin used "to finance revolution," Sanchez is equally willing to use Cuba and the corrupt, presumably right-wing, military ruler of Isthmus to serve his own ends. When Sanchez tells Bond shortly before he is apparently going to kill him "You could have had everything," he is referring to money and money alone. Bond replies "Don't you want to know why?" and sets Sanchez, then covered in gasoline, fatally alight with the engraved cigarette lighter he had been given by Leiter.

The personal quest had been fulfilled. Bond is to get his job back, but now the job itself is vindicated by his personal mission. It is not simply how Bond does it, but the fact that he chooses to do it for the government and for Britain, that in some way justifies both. In that respect, the film is closer to the issues of conscience raised in the novels, issues generally slighted on screen. In the film *Diamonds Are Forever*, Bond had arrived at Blofeld's offshore base with the lighthearted remark "The Acme Pollution Co. We're cleaning up the world. We thought this would be a suitable starting point." There was no comparable distancing humor in *Licence To Kill*.

Dalton succeeded against Sanchez, of course, but, although the right age, he was not suited to the task of rescuing the part. His expressed aim of moving back to a more "realistic" and grittier Bond closer to the books, which he indeed read, gave a violent edge to the acting and a dynamism to the narrative that focused on Bond rather than stunts. Dalton's brooding intensity also led to odd reflective comments in *The Living Daylights*, but, in practice, although less glib than Moore, Dalton was neither one thing nor the other. He tried to make Bond human, subject to pain and disheveled after combat, and this proved a mistake. Handsome and a good actor, Dalton appeared somewhat detached from the Bond persona, less humorous than Connery, let alone Moore, and compared to such contemporary film action heroes as Bruce Willis, he seemed effete and unthreatening, although *The Living Daylights* was more violent than earlier Bond films. Dalton lacked the physical authority of Connery. The tuxedo-clad Bond contrasted with the begrimed torso of Willis, and Bond seemed to some almost a puppet, at once unreal and flimsy.

Yet that, in part, was because style had changed and democratized. The stylish, gentlemanly conduct of the original Bond could now seem effete. Writing to the Columbia Broadcasting System in 1957, when it was considering Bond for television, Fleming had observed

In hard covers my books are written for and appeal principally to an "A" readership, but they have all been reprinted in paperbacks, both in England and in America and it appears that the "B" and "C" classes find them equally readable, although one might have thought that the sophistication of the background and detail would be outside their experience and in part incomprehensible.

However, although the details of the "sophistication" may have been unknown, the fact of sophistication was easy to observe and helped make the books attractive. Furthermore, the films offered a different, updated account of style. There was no role for complicated discussions of how best to cheat and win at bridge, no careful listing of the details of meals. Instead, style was suggested and defined in terms of the more accessible, yet still polished, consumerism and ethos of the 1960s. This was sustained during the Moore years, but it was, increasingly, problematic.

"You have class," Sanchez tells Bond, and he is not surprised to be told that he is a former British agent. However, by the late 1980s there was no longer a secure basis for the representation of class, either in terms of plot or of consumer appeal. This reflected, in particular, changes in style, not least in attitudes toward women, and in the presentation of bravery. The trailer for the film *From Russia With Love* (1963) referred to Bond as the "toughest, wiliest gentleman agent." In contrast, the trailer for the collected video edition of 1996 called him the "original action hero." The term *gentleman*, now difficult and contentious, had been dropped.

The social location of the original creation had been totally transformed. In the film *Goldfinger* (1964), the audience is assumed to know the "strict rules of golf," while Bond and Tilly Masterson, in her sports car, discuss sports for the leisured classes in Switzerland. Bond and his English caddy represent a benign and cooperative social hierarchy, contrasting with Goldfinger and his caddy, Oddjob. Now such images seem as dated as Agatha Christie.

10

The Brosnan Films

It's a New World. With New Enemies and New Threats. But you can still rely on one man. 007.

—advertisement for *GoldenEye*

Timothy Dalton was replaced by Pierce Brosnan, who has so far appeared in three films, *GoldenEye* (1995), *Tomorrow Never Dies* (1997) and *The World Is Not Enough* (1999). Dalton was due to continue in the role, but there was a long interlude after *Licence To Kill*, in large part due to a lengthy dispute over television and video rights to the films between Danjaq, the company of the producer Albert "Cubby" Broccoli, and MGM/UA Communications, the film studio that had backed Bond from the outset. By the time filming started on the next adventure Dalton had decided that he had had enough, and Brosnan had been selected to play Bond. He has been more successful than Dalton, and, indeed, was offered the role in place of him, but was at the time tied into a contract to lead in the American television series *Remington Steele*, a series designed to combine adventure and style. The correct age for the part, Brosnan appears to be enjoying the role and successfully fuses the roles of action man and actor. He is instrumental to the success of the adventure and a Bond closer to the Fleming novels than Moore had been, because he does not subvert the genre through humor. Yet he is also lighter and less intense than Dalton. As *GoldenEye* was the first of a four-film agreement, Brosnan will be Bond into this millennium. The positive response to *Tomorrow Never Dies* led many critics to suggest that Brosnan was the best Bond ever.

However, shifts in characterization are about more than changes of actors. There is also the question of how far and how successfully the Bond concept has been adapted to contemporary tastes, an issue that a change in actors obfuscates. Discussion of adaptation has concentrated on the attitude to women and sex. The latter plays a much smaller role in the 1990s films than was the case earlier. In part, this was a matter of the impact of AIDS and the consequent stress on sexual responsibility. This created problems for a character not associated with condoms, but, aside from sexual mores, in the narrower sense of venereal health, there was also a wider sense that attitudes to the role and position of women had changed, that emotional commitment was expected in relationships and that sexual behavior had to reflect this. The agenda set out, albeit for the villain, in Tom Jones's theme song for *Thunderball*—that he'll get any woman he wants—and for Bond in Dionne Warwick's original theme song for the same film—presenting Bond as a heartless ladykiller—had been discarded.

In many respects, the changing attitude toward sex returned Bond to the milieu of the novels, but there was a major difference. The women in the recent films have been achievers, rather than the emotional victims of the novels. Bond is no longer their first "real man," and they are not dependent on him. This could be seen in *Tomorrow Never Dies*, where the female lead was a Chinese spy, Wai Lin, played by the Malaysian actress Michelle Yeoh, a star of Hong Kong martial arts films. She was presented as resourceful, brave and effective, a match for Bond, and she was of course a Communist.

As both actress and character, Yeoh/Lin was different from earlier Bond female characters. She was able to do her own stunts and gets her own fighting sequence, although Bond appeared at the end to save her. The dynamic in her relationship with Bond was professional, not emotional. In *The Spy Who Loved Me* and *Moonraker*, Bond had been paired with spies—Anya Amasova and Holly Goodhead—but neither was allowed an action role equivalent to that of Wai Lin, and both were played by American actresses. The prominent role of an Asian actress in *Tomorrow Never Dies* was notable.

In previous films, the "good" female lead had been physically different from her "bad" counterpart. The latter tended to be darker physically and more worldly wise, as with Fatima Blush in *Never Say Never Again*, Xenia Onatopp in *GoldenEye*, or, most obviously, May Day in *A View To A Kill*, the latter played by the powerful African American Grace Jones. An Asian lead woman established a very different ethnic identification from that offered in the novels. It also contrasted with the previous Asian female character, Kissy Suzuki, the Japanese pearl fisher in *You Only Live Twice*. She was talented and brave, but also domestic and very much a support to Bond. The shift, in part, reflected the move from 1960s views of Asia to the 1990s image of the Tiger Economies.

There has also been adaptation in the Bond character. He no longer smoked or gambled. But for his association with the trademark "shaken, not stirred" line, he probably would no longer drink. It was as if the injunctions of the doctor at Shrublands in *Thunderball* (1965) about lifestyle and of Edward Fox's humorless M in *Never Say Never Again* (1983), about the need to avoid red meat, had been taken seriously.

This shift created problems for the Bond character, but they are, in part, averted by the continual emphasis on explosives. It was acceptable to have an agent who blew up and shot people at will (and without the concerns of Fleming's Bond), but he was no longer allowed to smoke or have sex, a contrast that reveals much about the nature and impact of modern political correctness. The action sequences clearly engage much of the audience's attention, but there is a danger, first, that they become a meaningless jumble and, second, that Bond loses any role other than as a link between such sequences and an activator of machinery, dangers already obvious in the Moore films.

Without his characteristics, especially his trademark mannerisms, it is not clear who or what Bond is. The introspection offered in places in the novels has not really been translated to the screen. There were limits to Dalton's "realism," and it has not been maintained. Bond has not been offered a character that can develop. Indeed, it is only through his relationships with women that Bond displays much personality. In the novels, there was a more multifaceted approach, for Bond's relationship with M was presented as crucial to his personality. This, however, was progressively lost in the films, and, with it, the issues of personal motivation and conduct discussed in terms of this relationship in the novels.

The Brosnan Bond will be no different in this respect, and, so, again, we are thrown back on action and plot. In large part, the latter is subordinated to the action, but it is still important to consider the extent to which the potency, even credibility, of the plot lends weight to the success of the film and the genre and to investigate the politics of the films as a way to approach the changing expectations and attitudes that focus on the Bond formula.

Directed by Martin Campbell, *GoldenEye* (1995) was designed to present the "Bond for the 90s." The publicity emphasized that Bond was not dated, but still relevant. The film was novel in several respects, most particularly the theme of betrayal, both personal and national. The film started with an astonishing opening sequence that included the apparent killing by the Soviet Colonel Ourumov of a captured 006, Alec Trevelyan, Bond's best friend, while they were on a joint Cold War mission against a Soviet biological warfare plant. It subsequently emerged that Trevelyan had defected and become head of the crime and terror group, Janus, dedicated to exploiting the chaos of post-Communist Russia. In particular, Trevelyan seeks to exploit the mismatch between Soviet weaponry and the political confusion and lack of direction within the former USSR, in order to seize the GoldenEye, a space-control weapon that can destroy Western communications through an electromagnetic pulse and, under its cover, permit the theft of the funds in the Bank of England.

Trevelyan is particularly angry with Britain, repeating the venom of Red Grant, and thus explaining why the country should be targeted for his anger. In a throwback to World War II, his parents were Lienz Cossacks who had supported Hitler and whom the British had turned over for slaughter by Stalin. This hearkening back to an unheroic act from a past war echoed Fleming's use of the war as a sheet anchor of values. A controversy over the alleged role of Harold Macmillan in the handing over of such people, and the related Aldington-Tolstoy libel action, increased British interest in and concern with the issue in the 1980s and 1990s. The device explains why Trevelyan aims to overthrow Britain, and not the far wealthier United States, and affirms Bond's role as the defender of Britain. This plot device would have struck few echoes, however, outside Britain.

Trevelyan's anger is matched by that of his ally, Ourumov, now a general and head of the Space Division. The KGB had been dissolved in 1991, and it was necessary to find new Russian villains. A would-be strongman who is not given a first name, Ourumov wishes to take over Russia and replace the confusion of the infant democracy with the introduction of authoritarian order.

At this point, the plot moves closer to the "real" world than is generally the case in Bond stories. It is also notable that the plot is very unsympathetic to the general. A harsher view of democratic chaos is offered by Bond in John Gardner's novel *GoldenEye*, a novel based on the screenplay, which appeared at the same time:

on arriving at St. Petersburg's international airport, he could almost smell the decay and the lack of direction which had come with the downfall of communism. Like many others, he felt that had the changes come from within the Communist Party, Russia would not have been in the freefall, crime and drug infested bankruptcy which stemmed from the sudden collapse of a ruling government.

The film lacks any comparable hostility to post-Communist Russia. Instead, the Defense Minister, Dimitri Mishkin, is presented as good, only for him to be killed by Ourumov. Trevelyan's plot is to use the GoldenEye to control *Mischa*, a Soviet satellite, from a ground station hidden underneath a Cuban lake, a repetition of a device from the film *You Only Live Twice*. As in that film, location beneath a lake ensures that American photo-reconnaissance did not spot the threat. There is no substitute for the man on the ground. This satellite was to fire an electromagnetic pulse at London, destroying the British computer system and everything using electronics. This would both return Britain to the Stone Age and cover the massive transfer of British financial resources from the Bank of England into banks under Trevelyan's control.

Indeed, in any future major war, it is likely that top priority will be given to destroying opponents' computer and communication capabilities, possibly by electromagnetic pulses. An American Defense Department panel on Information Warfare–Defense reported on 3 January 1997 that the American economy and military were very vulnerable to attacks on their information systems and that current precautions against such attacks were inadequate. More generally, public interest in satellites, radar pulses, advanced communications, laser-guided weaponry and anti-rockets had greatly risen as a result of the Gulf War of 1990–91.

GoldenEye linked themes traditional to the series, not least megalomania and rogue space vehicles, and offered a new site for much of the action: post-Communist Russia. Although the situation in Russia might be different, the danger from megalomaniacs, willing to use new military technology to their own ends, was unchanging. Bond was as necessary as ever.

The identification of the head of Janus and the discovery of his plans offers a degree of detection reminiscent of the more conventional spy story, rather than one focused on adventure. The contrast with *Diamonds Are Forever* is instructive. Las Vegas is as "real" as St. Petersburg—it is not a fantasy, like Drax's palace—but it offers a far less gritty setting and, in addition, the impact of the earlier plot is less threatening. The political etching of *GoldenEye* gives it a sense of reality absent in the more fantastical *Diamonds*.

The plot of *GoldenEye* demonstrates the validity of Bond's viewpoint expressed earlier in the story when he told the new female M that the Secret Service required agents as well as statistical analysis. M might regard Bond as a relic of the Cold War, a sexist dinosaur, but he is vindicated throughout the film. Bond both discovers and thwarts the GoldenEye conspiracy, he kills the three leading villains, and he wins Natalya's heart, as well as her body. The idea of a world as dangerous as ever is driven home.

GoldenEye presents the Secret Service in a more problematic light than any other Bond film. This is essentially due to a critical M and a traitorous Trevelyan, although Bond is also portrayed looking into the Caribbean in a meditative fashion. The exchanges between Bond and Trevelyan provide the latter with an opportunity to challenge what Bond does from a position of knowledge. Dr. No had called Bond a "stupid policeman" and there had been other slights from subsequent villains, but the clash of values is pushed furthest in this film. As 006, Trevelyan makes a sarcastic reference to the idea of saving the world, and his use of the phrase "For England, James" is ironic as he has already betrayed the mission to Ourumov. When Bond meets Trevelyan, now the head of Janus, nine years later, he is asked "Did you ever ask why. Why we toppled all those dictators," and his reply, that it was their job, is mocked. Duty is derided, as it had been by Octopussy, but the criticism is more biting. Trevelyan is given cause for his hatred of Britain. At the close, in a powerful line, Trevelyan asks if all Bond's vodka martinis had silenced the screams of those he had killed.

Valentin, Janus' rival as St. Petersburg godfather, who, as a KGB agent, had been an opponent of Bond and was wounded by him, now asks him if he is still working for MI6 or if he has joined the twenty-first century and gone freelance. Bond's sense of purpose is also challenged by "the evil Queen of numbers," the new M. Reliant on analysis, M is convinced that the Russians cannot have a Golden-Eye program and has to be persuaded of the need to send Bond on a mission. Natalaya, the Russian space-programmer who escapes from the destroyed Severnaya Space Weapons Control Centre, criticises Bond and the Russian minister of defense for squabbling like boys, and later refers to Bond as a destructive boy with toys and is not impressed by the struggle between Bond and Trevelyan.

Bond's role is thus challenged from a number of quarters. His reply to Natalya—that he does a necessary job—is matched by the exchanges with Trevelyan as Janus, in which Bond's emphasis on trust contrasts with Trevelyan's hatred for Britain and desire for power, especially in the form of wealth. Trevelyan is witty, but wicked and callous, and, thus, the views he outlines are not probed. Instead, there is the traditional theme of Bond as the crucial individualist. He is up against not only M's reliance on analysis, but also Trevelyan's belief in planning. Thus, aside from the meticulous planning of his proposed coup, Trevelyan tells Bond when he breaks into his armored train, "Situation analysis hopeless. You have no backup." Furthermore, Bond and Natalya's conviction that there is a secret satellite tracking station in Cuba is challenged by the CIA contact, Wade, who tells them that you can't light a cigar in Cuba without the Americans knowing about it, an example of foolish presumption given American inability over three decades to change Cuban politics. M and Wade are wrong and Trevelyan is defeated. Individualism has triumphed, but it is an individualism of selfless dedication and loyalty, not the selfishness proposed by Trevelyan and Valentin.

The theme of anger with Britain essentially stemming from psychological maladjustment also arose with Elliot Carver, the villain of *Tomorrow Never Dies* (1997), which was directed by Roger Spottiswoode. A billionaire media mogul, Carver seeks to set off a war between Britain and China in order to provide him with marvelous copy. To that end, he sinks a British warship. "You give me the pictures. I'll give you the war," says Carver, repeating words attributed to William Randolph Hearst, owner of the *New York Journal*, as he successfully sought to lead the United States into war with Spain in 1898. War between China and either Russia or the United States would be more feasible but would not give Bond a role. Again, Bond is Britain's defender.

According to the novel based on the film, Carver's anger is particularly directed against Britain because of his origins as the illegitimate son of a perverted British media lord. This leaves him with a distaste and contempt for Britain that Bond challenges. Thus, Carver's worldview requires the absence of characters such as Bond. Instead he needs a Britain ruled by the stuffed shirts whom Bond cannot abide, such as Roebuck, the stiff, arrogant British admiral in *Tomorrow Never Dies*, who is not given a first name. According to M, Roebuck thinks with his balls, striking a note of interdepartmental rivalry that was new to the Bond films.

The theme of illegitimacy captures the notion of the villain as maladjusted, an aberration whose destructive anger is readily understood. Nena Blofeld, the villain of John Gardner's Bond novel *For Special Services* (1982), is illegitimate, although she loves her father. The idea of the villain as maladjusted from birth also echoes Fleming's emphasis on racial characteristics and his belief in the pernicious consequences of "cross-breeding."

Carver seeks not only copy, but also global coverage. He wants his media empire accessible to everyone in the world and to that end plans, as part of the Anglo-Chinese conflict, an attack on Beijing by a cruise missile he has taken from the British warship he has had sunk at the beginning of the film. This missile is designed to destroy the Chinese leadership, permitting his ally, General Chang, to seize power and then to open China to the Carver communications empire. However, Chang is not developed, as a character or theme, especially in the film. He plays a far smaller role than Ourumov in *GoldenEye*.

The plot presents Britain as still powerful. She is able, thanks to her navy, to project power across the world. Thus, at the outset, a cruise missile is fired by a warship at a terrorist arms bazaar in the Hindu Kush: Afghanistan is now a locus of freelance menace rather than Cold War rivalry. By this action and Bond's intervention at the site, Britain is presented as the global foe of terrorism. Another British warship, HMS *Devonshire*, is soon after sunk while on patrol in the South China Sea, apparently due to Chinese action, but in fact due to Carver's stealth boat that cannot be seen on radar. The British fleet is then sent to confront China, a gross exaggeration of British capability. Bond also begins the story in the Hindu Kush and ends it off China.

Bond's cooperation with Chinese agent Wai Lin is a world away from the fears voiced in the novel *Colonel Sun* (1968) and, less forcefully, in the films *Dr. No, Goldfinger* and *You Only Live Twice*. In the 1950s China had supported the Communist insurgency in Malaya. Indeed, in *Tomorrow Never Dies* there is a theme of cooperation with former enemies. At the outset, the surveillance of the terrorist bazaar is watched in the British situation room by a Russian general as well as Roebuck and M. The options for action are not only a British cruise missile, but also a Russian army assault. This is the limit of Anglo-Russian cooperation in the film, but it indicates the development sketched out by the favorable portrayal of the Russian minister of defense in *GoldenEye*. The Chinese agent sees Bond as a decadent Westerner, but they join forces. Carver and Chang are as much a threat to China as Janus and Ourumov were to Russia.

The Americans also play a role in the film, but, as in *GoldenEye*, it is a minor role. While pretending neutrality in the Anglo-Chinese confrontation, the Americans provide Bond with a likely location for the sunken British warship and with the plane from which he parachutes onto the site. That, however, is the limit of American intervention. There is no mention of the American provenance of cruise missiles. More seriously, the unlikelihood of the Americans permitting Britain and China to wage a war is ignored.

Thus, the plot essentially repeats the politics of *From Russia With Love*. A secret third party engineers, and seeks to benefit from, a serious dispute between two traditional enemies but is finally revealed and vanquished. Carver embodies, in his own person, the new world disorder, a megalomaniac plutocrat benefiting from traditional and new divisions, and able and willing to use techno-terrorism to his own benefit. Such a threat throws powers together in an unlikely alliance.

Within Britain, the Secret Service repeats its role in Anglo-Soviet relations, shown from *You Only Live Twice* on, of opposing the automatic assumption of Soviet enmity. Roebuck's trigger-happy dispatch of a cruise missile comes close to causing an unintentional nuclear conflagration at the outset, and, later, he nearly causes war with China. The minister of defense lacks the pragmatism and steadiness of the Freddie Gray character, and, indeed, is not given a name. The character of the minister suggests that not all is well with Britain's government. It cannot be relied upon. Instead, it is the Secret Service that saves the day by revealing that China is not responsible for the sinking of the British warship.

Carver is cast as the villain as twitcher, the unbalanced evil mastermind who relies on others to do the fighting. His principal heavy, Stamper, a tall blond, fulfills the stereotype of Aryan sadist, echoing, without direct reference, the notion of Nazi villainy. His sort of masculinity is presented as unreal and perverse, as in Fleming's description of Red Grant and the film portrayal of Zorin in *A View To A Kill*. Stamper is cold, if not robotic. His is a role very similar to that of Hans in *You Only Live Twice* and that of Eric in *For Your Eyes Only*.

In the wider sense, the politics of *Tomorrow Never Dies* is very different from that of the early Bond films. This is signaled from the outset, when Bond refers to smoking as a "filthy habit" while knocking out a smoking thug. Bond and M both drink, but the movie portrays very little sex. Aside from Inga Bergstrom, the improbable Danish professor in Oxford at the outset, Bond has sex only with Paris Carver, the wife of the villain, but this is not presented as an adulterous one-night stand. Instead, she and Bond were former lovers, while Elliot Carver is revealed as a sadist no longer worthy of

Paris's love. This change in the depiction of Bond's relationship with women was an aspect of the extent to which the Bond films, while reassuring people about stability and stereotypes, also registered changes in stereotypes, conventions and ideas.

In place of sex, however, there is massive violence. Indeed, violence essentially provides the story line in a plot that is largely free of humor and suspense. The violence pitches Bond against masses of villains and, in terms of fights per half-hour, *Tomorrow Never Dies* is very different from the early films. Thus, Bond becomes a stylish automaton, an identity hinted at by Fleming, but one that the author chose not to develop. The greater complexity of the Bond persona in the novels is totally neglected. Yet this Bond is popular. *GoldenEye* made more than the two Dalton films combined, and *Tomorrow Never Dies* was more successful than the film versions of *The Saint* and *The Avengers*, 1960s television spy series that were turned into films in the late 1990s.

An absence of complexity in the portrayal of Bond was also, on the whole, true of *The World Is Not Enough* (1999). However, his anger with the villain Renard for "breaking in" Elektra was not that of an automaton, while his response to her was given variety in what was a more complex and interesting plot than *Tomorrow Never Dies*. As with Alec Trevelyan in *GoldenEye*, there is betrayal, which helps drive the plot and ultimately gives the central relationship in the film—that of Bond and Elektra—its tone. Furthermore, the relationship between Elektra and Renard is complex: he is the manipulator, manipulated, and her will is the dark center of the film. This moves the "bad girl" onto center stage.

The politics of the film relates very much to the real world, both in its setting in a volatile part of the world, the Caucasus, and in its plot: control over oil and its movements. The conflation of geopolitics and resources is handled deftly. The commercial and critical success of *The World Is Not Enough* indicates that the cinematographic Bond is still alive and healthy.

11

The Films Reviewed: Villains and Plots

The contrast is less with the original Bond, the real Bond of the Fleming novels, than with the Bond of the films, that rakish non-entity who drops yobbo-style throwaways out of the corner of his mouth before or after escaping by personal jet-pack or submersible car fitted with missile-launchers or (at any moment) a reactor-powered iceberg.

Kingsley Amis's 1991 introduction to a later edition of his *Colonel Sun* (1968) repeated some of the criticisms he had already expressed in *The James Bond Dossier* (1965). To Amis, Bond was a recognizable human being, a person, not an adolescent fantasy. His attack on the films was more fundamental, more wide-ranging, than either the discussion of whether Connery was better than Moore or the other comparisons of actors, films and scripts. In a study concerned with the politics of the books and the films, the contrast between the two may not appear so abrupt. The Drax of the film *Moonraker* might desire to destroy life on earth, while his novelish counterpart wished to destroy "only" London. Both were improbable. So, arguably, was

SPECTRE, which featured in both the books and the films. In both the books and the films, there was a problem of credibility affecting the character, his feats, his task and the reasons for the task. To isolate the last from the general suspension of disbelief might appear inappropriate, but it is important to consider how far they contribute to the general impression and how far they are an extraneous factor.

By focusing on SPECTRE, and, subsequently, on independent plutocrats, such as Stromberg and Max Zorin, the stories were made more free-floating politically than if the emphasis had been on the Cold War, although, insofar as SPECTRE and the independents have a political purchase, it tends to be non-Western. Goldfinger in the film (although not the novel) plans to take refuge in Cuba. More generally, the visual note is usually of individuals who are not classically Anglo-American, although political correctness in Hollywood leaves few but the British eligible to play villains. The wily Oriental is matched by the untrustworthy Continental in the depiction of villainy. Thus Fleming's racialism is repeated on screen, although Carver, significantly the villain of a recent film, is an exception. He has an English name and is played by a British actor. Sensitivity to charges of racial and national prejudices may ensure that future films have villains who are presented as British or American. The ethnic/physical visual note of the earlier films was repeated in satirical treatments. Thus, in *Carry On Spying*, STENCH deployed Milchmann and the Fat Man, as well as Dr. Crow.

The emphasis on the Cold War was frequently slight in the film plots. Their politics appeared timeless, part of a universal morality story in which the pride of bad people had to be restrained. In terms of this axis, the adventure and the technology were dominant and the plot a mere device, in part, indeed, an adventure of technology.

This can be seen in *A View To A Kill* (1985), one of the films that is frequently overlooked. Moore's formulaic presentation of the character was palling, he no longer looked the part of Bond, only of Roger Moore, and this was his last outing as Bond; while the female lead, Stacey Sutton, an American geologist played by Tanya Roberts, contributed relatively little, and the villains were less cinematographic than Jaws. Nevertheless, the film has much to commend it. Although lacking the intensity of, say, Michael Lonsdale's Drax, Christopher Walken offered an interesting portrayal of the psychotic Max Zorin and Grace Jones was a powerful partner as May Day, continuing Fleming's taste for silly names for women, which was an aspect of his jokiness, although of course disparaging to women.

Yet to illustrate the point about the dispensability of the plot, Zorin's scheme of profitable mayhem could have been located anywhere and anytime. In some respects, it echoed the film *Goldfinger*. Zorin is a manufacturer of microchips who plans, in Project Main Strike, to destroy Silicon Valley, the area where 80 percent of world production is said to come from, in order to make a financial killing by enhancing the value of his own stockpile and the profitability of the producers' cartel he forms. As in *Goldfinger*, the one producer who dissents is killed, in this case thrown from Zorin's airship as stairs are transformed into a slide, another impressive device. Again, as in *Goldfinger*, there is a tenuous link to a wider struggle. Zorin had been a KGB agent and had been set up with KGB funds, but this is not a Cold War film, despite initial appearances to the contrary.

The film supposedly begins in Arctic Siberia (in fact, the scene was shot in Iceland and Switzerland), with Bond finding a microchip stolen from a Siberian research center on the body of 003, a dead British agent. Bond then evades Soviet pursuit in a spectacular chase scene that echoes the ski chase at the outset of *The Spy Who Loved Me* and sails away in a submersible iceberg with the Union Jack on the inside of the submarine hatch. The microchip is revealed as a copy of one being made by a British private company that would be capable of resisting an electromagnetic pulse set off by an atomic explosion over Britain, the latter an idea developed in *GoldenEye*. This section of *A View To A Kill* is very much located in the Cold War, part of a technological race between West and East. Who else could aim atom bombs at Britain?

Thereafter, the plot departs from the Cold War setting, a process dramatized when Zorin, owner of Zorin Industries, which had bought the British manufacturer, rejects General Gogol's attempt to reimpose Soviet control. "No one ever leaves the KGB," says Gogol, an argument that anticipates M's views in *Licence To Kill* (1989). Zorin, however, does, and the plot already has. Zorin's independence is very different in its intention and character from what Bond was to display in *Licence To Kill* when he leaves the Secret Service.

The setting at Zorin's stud farm, filmed at Chantilly, was a world away from East-West confrontation. In one respect, this is what makes villains like Zorin so threatening and dangerous. They are not restrained or confined by political considerations or international boundaries. As such, they can seek the destruction of humanity, as did Drax and Stromberg, or its domination, as did Blofeld, or exploitation, as did Sanchez and Carver, or can operate successfully within the West, as did Goldfinger, Zorin and Carver. Great wealth acts as a solvent of reality and sanity: "What he [Drax] doesn't own he doesn't want." Drax had purchased the Eiffel Tower, but the

French government refused him an export permit. Capitalism provides opportunities for an individualism of enterprising power.

Zorin indeed is a "rags to riches" figure, like Dr. No, Goldfinger, Drax and Carver. Of obscure origins, Zorin is a leading French industrialist, and, according to the British minister of defense, a staunch anti-Communist. The last is, in one respect, ironic, a product of Zorin's successful cover as a KGB agent, but it also reflects the free-floating nature of the story's politics. From the point of the plot, it would not matter greatly whether Zorin was a staunch anti-Communist. Indeed, at the close of the story, the politics come full circle. Gogol is seen with M and the minister of defense, presenting to them an Order of Lenin designed for "Comrade Bond," the first time ever it has been given to a non-Soviet citizen. Gogol explains that Soviet research depends on Silicon Valley. The USSR can benefit more from the interchange of industrial espionage than from the maverick destructiveness of Zorin.

Zorin constitutes a challenge to both superpowers. He had already dramatized his break with the KGB by cruelly killing a Soviet agent sent to blow up his oil-pumping station in San Francisco Bay. Bond then relives a former romance with this agent's colleague, Pola Ivanova, but they are really competing to see who can discover more about Zorin. Thereafter, the KGB fades from the story, until Gogol's appearance at the close. There is nobody to match Anya Amasova in *The Spy Who Loved Me*.

Zorin was outside anyone's control, possibly a metaphor for a cruel anarchy that threatened a whole world of which the Cold War was simply part. Although Zorin intends to destroy only Silicon Valley, rather than humanity as a whole, he is presented as an inhuman threat to all. This is traced to his origins in a cruel Nazi genetic experiment that produced intelligent psychotics and is seen in his amoral ruthlessness. Having prepared an atomic explosion under the San Andreas Lake, which will destroy "the key geological lock that keeps the faults from moving at once," Zorin kills his loyal workforce, a totally unnecessary act. Zorin plans from his airship to have a view to the massive killing he aims for in Silicon Valley.

Laughing as he machine-guns the workers, Zorin is a satanic figure, rather like Jack Nicholson's portrayal of the devil in *The Witches of Eastwick* (1987). A similar callousness to employees also characterizes other villains. Both Stromberg and Blofeld dispense with helicopter pilots—by explosion and electric shock, respectively, Blofeld telling Bond that the pilot was "one of my less useful people." The price of failure is even higher. In *Thunderball*, Largo has a henchman—who has been bested by Bond, but not shot by him, as the henchman had feared—thrown alive into his shark pool. Count Lippe has already been dispatched by SPECTRE thanks to a rocket-firing motorbike. In *You Only Live Twice*, Blofeld has Helga Brandt tipped into his piranha pool and shoots Osato himself.

Zorin is also seen as in some way a product of planned society. This is sensed not only in the account of his origins, but also in the killing scene. Zorin begins by asking for some spare cartridge clips and closes, after slaughtering everyone in sight, by saying "Good. Right on schedule. Let's go."

This is a much-repeated theme in the films. The villains believe in planning and, indeed, represent a conflation of plutocratic and bureaucratic man, the last understood by Fleming as a characteristic of Communism. In Weberian terms, Bond represented the persistence of charisma against the iron cage of rationalism and bureaucracy. Planning is necessary, not only for the villains' schemes, but also because they are control freaks, seeking order even as they pursue disorder. Thus Kronsteen, the Czech chess master who is also SPECTRE's No. 5 and its director of planning, is convinced that his plan in *From Russia With Love* is foolproof. Goldfinger greets Bond at Fort Knox, "Morning, Mr. Bond. For once you are exactly where I want you." In *Thunderball*, Largo tells Domino "There's no escape for you" and, later, "Do not live in hope, my dear. There is no one to rescue you." "There is nothing that can stop us any more," declares Blofeld in *Never Say Never Again*. He had already declared in *You Only Live Twice*, "We are now impregnable. Interception will take place in eight minutes. Nothing can prevent that." In *Moonraker*, Drax addresses his followers in space: "First there was a dream. Now there is reality." He is, repeatedly, certain of Bond's fate; "I shall be leaving you in your own private crematorium. . . . observe, Mr. Bond, your route from this world to the next. . . . at least I shall have the pleasure of putting you out of my misery."

The role of planning in the schemes is naturally stressed, because it provides the drama for the action. It is not just that Bond has to save civilization, but also that it has to be done in less than ten seconds, as the bomb ticks away (*Goldfinger, A View To A Kill*) or as the germs approach earth (*Moonraker*) or as the rockets or lasers come toward the target (*Thunderball, You Only Live Twice, The Spy Who Loved Me, Diamonds Are Forever, GoldenEye, Tomorrow Never Dies*) or the time to switch on the rocket-toppling beam approaches (*Dr. No*). In *Octopussy* Bond stops the timer on the atom bomb with less than a second to go. The last-minute cliffhanger is also a feature in the books, but it is taken further on screen. There it meets the demands of the cinema for a filmic crisis. This can be seen by contrasting the close of both versions of *Dr. No.* Bond is up against technology, increasingly so. In *A View To A Kill* Zorin penetrates Bond's disguise by employing computer identification, and controls a steeplechase course in which Bond takes part by radio controls that alter the obstacles.

Thanks to technology, Bond can be made to appear embarrassingly incompetent, but, nevertheless, he is always resourceful enough to cope when it matters most. Pursuing the germ-laden globes in the space shuttle *Moonraker 5*, Bond is able to destroy the first two thanks to the automatic laser firer, but the automatic controls are knocked out by the heat engendered by the very steep angle of the shuttle's approach to the Earth's atmosphere. Ignoring his own safety, as the wings begin to glow, Bond switches to manual in order to destroy the third and last globe. He misses at first, but, at the last moment, destroys the globe as it enters the world's atmosphere. Thanks to Bond's determination, 100 million people have been saved.

In the characterization of the villain, there is more than technology and an evil plot. There is also an evil person. The villains can be so exaggerated that they are easier to satirize than the hero, as seen with the presentation of Dr. Evil in the films *Austin Powers: International Man of Mystery* (1997) and *Austin Powers: The Spy Who Shagged Me* (1999), which were spoofs of Bond and the 1960s. Bond declares Largo "certifiable" in *Never Say Never Again.* The inclusion of life-threatening pain as a central feature in Largo's competitive game, Domination, and his ax attack on Domino's dance room after she kisses Bond, reveals that Largo is, indeed, deranged. He cannot bear the idea that someone he sees as his can have any independence.

The evil of the villains can be seen in the utter ruthlessness with which subordinates are used, as in *The Spy Who Loved Me,* and in the reliance on torture, and in a sadistic delight in cruelty, as with Sanchez in *Licence To Kill*: "What did he promise you? His heart? Give her his heart"; and "Red" Grant in *From Russia, With Love.* "The first one [shot] won't kill you, not the second, not even the third, not till you crawl over here and you kiss my foot"; and Stamper in *Tomorrow Never Dies.* In *Never Say Never Again,* Fatima Blush, SPECTRE's number 12, tells the captive Bond to spread his legs and taunts him "Guess where you'll get the first one?" She has had Bond and does not need him, although, in a moment of forced humor, her demand for a signed reference for her sexuality leads to her demise from Bond's explosive-firing pen. In *The World Is Not Enough,* Renard has literally lost his feeling.

A perverted sexuality is also a characteristic of some of the villains. Scaramanga has sex before he kills, a characteristic the theme song stresses. His third nipple also marks him out as abnormal. Zorin kisses May Day while they watch the Rolls Royce in which Bond is due to die sink to the bottom of a lake. In *Never Say Never Again*, Fatima Blush is sexually excited by the prospect of killing. At one point, she ecstatically dances down the stairs of the Monte Carlo casino, jubilant at the prospect of killing Bond. She adds the gratuitous murder of the inexperienced MI5 agent Nicole, showing that she is as much a threat to women as to men.

Bond's sexual freedom, an important part of the character's appeal, is carried to excess by some of his opponents, but this is clearer in the novels than in the films. In part, this reflects what can be shown on the screen, but it is also linked to the mechanistic megalomania of many of the villains. Their desire is focused on life-denying schemes for global control. Although Drax listens to classical music, he, like other villains, seeks the intoxication of the idea, not the more balanced sensuality that Bond pursues with virility and humanity. The latter is a male fantasy, but it is central to the image of Bond's sexuality that he gives as well as receives pleasure. That can be imagined of few of the male villains, with the exception of both Largos. Of the villains, only women are shown having sex and then only with Bond. He is the phallic center.

As in the novels, Bond is established as a hero not only by his actions and style, but also by the contrasts between him and the villains. Style is crucial, because few of the villains have any, although Adolfo Celi as Largo in *Thunderball* both is an action man and looks good in a tuxedo. However, the master of the tux is Connery at the start of *Goldfinger*, when he takes off his frogsuit to reveal a dinner jacket, a move echoed by Arnold Schwarzenegger at the beginning of *True Lies*.

Connery also displays style at the close of *Diamonds Are Forever*. In a scene reminiscent of *From Russia With Love*, Bond identifies the wine waiter as a fraud on the ocean liner when he tricks the killer into revealing that he does not realize that a Mouton Rothschild is a claret. This scene lacks the social edge of *From Russia With Love* and Bond's superiority is not presented with an uncomfortable snobbery. Furthermore, the style here helps to save, as well as define, him. Style also locates Bond socially. Unlike Michael Caine's Harry Palmer, the hero of the films of the Len Deighton stories, Bond does not cook. With his black horn-rimmed glasses and raincoat, Caine's Palmer was a working-class character played by a working-class actor, unlike Connery, a working-class actor playing a stylish char-

acter, an individual with class. The confident independence of
Connery's Bond became with Palmer an edged insolence and cyni-
cism.

The timelessness of evil gives Bond an inexhaustible number of
enemies. In the novel *Moonraker*, where he surveys his career, and
its pluses and minuses, an introspective approach not taken by the
screen character, Bond assesses how many missions he is likely to
have left before he reaches retirement, if he indeed does so. Furthermore, the novels are linked, however tenuously, to provide some
sense of chronological development and placing. Nevertheless, Bond
does not age in the novels.

On screen, Bond has long outlasted any realistic chronology. There
is no sense of retirement; or, indeed, as in the novels, interest in
remuneration or tax, the details of which readily date a character.
Instead, Bond is saved from retirement by the succession of new
actors, a development that attracts considerable media and public
attention and that dramatizes the timelessness of the Bond character,
while permitting some development—a paradigm shift with each
new actor. In the spoof *Austin Powers*, Bond returns after being cry-
ogenically frozen for thirty years to fight Dr. Evil. No such pseudo-
science was possible for the "real" Bond.

The conventions of the films remain the same: Bond will survive
and the villain will be defeated. Unlike in the novels, Bond is physically and mentally unscathed. This is a central aspect of the treatment of violence in the films. For a long while, this was totally
unreal, especially in the Moore films. Bond would be involved in
a massive punch-up, with all the furniture in the room getting
smashed, from which he would emerge unscathed, still elegantly
groomed and without a hair out of place. This contributed to the
woodenness of the later Moore films. After Moore left, the policy
changed. *Licence To Kill* (1989) was a very violent film with no holds
barred. This was a paradigm of the handling of violence on television
and by the media more generally.

The handling of violence is an aspect of the delicate balancing act
that is a key element in the success of the Bond films. This balancing
takes place at several levels. The extent of the escapism offered is
one such. On the one hand, the films take the viewer into an exotic
fantasy world; yet, on the other, they have to be sufficiently
grounded in daily reality to carry conviction. There is also the problem of resonance with the audience. On the one hand, the filmmaker
has to include all the regular items the audience likes and expects,
such as the meeting with M, the visit to Q's laboratory, the car chase
and the face-to-face encounter with the villain; but, on the other,

something new has to be put in each time; and each film has to go a bit further than the one before. The success or lack thereof of each film has much to do with how well this balancing is accomplished.

The viewer is assured by the conventions of the Bond films; as, indeed, by the more specific continuities provided by the roles of M, Q, Moneypenny, Leiter and General Gogol, continuities underlined by the use of the same actors for many of the films. Walter Gotell was Gogol throughout, and Lois Maxwell created Miss Moneypenny. Desmond Llewelyn was Major Boothroyd—Q—from *From Russia With Love* on. Bernard Lee was M for many of the films, but his death ensured that he had to be replaced in *For Your Eyes Only*. Other actors, such as Geoffrey Keen as Freddie Gray, the minister of defense, and Robert Brown as M, had shorter runs but still offered continuity. Similarly, Shirley Bassey sang the title song for three of the films, helping with her song for *Goldfinger* to create a pattern for lyrics that were at once joking and gritty. The 007 theme music also activated familiar responses. This process was important as the actor playing Bond changed. It has been made more uncertain by the death of long-standing actors, such as Gotell and Llewelyn.

By moving Bond away from conventional power politics, he is also freed from the constraints of place. Action can occur wherever seems photogenic. There is no need to consider plausibility, although the Bond plots are far more plausible than those adventure films reflecting contemporary interest in the occult, such as the Indiana Jones films. The occult, indeed, is mocked in *Live and Let Die*: the villains manipulate voodoo beliefs, while Bond responds to the tarot reading powers of Solitaire by having an entire pack composed of "The Lovers" card, thus tricking her into fulfilling her desire and destiny to be a Bond girl. Religious cults are mocked in *Licence To Kill*.

Bond has become timeless and universal. As a film character, like Tarzan, Batman and Philip Marlowe, who can sustain changes in actors (just as the theme songs have been recorded by new artists), he has bridged the gap between generations of filmgoers and also that separating Britain from the wider world. The sole constraint is that of profitability, although that is helped by Bond's role as a multimedia phenomenon. A Bond film is very costly, necessarily so given its very nature: expensive stunts and exotic locations, both arising from the need to make each film better than the previous one. Bond will continue "developing" while the financing exists for new films. Thereafter, he will be trapped in time, a figure in video stores and television repeats. As an icon of late twentieth-century adventure consumerism/consumer adventurism, such a shelving will be deadly. Just as sales of the novels benefited greatly from the films, so the appeal of the past films depends, in part, on the continuity of the iconic character. Without this, Bond may be treated as a conceit, a historical figure no longer amusing, exciting or relevant, other than as a figure from the past.

PART III

THE BOND LEGACY

12

The Later Bond Books

"[T]he situations are about as real as the heroes. You know what I mean? The hero's a superstar. Former Green Beret, CIA, KGB double agent, colonel in Army Counter-Intelligence. Can speak about seven languages including Urdu and Tamil. Expert with any kind of weapon ever invented and has a black belt in Tae Kwon Do. His hands are lethal weapons, ah, but manicured. You know the kind of guy I mean?"

"Sure, very cool. Has all these broads around—"

"But grim," Robbie said. "The serious type."

Walter was nodding. "Yeah, dedicated. Never looks around."

—Robbie Daniels and Walter Kouza
in Elmore Leonard's novel *Split Images* (1981)

[N]obody believes all that stuff about guns being phallic symbols any more.

—Ann Reilly in John Gardner's *Licence Renewed* (1981)

Fleming's death in 1964 did not lead to the end of the Bond novels. Indeed, for legal reasons, there was pressure to continue the product and write a 007 sequel. As the character Bond could not be copy-righted, the best way to deal with the threat of imitations appeared to be for Glidrose, who owned the Bond publishing rights, to com-mission a sequel.

The first choice was Kingsley Amis, a prominent writer and fan of Fleming's novels who had advised on *The Man With the Golden Gun.* Ann Fleming was hostile toward the idea and disliked Amis anyway, but the latter was commissioned by Glidrose to write *Colonel Sun* (1968), the book appearing under the pseudonym Robert Markham and dedicated to Fleming's memory. In *Colonel Sun,* the villains are the Chinese, out to wreck a Soviet diplomatic initiative in the Middle East and to blame it on the British. This was indeed a period of growing worries about China, which had first test-exploded a hydro-gen bomb in 1967. The spread of Chinese influence in Africa and the Middle East aroused concern in the West, while the Cultural Revolution, which had begun in 1966, suggested a dangerous vola-tility in Chinese policy and dramatized the split with the Soviet Union. Furthermore, the Arab-Israeli Six-Day War of 1967 had un-derlined the instability of the Middle East and its prominence at the front line of the Cold War. The Chinese menace was also highlighted in *River of Death,* a Bond cartoon that ran in the *Daily Express* in 1969. The villain, Dr. Cat, chief torturer and inquisitor for China, was seeking to create a revolutionary native movement in the New World.

The plot of *Colonel Sun* permits Amis to bring the Soviets and Brit-ish together, but the scenario faces skepticism from Colonel-General Igor Arenski, the KGB official responsible for supervising the secu-rity arrangements for the Aegean conference. Arenski tells Ariadne Alexandrou, the female Greek Communist whom Bond has won over, that despite errors in ideology, the Chinese would never resort to violence to disrupt the upcoming conference. "That would be gangsterism . . . and gangsterism is the typical resort of Western war-mongers." Arenski is wrong. The cruel Chinese Colonel Sun is the villain, not Bond, and, indeed, in 1969 longstanding Sino-Soviet bor-der disputes were to deteriorate into serious clashes.

In an echo of Fleming, Sun is assisted by a Nazi, von Richter, responsible for a serious atrocity against Greek civilians during the occupation. At the close, Bond is congratulated by the high-ranking Mr. Yermolov from Moscow and is told that Sun's failure will be exploited by the Soviets; although this is, in part, a measure of British weakness. A sullied Chinese reputation will be of more benefit to Moscow.

The entire episode, more generally, indicates a shift in world politics: Yermolov offers Bond "the Order of the Red Banner for services to peace," an offer Bond has to decline, but he has had his role, the role of an individual, rather than a historical process, extolled. Bond's actions have unmasked China as the "real enemy" and have revealed "future friends" in the West.

This looked toward a theme that was to be increasingly sounded in the 1990s, that of the need for a wide-ranging alliance against China, including post-Communist Russia. It also looked back to racialist literature of the early decades of the century with its theme of the "Yellow Menace."

Notwithstanding such international progress toward a better understanding with the Soviets and the realization that human endurance and resilience could triumph, while technology—the products of the Q workshop—was irrelevant and useless, there was also a powerful sadness in the book. This was both emotional and social.

At the close of the book, Ariadne can't come to London with Bond, because she is stuck with "middle-class respectability" and also because of her work. The last sentences are far more in keeping with the Fleming novels than with the films. About their work Ariadne says "People think it must be wonderful and free and everything. But we're not free, are we?" "No," said Bond again. "We're prisoners. But let's enjoy our captivity while we can."

The social sadness was one of reaction against the modern world, a theme that echoed some of Fleming's writing, as in his account of Paris in "From A View To A Kill" (1960). The closest film presentation of any despair with modernity was in the very different and richly comic *Never Say Never Again* (1983). To Amis, in *Colonel Sun*, the world had become a scene depicting mediocrity and tastelessness, vulgarity as opposed to class. Soon after the opening of the book, Bond drove across a part of England, in this case Berkshire, and Bond notes "the ugly rash of modern housing . . . the inevitable TV aerial sprouting from every roof." Overhead, planeloads of tourists set forth for destinations as far as Spain and Portugal, exporting their "fish-and-chip culture."

Amis continued: "But it was churlish to resent all this and the rising wage-levels that made it possible. Forget it," but it was the bitter criticism that struck: more means worse. The same passage also identified Bond with a sense of true nature. Bond drove past productive farms and ancient forests that would long stand "as memorials of what England had once been," a passage that could also have been applied to Bond, although he was of Scottish-Swiss parentage. Later, in Greece, in the international atmosphere of Constitution Square, Bond reflects on a similar theme, although it is developed in a surprising fashion:

What Adriadne Alexandrou had said about the decreasing Greekness of Greece came to Bond's mind. In thirty years, he reflected, perhaps sooner, there would be one vast undifferentiated culture . . . stretching from Los Angeles to Jerusalem; possibly, by then, as far as Calcutta. . . . Where there had been Americans and British and French and Italians and Greeks and the rest, there would be only citizens of the West, uniformly affluent, uniformly ridden by guilt and neurosis, uniformly alcoholic and suicidal, uniformly everything. But was that prospect hopelessly bad? Bond asked himself. Even at the worst, not as bad as all that was offered by the East, where conformity did not simply arise as if by accident, but was consciously imposed to the hilt by the unopposed power of the State.

This was the consolation of a depressive. The notion of an "End of History," of a uniform, deracinated, decultured West located in 1998, was presented not as triumph, but as a source of despair, only for the consolation to be offered that the alternative was even worse. This was a deeply pessimistic, skeptical conservatism. There was no sense of national survival and success, nor of the triumph of capitalism. Bond's villains themselves expose the triumphs of capitalism.

A sense of placelessness had earlier been expressed, albeit in a different context, by the Secret Service's chief of staff, Bill Tanner, who had referred to the new "international" criminal "without a traceable history" who seems to appear "out of thin air." Thus, placelessness was more than a challenge to identity; it was also a threat. Goldfinger had been such an individual.

The forecast end of the "British" was a particularly sinister anticipation for Amis, as for Fleming, because both were keen on the idea of national character. Thus Amis described the Albanians as "much less a race than the end-product of successive admixtures with the native stock," and wrote of Doni Madan, "Asia was in her cheekbones and the strong planes of her jaw, Asia Minor in the all-but-black brown of her eyes, Venice in the straight but fully-moulded mouth."

Amis also caught Fleming's mood in Bond's attitude to politicians, women and force. Sir Ranald Rideout, the minister responsible for the Secret Service, is revealed as arrogant and stupid, adopting "an air of superiority in the presence of men worth twenty of him." He wears a "frilled azure evening shirt," unfairly criticizes Bond for abandoning M, and hates smokers, a trait Amis describes as psychopathic and associates with Hitler. Scarcely improved, Rideout turns up at the close, less tactful and attractive than Yermolov. This portrayal reflects a hostility toward politicians as complacent and duplicitous that was commonplace in spy stories, although not so much in those by Fleming, as his M had been all powerful, especially in the early novels. In Anthony Price's *For The Good Of The State* (1986), "Garrod Harvey couldn't bring himself to recall 'the good of the state' as an ally, even though it had to be their only true good, for what he envisaged; because the Minister's Special Adviser would only be concerned with the good of his Minister." Bond, however, is not a player in the cold corridors of governmental duplicity. His ironies are warmer, his deceits aimed at recognizable enemies. This is all part of his virility.

Bond's success with Ariadne contrasted with Colonel Sun, who was "unmoved by women," harshly treated the Albanian women in his service as contemptible whores for his men and was stabbed by one, Luisa. She thus saves Bond. He, in turn, is unwilling to stab the motionless Sun to death and is nearly killed as a consequence. As with Fleming, this is a case of fairness, a central theme in his stories, for all their presentation of Bond as ruthless. *Colonel Sun* was a fitting echo of Fleming in terms of content and was the best of the post-Fleming Bond novels. It reflected Amis's deep understanding of Fleming's Bond and was a mature attempt to write in his style. *Colonel Sun*, however, lacked the tautness and suspense of the original. Furthermore, it was unfairly criticized by Ann Fleming as the beginning of a decline toward a "petit bourgeois red-brick Bond" who would end by betraying Britain to SPECTRE. A self-depreciating Amis acknowledged his failure to "follow worthily," but this was largely a matter of style and pace. Ann Fleming's remark was inaccurate as analysis and prognosis. There is no sign of a Bond being harassed about his expenses.

Amis's was not the last of the continuation volumes, although there was a gap for many years. A novel commissioned by Glidrose from Geoffrey Jenkins, a thriller writer who persuaded the company that he had worked on a plot with Fleming, was finished in 1971, but Glidrose decided not to permit its publication. Christopher Wood produced two novelizations of film screenplays, *James Bond, The Spy Who Loved Me* (1977) and *James Bond and Moonraker* (1979), but between 1968 and 1981 there were no new Bond stories. In 1981, however, appeared the first from John Gardner, who has hitherto proved the most prolific and successful continuator, at least in terms of sales and longevity. Gardner attempted, as he put it, "to bring Mr Bond into the 1980s." A Cambridge-educated ex-Royal Marine officer and established thriller writer, his Bond characterization began with *Licence Renewed*. This introduced Anton Murik as a freelance villain out to blackmail states, with his threat to cause a nuclear meltdown in six of the world's nuclear power plants, into funding his own plans for nuclear power. This drew on the serious nuclear accident at Three Mile Island, Pennsylvania, on 28 March 1978 in which thousands of gallons of radioactive water were released. Anxiety about nuclear power rapidly increased.

Apparently a wealthy Scottish laird, Murik had, in fact, had the rightful laird, his half-brother, killed and was trying to arrange the same fate for the latter's daughter. Legitimacy and displacement were at issue. Murik was presented as a crazed fanatic for whom the end justified the means. Meanwhile, Britain was in a mess, affected by political and economic lethargy and a short-term attitude to problems, a charge that could be directed against both the Labour governments of 1974–79 and their Conservative successor. Q branch was under severe financial restraint, such that Bond, himself, had financed the security devices installed in his car. The 00 section had been abolished, as financial exigency led to a reassessment of the Secret Service, producing a "Realignment Purge."

A sense of passing values was provided by Bond's visit to Royal Ascot. He was inspired by the sight of tradition as the royal family came down the course in their open carriages, but it was "a ceremony from another age." M's office was dominated by a painting of a naval victory, but it was off Cape St. Vincent in 1797, another echo of past glories. (Similarly, in *Nobody Lives Forever* [1986], M repeats Nelson's message, "England expects.") Even Bond had to be protected from the charge of snobbery with the defense of his right to "certain pleasurable idiosyncrasies"—his particularity about breakfast.

The following year, SPECTRE returned in *For Special Services* (1982). It was now extremely wealthy, holding at the outset $150 billion—$140 million and £50 million. Bond was seen as SPECTRE's particular foe, offering the element of the duel that had been so powerful in the Fleming novels. In this story, Bond was placed on special duty, in order to provide "Special Services to the US Government," paired with Felix Leiter's daughter, Cedar, and sent to investigate an American plutocrat, Markus Bismaquer, a wealthy Texan, who, in an echo of Fleming's concerns, was "a firm and convinced member of the American Nazi Party." M presented a picture of a world that was far from stable:

[T]here's enough danger . . . with the governments, unrest, political ineptitude, recession, and the draining of resources—on an official level. Some big freelance operation could be catastrophic.

The plot involves three puzzles. Has SPECTRE been revived? If so, who is Blofeld—Bismaquer or his right-hand man, Walter Luxor?—and what are SPECTRE's objectives? Bond is correct to suspect a revival of the organization but totally wrong about the identity of Blofeld, and only able to thwart SPECTRE's immediate objective—taking over the American NORAD (North American Air Defense Command) command complex—because he had been given an antidote pill by the squeamish Markus, who turned out to be Blofeld's sexually ambivalent husband. Blofeld was a woman, the daughter of Ernst Stavro Blofeld. Generations change, but not Bond! Like other villains, Nena Blofeld was distorted in mind and body. She had been born with the potential for only one breast, and, as with so many of the Bond villains, physical difference served as a sign of spiritual illness. Her sexual appeal to Bond also placed her in the line of female deceivers whom he has sex with. Having the "bad" woman as the villain, rather than the villain's assistant, altered the pattern of so many of the Bond stories. Unlike in *Goldfinger*, there was no possibility of Bond's heterosexuality resolving the plot. Instead, Nena suggests to her husband before she shoots him that he was attracted to Bond, a hint of a homoeroticism not generally associated with Bond.

Responding to new developments in the arms race, SPECTRE aimed to thwart President Reagan's plans for Star Wars, to gain computer information about the Space Wolves, the American laser-equipped killer satellites disguised as weather satellites, and to sell it to the Soviets. This was to be done through doctoring the ice cream eaten at NORAD with a drug that induced euphoric obedience to instructions. NORAD was to be given a surprise inspection by a new inspector general, none other than a drugged Bond. Just in case the readers missed the point, Bond reflected that "the United States—possibly all the Western powers—needed the Space Wolf satellites, for they gave the real edge over any aggressor . . . the one person in all the West who might yet be able to avert disaster was James Bond."

Gardner published at Fleming's pace. *For Special Services* was followed by *Icebreaker* (1983), a story that echoed Fleming's concern with the Nazis but had relatively little to offer in terms of plot. Count Konrad von Glöda, the villain, and his National Socialist Action Army sought to bring about a Fourth Reich but were thwarted by Bond in some icy scenes. A role for the Nazis in novels of the 1980s was frequently the sign of a somewhat stale story line. They did not have the proximity that they had had for Fleming's readers. In another echo from the past, SMERSH also plays a role in the plot, and

Soviet spying on Britain at GCHQ is mentioned. This was a sensitive issue in the early 1980s. Bond is revealed to have played a role in the Falklands conflict of 1982.

SPECTRE returned in *Role of Honour* (1984), a story with conventional Bond settings—England, Monte Carlo and Switzerland. Tamil Rahani, an electronics mogul and the new head of the organization, sought to destroy American nuclear weapons. In this novel SPECTRE sided with the Soviets. Rahani reappeared in *Nobody Lives Forever* (1986), sponsoring a competition for Bond's head. Unlike in the Bond films of the period, there was a traitor working for the KGB within the Secret Service, Steve Quinn, the service's resident in Rome. One of the villains, Der Haken, a corrupt and sadistic Austrian detective, also combined two standard features of the Fleming demonology— Nazi background and physical oddity. Rahani was killed at the close.

The KGB replaced SPECTRE in *No Deals, Mr. Bond* (1987), with General Konstantin Chernov seeking to wipe out all those involved in a defunct British espionage operation. As with Fleming, Communism was equated with Nazism. Unlike in the films, there was a sense of a divided Britain. The Foreign Office had been responsible for the end of the 00 section and there was pressure from it for M's resignation. He felt under siege, and Bond had to save him from his domestic critics. Lt. Commander Alec Stewart, the commander of the nuclear submarine taking Bond to the East German coast, disliked covert operations and his relationship with Bond was tense.

As elsewhere in Gardner's novels, there was also a sense of Britain on the slide. Murders were becoming more common, the elegant club Blades now needed money from foreign gamblers, Chernov claimed that the decadent British would fall because of self-indulgence and laxity and Bond offered an ironic paean to Britain: "the click of willow against a villain's head, the roar of the riot, the scent of new-mown grass snakes."

In *Scorpius* (1988), it was the turn of a freelance villain, Vladimir Scorpius, posing as Father Valentine, who used drugs and hypnotized religious followers in his English-based Society of Meek Ones in order to try to assassinate major political figures, including the American president and the British prime minister. This drew on concern about religious cults.

Win, Lose or Die (1989) was one of Gardner's better-plotted novels. It had an explicit political theme, the habitual one of the clash between order and anarchy, more specifically an anarchist attempt to disrupt a great power summit. The anarchists, BAST, the Brotherhood of Anarchy and Secret Terror, led by Robert Besavitsky, sought to benefit from the disaffected of the world. A New Yorker who had killed his two wealthy wives and made money with stock-market frauds, Besavitsky had become a good friend to Yasser Arafat and an arms supplier to the PLO (Palestine Liberation Organization). Enjoying a luxurious lifestyle, he sought by one major coup to earn enough money to permit him to retire.

Besavitsky decided to accomplish his aim via terrorism and created BAST to that end, recruiting over 400 terrorists. His selfish ruthlessness extended not only to the intended victims of his major coup, but also to his own organization. Besavitsky was an opportunist not interested, as they were, in assisting "the cause of true freedom." He thought the password "gobbledegook" and "laughed out loud, thinking of the fanatics who would have given their souls for an opportunity like this, and how they would have wasted the money [he intends not to pay them] on guns and bombs, bringing more danger to their lives." Similarly, in *Nobody Lives Forever*, Bond noted how many violent criminals had become mercenaries for the terrorist organizations.

Aside from the hostile portrayal of the villain in *Win, Lose or Die*, Gardner has little time for the anarchists. The beautiful Clover Pennington explains to Bond "Our kind of anarchy is positive. We want a fair and open society throughout the globe." Bond replies

You're just like all those pipe dreamers, Clover. There'll never be a fair, free and open society in this world. You see, people get in the way. Ideals are for idealists, and all idealists fall from grace. No ideal works, simply because human beings cannot cope with it. . . . [P]ower tends to corrupt; and absolute power corrupts absolutely.

Descending to specifics, Bond was also convinced that the BAST scheme would make little difference to the world. Besavitsky proposed to seize HMS *Invincible*, while the British warship was the site of a summit conference of George Bush, Mikhail Gorbachev and Margaret Thatcher, and to hold them for ransom. Bond pointed out to Clover that this would simply provide opportunities for politicians who opposed these leaders. Gorbachev would be replaced by anti-glasnost politicians, Bush by the vice president (the unmentioned Dan Quayle) and Thatcher by whomever the Cabinet chose. The purpose of the summit was to establish new policies on antiterrorism, the global economy and the reduction of the nuclear arsenal. The membership and setting were a somewhat implausible statement of British importance, although Thatcher had played a major role in the positive response to Gorbachev's initiatives for *glasnost* and détente. Twice the leaders in the novel were described as "the

three most powerful" in the world, a curious phrase given the absence of China. The setting anyway permitted Bond, as head of security for the meeting, to play a major role, indeed a continuing one,
as Thatcher points out that he had already saved her life and that of
Ronald Reagan. Furthermore, the last confrontation in the book is in
another relic of empire, Gibraltar. It had been used two years earlier
as the setting for the sabotaged training exercise at the outset of the
film *Living Daylights*.

The declaration of British importance was in line with the Fleming
novels but seemed, increasingly, inappropriate in a changing world.
So, arguably, was Gardner's views on society, race and women, or,
at least, those that were expressed in the novel. Bond goes for a stroll
in Woodstock, noting with disdain the aromas of cheap "Pub Grub."

He would, if pushed, like to see the countless young people crowding those very
bars banished to some kind of National Service—preferably in the armed forces.
That, he considered, would take violence off the streets of country towns, and
make men out of the louts who littered pavements and got drunk at the sniff of
a barmaid's apron.

This dyspeptic response was maintained in the next scene, a very
critical portrayal of Naples as Bond traveled by ferry to Ischia where
he found only shabby buildings and other such depressing sights.

In part, this was a matter of Christmas blues—of families gathering
when he had none. But there was more than that. "The thought of
age and decay, of lost glory and of the current world tensions" that
Bond experienced was part of a persona disenchanted with his society and hostile to change. The settings of the novels had to be
exotic, in part because the readers and genre anticipated it, but also
because the escapism was not only that of resilience and success
against the odds, but also that of setting.

Yet, as elsewhere in the Gardner novels, a characteristic of the
Fleming approach, in this case disenchantment with the ordinary
world became ugly in the new guise. In part, this was because attitudes that were widely accepted in the 1950s, and, thus, could be
accepted by later readers, seemed misplaced in a different world.
But, in part, this was also a matter of heavy-handedness, a facet that
extended to the failure on Gardner's part to emulate both the irony
and the style that had been so important in the Fleming novels.

The changing world was also captured in the emphasis on ELINT,
the electronic collection of information. Bond reflected

We're T. S. Eliot's "Hollow Men"; we are also rust-stained dinosaurs. Our day has come, and gone. I give us a decade more. After that, well we could be sitting in front of computer terminals all day and most of the night.

Necessarily, for both plot and persona, Bond is, in fact, crucial to the defeat of BAST, but this reliance on individuality is throughout circumscribed by an emphasis on intrusive technology, particularly in the field of information gathering.

Race as a factor in a threatening world was suggested by the Arab background of BAST. Although Besavitsky and Pennington are not Arabs, they have Arab cover names, and both they and their two leading associates are one-time members of Middle Eastern paramilitary political groups. It is unsurprising that one of the villains was "olive-skinned," that Abou Hamarik, the strategist of BAST, had an "oily smile" that "greased over his face," and that the traitorous pilot on the Harrier training course at Yeovilton was not British or American, but a Spaniard, Felipe Pantano. That alone did not suffice. He was a "swarthy little pilot" with "a small goldmine of fillings." Race was also present in the hostile presentation of Besavitsky's background: a father of "mongrel immigrant stock, part Russian, part Rumanian, with a strange dash of Scottish via his great-great grandfather on his mother's side" and a mother of "a similar mixture." This made Besavitsky "the product of a half a dozen other mongrels."

At one level, this was simply a continuation of Fleming's distaste for what he perceived as deracination, but, given the very different nature of British (and indeed American) society by the late 1980s, this was a more reprehensible attitude and one that more obviously clashed with contemporary attitudes. Furthermore, in other respects, Gardner was willing to have Bond depart from the Fleming model. In this adventure, he foregoes his ritual martini, vowing to abstain until the mission achieved its goal. Although Gardner does not mention it, the name, the origins "in the old Hell's Kitchen area of New York," and such cover names as Bennie Benjamin and Ben Brostov, were presumably designed to suggest that Besavitsky had a Jewish background. This added a fresh twist to his exploitative relations with Middle Eastern terrorists.

Aside from race, there was the issue of gender. Bond was worried about women on the *Invincible*, and the touchstone of probity, M, describing himself as "a solid male chauvinist pig," regarded their presence as bad luck. Women were a source of confusion. The evil Clover taunted the captured Bond, "You see how easy it is for women to do the job of men?" She did not carry any sinister visual

indications: an "attractive" smile, "without menace, or phoney evil."
She resembled "any other, nice, well-brought-up girl with a future."

The gender lines were not all clear. Donald Speaker, an avaricious
villain whose views are presumably not intended to attract approval,
claimed that "girls can't do a man's job." Beatrice Maria da Ricci,
the female lead, saves Bond in the denouement by killing Besavitsky.
Nevertheless, the general tone was anachronistic and unappealing,
and without humor to rescue it.

Ultimately, *Win, Lose Or Die*, like so many Bond plots, was about
maladjustment, specifically a failure to accept station. Besavitsky,
unsatisfied with his own background, was using his terrorist gains
to "buy himself into the aristocracy." At a less exalted level, Petty
Officer "Blackie" Blackstone, who is blackmailed by BAST into sab-
otaging one of the *Invincible*'s turbines, had been told that the driving
force behind the operation was Greenpeace, who hoped to embar-
rass the British, Americans and Russians. Blackie had long viewed
Greenpeace as a sympathetic cause. Aside from this slur on Greenpeace—a case of guilt by association—the implication was that people like Blackie should not have opinions. The working-class
member of the cast, he was presented as gullible and weak. The slur
on Greenpeace can be seen as an echo of earlier criticism of sup-
porters of nuclear disarmament in the Bond novels and films, but
Gardner pushed this too far and thus weakened his political thrust.

Win, Lose Or Die was followed by the novel *Licence To Kill* (1989),
based on the film of that year, and then by *Brokenclaw* (1990). Set in
the United States, this had Bond battle Brokenclaw Lee Fu-Chu, yet
another villain with a diverse racial background: "a monster who
claimed two sets of ancestors, two traditions and could slip between
them like someone infected with a multiple personality." A Native-
American-Chinese, with great power in the San Francisco under-
world, Brokenclaw had schemed to acquire the plans of an American
submarine tracking device and its antidote for China and, also, to
break into Wall Street's computer system and devastate the West's
financial system. The former threatens "the whole safety of the
United States' and our own fleets," an echo of the frequently reiterated Chinese menace to the West. The financial strategy, Operation Jericho, was originally a Japanese-initiated plot against the
United States which sought to destroy the New York Stock Exchange
through computer hacking. This scheme was taken over by the Chinese, computer fraud becoming a tool of geopolitics in order to produce the intended crash of 1990, rather as drugs had been used by
Communists in earlier plots. Brokenclaw himself would be safe from
the consequences as he intended to shelter his money in Switzerland

and Luxembourg. Gardner's plot offered a nasty recycling of racist ideas on Chinese subterfuge and Japanese aggression. Fleming's hostility to Switzerland was also echoed.

In saving the American economy, Bond is dependent on American resources and technology. However, the continued skill of the British Secret Service is also important. M reflects that it "shows we're not the dinosaurs the press would have people believe," a remark that reflects the challenge, to both Britain and her Secret Service, of being seen as still relevant, and the specific problem of press criticism. This was a typical conservative response to the idea of public accountability. Bond's foes in *Brokenclaw* include traitors in the FBI, operating for cash, an aspect of the pervasive impact of corruption and crime that creates the impression that the ordinary processes of law enforcement will not suffice to defeat Brokenclaw. This is part of a diatribe against the modern world, specifically the United States:

[H]e thought the world had gone crazy . . . they were happy about heading for a smoking-free society, yet doing little about the thousands of alcohol-related deaths in the home, on the roads and in hospitals. The anti-smoking lobby appeared to gratify that other guilt which knew little headway was being made against drug abuse.

The contrast between revolting junk food and the public stress on health also led to critical comment. The popular music industry, the use of English and alternative lifestyles, also, all come in for criticism, while, at the conclusion of the novel, the *O-kee-pa* ritual, in which Bond and Brokenclaw pitted their resilience against each other, is applauded as an alternative to the ways of the world. Bond prefers that to a high-tech mass assault on Brokenclaw's hiding place:

[Y]ou deserve to die, Brokenclaw Lee, and I fear that, though the authorities will eventually catch up with you, they will only imprison you. Prison is too easy. Your way is good. It is a test of manhood, leadership and courage. You merit death.

This leads to a somewhat ridiculous ritual contest, won, of course, by Bond. It is a later equivalent of the duel in the film *The Man With the Golden Gun*, and, indeed, a duel of sorts is part of the formulaic climax of the films. It personalizes the struggle, and victory goes to Bond, the knight of honor and nobility. He immediately rescues the maiden, or gets the girl in modern terms.

Far from romanticizing the Native Americans, Gardner depicts
them as part of the conspiracy:

We figure [Brokenclaw] only took in the most basic types, those who would
return to the old brutal ways. No reservation Indian would ever think of per-
forming the O-kee-pa torture rite nowadays. We're pretty sure he had some
reason for building a private Indian army that had nothing to do with peace.

One tries to shoot Bond in the back. Thus "primitive" society offers
no real alternative to the modern world, and Brokenclaw is not an
equivalent to Bond. Indeed, as throughout the corpus, the villain is
seen as lacking limits, while Bond is presented as balanced and the
exemplar of moderation and poise: "Bond did not aspire to be a hero,
it was just something that came with the job." An instructor once
cautioned Bond to keep in mind his gentleman status—"live like a
gentleman and for God's sake die like a gentleman."

The gender issue is handled with somewhat more tact than in some
earlier novels. Bond thinks women operatives good only if free of
"emotional baggage," and he rescues the captured CIA agent, Chi-
Chi, thanks to the O-kee-pa, but Bond, himself, is not able to avoid
capture by Brokenclaw. Chi-Chi has quite a liberated manner, Bond
notes, but she lacks "those abrasive bad manners so often used to
force women's rights down the throats of men who exhibited a particular kind of chauvinism." Furthermore, she is not immune to
Bond's charms. As in earlier novels, the villains treat women far
worse. Wanda Man Song Hing of Naval Intelligence is slapped hard
by her father, the blackmailed gambler Tony, because she initially
defies his attempt to break her will. His "fatherly demand" is that
she should prostitute herself to settle his debts, and his use of the
notion of "love and respect" for parents condemns the concept. A
similar distancing from traditional images was provided when Bond
and Chi-Chi parted from their controllers on the American aircraft
carrier off San Francisco:

They all shook hands rather soberly, and Bond was reminded of all those stiff-
upper-lip, ludicrous scenes from old war movies where the suicide mission vol-
unteers were told what a good thing they were doing for their country and for
the world.

Brokenclaw was followed by The Man From Barbarossa (1991), a book
that returned Bond to a European setting and had a more political
thrust than most of the Gardner novels. Indeed Europe was central

in the next four of Gardner's novels. This took up an observation of M's in *Brokenclaw*:

Europe—the world come to that—is at a crossroads. What with the wind of change blowing among the Eastern Bloc countries, and *perestroika* running amok in the Soviet Union, we need cool heads . . . never since the early days of the cold war have we been so in need of human intelligence—HUMINT. The map of Europe is being changed. For good? Maybe. Who knows? Those countries are unstable. The Soviet Union is unstable. We're recruiting, establishing old networks so that, should the problems return, we shall be ready.

The stability of the Cold War was thus challenged by the fall of Communism and the Soviet Union, a very *realpolitik* attitude. Later in the book, the Secret Service's chief of staff, Bill Tanner, remarked "we desperately need agents to cope with the turmoil of transition in Europe."

In *The Man From Barbarossa*, the authoritarian General Yevgeny Yuskovich seeks to overthrow the Russian government and reinstate Communist rule, to use atomic weapons to help the Iraqis in the Gulf War, both contemporary issues, and to launch a nuclear attack on the United States. Masquerading as a Russian officer, Bond, in league with the KGB and the Israeli Mossad, thwarts him, gaining an Order of Lenin from President Gorbachev. Several of the themes from the book were also seen in *GoldenEye* (1995).

Death Is Forever (1992) opens with two quotes, locating the novel in genre and time. The first is from *Diamonds Are Forever*, the second by Markus Wolf, the former chief of the East German Foreign Intelligence Service, responding in November 1991 to a question about the risks posed by former East German agents: "some adventurers might try to profit from their knowledge." A warning about the dangers of relaxed vigilance is offered at the outset of the first chapter. Ford Puxley, "all of his lifetime security habits" put to sleep by his subconscious after the collapse of the Soviet Union, is killed by Cold War experts in Frankfurt. Later Bond is asked

Do London and Washington not realise that there are men and women in Europe—especially in the old Eastern Bloc—who've given their lives to the religion? To the ideology of Communism? . . . [T]hese people are organised and ready to fight back . . . for some major destabilisation of Europe. . . . They also have a lot of hardware: weapons, transport, aircraft, helicopters.

The leader Wolfgang Weisen, "The Poison Dwarf," formerly the second in command of the East German Foreign Intelligence Service, was a protégé of Stalin who wanted to return Stalinism to Europe with himself as the new dictator. After wiping out most of the Anglo-American Cabal spy network, Weisen plans the destabilization of Europe by hijacking the first train to pass through the Channel Tunnel, a train carrying the leaders of the European Union and their advisers, including M. They were to be killed. This would "create the ultimate political vacuum," although Gardner exaggerated when he claimed that "the result could be far worse than anything that had happened in war-torn Europe during this century—or any century in its long history."

Bond thwarts Weisen in a story in which his conscience about killing is referred to frequently, while, in another departure from the carefree image of Bond, there are two references to the threat from AIDS. An authoritarian note is struck by Bond's support for identity cards, "given the criminal and terrorist rate," while skepticism about the European Union is reflected in reiterated comments about distrust among allies, although in the end Bond receives the thanks of the prickly colonel of the French Special Forces and the Croix de Guerre.

The killing of Bond's partner and lover in the story—the American agent Elizabeth "Easy" St. John—leads him to shout "kill those two bastards." Bond accepts that there are casualties in any war, that that is "the law of the jungle of secret Europe," and he is able to keep his mind "apart from the reality" of the "brutality of killing," concentrating only on the technique. However, he is soon sickened by the realization that death is becoming part of his life, and, more generally, is reluctant to kill, rejecting the suggestion that he should slaughter the unconscious Giorgio. Furthermore, while saying that killing is "constantly inevitable" Bond sees it as basically immoral and presents doing his "country's dirty work . . . pest control" as an "unpleasant occupation."

At a more emotional level, the death of Easy greatly moves him, and the "guilt and pain" of the death of Tracy in *On Her Majesty's Secret Service* is a constant pressure. There is no romanticization of Bond's job. More generally, betrayal is even more insistent in this plot than in most Bond stories. Double-crosses are continuous and give the presentation of Berlin an almost Deightonesque feel. The sense of ambiguity, of nothing being what it seems, is descriptively present in the nightime mists of Venice.

Death Is Forever was followed by *Never Send Flowers* (1993), in which David Dragonpol, a psychopathic actor, sets out as a serial killer to assassinate celebrities. EuroDisney is the scene of the denouement, with Bond thwarting Dragonpol's attempt to kill Princess Diana and her two sons. The Bond girl in the novel has a name from a trashy celebrity magazine: Fredericka (Flicka) von Grüsse. In *Sea-Fire* (1994), a more wide-ranging plot is offered, as the action spans the West Indies, England, Spain, Germany and Israel. Sir Maxwell Tarn, a plutocratic businessman, sees himself as the new Führer of a revived Nazi regime. Flicka returns and receives a marriage proposal from Bond. Tarn is helped by a junior minister on the Watch Committee in charge of British Intelligence.

Based on the screenplay, Gardner wrote *GoldenEye* (1995), and the differences are instructive. Much naturally relates to what can be provided in the different media. Thus, the scene, near the beginning, in which Bond races a Ferrari on the Grand Corniche is preceded in the novel, but not the film, by an angst-ridden passage revealing a nostalgia for the past and a concern, if not detestation, of the present:

The south of France, Bond often reflected, was not what it used to be. The coastline . . . was packed to capacity during the season. The once leisurely Promenade des Anglais in Nice was even more leisurely, but today it was because of the steady, slow-moving stream of traffic. . . . Bond detested the crowds, the traffic and the obvious growth of pollution, not only in the air, but also in the sea itself. There was trouble in what used to be paradise.

In his last Bond novel, *Cold* (1996), Gardner had Bond thwart General Brutus Clay's attempt to stage a Fascist coup in the United States on behalf of COLD, the Children of the Last Days. Clay plans to stage *Operation Blizzard*, a massive and widespread series of terrorist explosions that will provide an opportunity for COLD to seize power in order to maintain order. Clay is a power-crazed political fundamentalist, seeking to exploit disenchantment with the American political system and its constitutional gridlock:

The American people have pleaded again and again for strong leadership; for something to be done about the blot that lies over our country. A serious and sensible solution to our method of government where a President from one party can be held to ransom by a Senate ruled by a different faction. This is an idiotic situation, and we must stop it, change it. We must also be ruthless. We must do the unpalatable things that have required doing for decades. The problem of drugs and serious crime—in particular street crime—is to be dealt with from the word go. Anyone in possession of drugs will be shot out of hand.

Gardner presented Clay in a very unsympathetic light, but he also has a low view of the British. M is first circumscribed by committee and then replaced by a woman. The old world is cracking and change is unwelcome. This is seen in miniature in Gardner's presentation of Switzerland, "a country displaying the less pleasant aspects of the drug subculture. . . . A few years ago, graffiti would have been unthinkable. Now it was the norm, as were the ragged unwashed teenagers who would never have been seen a decade before. In modern Switzerland the order and cleanliness were now only skin deep." This is more insidious than Fleming's portrayal of Swiss selfish secrecy as a cover for Blofeld in *On Her Majesty's Secret Service*.

Raymond Benson, an American Board member of the Ian Fleming Foundation, and the author of *The James Bond Bedside Companion* (1988), produced three Bond works in 1997. "Blast from the Past" appeared in the January 1997 issue of *Playboy*, an echo of the appearance of Fleming's "The Hildebrand Rarity" in the same magazine. Irma Bunt, Blofeld's relict, seeks revenge, among her weapons a poisoned razor, but is killed. This echo of the Blofeld trilogy was a successful revival of the Fleming style, more so than Gardner's deployment of Nena Blofeld. Bunt mounts the attack in New York, thus underlining the Americanization of the stories.

Benson also wrote the book of *Tomorrow Never Dies*, as well as *Zero Minus Ten* (1997), in which the villain, Guy Thackeray, the drunken head of a trading corporation, plans a nuclear explosion in Hong Kong as it is handed over to Chinese rule, in order to cause war between Britain and China. Excerpts from the book appeared in the April and May issues of *Playboy*. Again, there were more echoes of Fleming's style than in the Gardner book, but there was also a crudity generally lacking in Fleming. Captured by Carver in *Tomorrow Never Dies*, Bond deliberately taunts him "you're still the son of a whore, a bastard, raised in the gutter," hardly the wounding bite of stylish satire. In *Zero Minus Ten*, the squalor and corruption of China are used to vindicate Bond's anti-Communism. Bond justified his reluctance to commit himself to a woman by reflecting on the fate of women to whom he had done so, and the Triad leader, Li Xu Nan, dies helping Bond against the villain. As so often, the apparent villain—in this case Li—is presented as a man of true honor.

The Facts of Death followed in 1998. The Decada, a mysterious secret body seeking to provoke war between Greece and Turkey, uses the Suppliers, a terrorist group that employs poisons such as ricin and sarin. The Decada itself is split, with a group of three female members led by the deadly assassin Hera Volopolous, seeking not war, but instead to exploit the poisons.

The Benson book for *The World Is Not Enough* (1999) stuck closely to the screenplay, but there was a note of Fleming, absent from the film, in the description of the Greenwich Dome and the MI6 headquarters, two leading London examples of modern architectural style, as eyesores.

Any reading of the post-Fleming stories reveals that the Bond genre still has considerable staying power in novel form, although clearly it is the films that sustain the public interest. There is a degree of interplay between novels and films, aside from those books that are directly based on screenplays. As in the films, the general drift has been away from the 1950s world that Fleming portrayed, but many of his themes and narrative conventions have been maintained, although Gardner and Benson never matched Fleming's writing. The handling of gender clearly creates problems for the continuators, while the notion of Britain as a major global player can strain credibility. There has been some tempering of the clearcut right and wrong of the Fleming novels, but, compared to the ambivalence of much spy fiction, the Bond novels are still adventure stories operating within a readily grasped context.

13

The World of Bond

With Bond we are back to barbarism. He has the virtues of courage and loyalty, but few others. He is a high technology killer, a sadistic womaniser and a pseudo sophisticate. If one met him, he would seem a sinister bore. Perhaps he is a natural hero for an age of technological liftoff but cultural confusion. Yet it is absurd that the Achilles of our thoroughly modern age should be a man born in the reign of King Edward VII. The Bond cult suggests that our age may not be as modern as we like to think.
—William Rees-Mogg, *The Times*, 29 December, 1997.

I never fantasise any more about driving along the Grande Corniche in my supercharged Bentley, one of my triple gold-ringed Morland Specials clamped between my fingers, and my Walther PPK automatic in its customised holster underneath my immaculate white tuxedo. No, the charade is now a load of sad cobblers as far as I'm concerned. I can think of few other fictional characters whose stock has fallen as low—in my estimation—as Bond's.
—Will Self, *The Times Magazine*, 28 March 1998

The appearance of *Tomorrow Never Dies* in late 1997 and *The World Is Not Enough* in late 1999 stimulated a mass of publicity and hype and a limited amount of analysis of the run of the Bond films. Most of the latter was celebratory, a case of dusting off the film footage and producing a lightly scripted ensemble on television. There was also criticism, as in the articles in the *London Times* quoted above, although some might say that the decline in quality of that newspaper is a more accurate reflection of barbarism than a Bond series nearly forty years old. The sense of Bond as anachronism, and a very unwelcome anachronism at that, was directed at the values apparently central to the persona, values that were presented as outdated.

As so often, criticism is self-validating. Classification in terms of a set of values is presented as readily apparent, and these values are shown as obviously undesirable. The clarity and conviction of such an approach can, however, be misleading, the classification invalid and the presentation flawed. That is the case with much of the criticism of the Bond persona and corpus.

There are naturally variations in this corpus. These are not due simply to different writers and to the differences between novel and film. Prior to that, there were contrasts in the Fleming novels. Nevertheless, there is a fundamental consistency. In part, as Umberto Eco showed in *The Bond Affair* (1966), this is a matter of repeated narrative structures and of Bond's mythic status. In part, the consistency was a matter of maintaining a successful model and preserving him for a series of profitable bouts.

Consistency aside, there is the question of judgment. Bond's status as a consumer product, icon of adventure and male style, and role model, as the character summarized by his Japanese nickname "Mr. Kiss Kiss Bang Bang," invited repeated criticism. Much of this is a matter of ignorance and condescension. Ignorance is readily manifested because many of the critics have clearly read and viewed, or, at least, remembered, only part of the Bond corpus. Much of the specific criticism is also misplaced. The Fleming novels are not great literature, and to judge them by such standards is unhelpful. Yet the very success of the novels as adventure stories suggests a degree of potency that is worth probing. Compared to the films, the novels devote relatively less space to fighting (and stunts), and more to description and dialogue. Indeed, relatively few people were killed in most of the novels, and the films represented a major departure in this respect.

The characterization in both films and novels can be regarded as limited. This is particularly true of the villains, who are generally grotesques, while many of the other characters are one-dimensional, clearly devices to move the plot along, rather than fully realized individuals. This is especially true of the "goodies," many of whom are either dull (males) or implausible (women). Attractive male supports to Bond, such as Kerim Bey, in both the novel and the film of *From Russia, With Love*, are infrequent.

Yet this is no different from much fiction, especially adventure fiction. Agatha Christie, the most successful detective novelist of the century, was not noted for her characterization. Furthermore, the depiction of people as grotesques or characters has a long history: Fleming is somewhat Dickensian in his villains. Lastly, the Bond of the novels is far from a one-dimensional figure, and, as he is the narrator in all the novels, except *The Spy Who Loved Me*, that gives them a welcome depth.

"Most of their strength lies in the myth—in the myth of Scotland Yard, of Sherlock Holmes, of the Secret Service." General Vozdvishensky's comments, in the novel *From Russia, With Love*, offer a parallel for Bond. Holmes had been translated to the screen in midcentury with brilliant effect by Basil Rathbone. In a series of fourteen films, the Holmes corpus was brought up to date, Holmes taken to new destinations—Canada and the United States—and given contemporary concerns and foes. The series asserted that he was a "timeless" figure, and, as such, in particular he battled the Nazis. Moriarty, however, was still a foe, his struggle with Holmes a duel to match that of Bond and SPECTRE.

In some respects, the transfer from print to picture, in the Rathbone Holmes films, matches that of Bond, although the chronological gap was far larger, and thus the challenge of topicality greater. Holmes was an individualist, trusted by the government, but essentially a loner, forced to rely on his own skill to thwart nefarious conspiracies that knew no boundaries. Thus, in *Sherlock Holmes and the Voice of Terror* (1942), Holmes thwarts a Nazi program of sabotage and an attempted invasion whose mastermind is the head of the British Intelligence coordination committee, Sir Evan Barham. As with Bond's villains, Barham is callous and cruel and despises ordinary people. He is also overconfident: it is Barham who brings Holmes onto the case in order to appear to be doing everything possible to thwart the Nazis. In another parallel, Barham himself is not really the Home Counties gent he appears to be. Instead, Holmes discovers that the real Barham was killed in World War I and replaced by a German agent. He is a phoney, like Fleming's Drax. To underline German villany, the real Barham was shot in cold blood while a prisoner of war.

Holmes's addiction to narcotics and his solid location in a home are just two facets virtually alien to Bond: the weakness of addiction and the strength of location. Although in the novel *Moonraker* Bond takes benezdrine pills to keep going and seconal to sleep, a need for such pills is not a strong feature of the characterization. There is no equivalent to Baker Street or to the repeated appearance of London and the Home Counties in Doyle's stories. Holmes lacked Bond's sexuality and was scarcely surrounded by a bevy of beauties, and the contrast is important in the image of both characters, but less so than might appear. Despite episodic emotional commitments, Bond is not possessed by love, or for that matter lust, nor, as he recognizes, can he afford to be. The mission is central, and he is a dedicated servant of the right cause, a process eased by a lack of ambiguity about cause, rectitude and service. Bond, like Holmes, breaks the rules but can be trusted, and trusts himself, to pursue the quest. Both are gentlemen and each is important to the development of the British adventure detective genre. Unlike the "Queens of Crime"— Agatha Christie, Dorothy Sayers, Margery Allingham, Patricia Wentworth, Ngaio Marsh, Ruth Rendell and P. D. James—with their emphasis on domestic settings, there was a strong interest in a wider world in both Doyle and Fleming.

Holmes gets to Algiers in one of the last Rathbone films, but his foreign travels are limited, and Doyle's Holmes knows and dominates London in all its facets in a manner that Bond never attempts for any location. The politics of the Rathbone films focused on the enemy within, and that encouraged the setting in Britain and North America, the latter provided by backdrops. The Bond novels ranged further afield, but less so than the films. The contrast between the two is instructive. The adventure of Bond's travels was also captured in satires such as *Carry On Spying*. There episodes were set in Vienna and the Casbah and on the Orient Express.

To note, however, that the Bond films offered a more farflung itinerary than the novels, and also a world bonded by air travel, does not imply that all parts of the globe were equally treated. Instead, the southern hemisphere received far less attention. Rio de Janeiro and Amazonia featured in the film *Moonraker*, but Africa was ignored in the films, with the exception of Mediterranean Africa: Egypt, Tangier and Palmyra, Largo's holiday fortress on the North African coast in *Never Say Never Again*. Australasia and Antarctica were also ignored.

These omissions do not reflect the location of the novels, as they have long ceased to be significant. In part, the locations reflect factors of cost and accessibility, but there is also the issue of familiarity and tourist appeal. Rio, the first Bond setting in mainland Latin America in book or film, offers a recognizable presence. Both the carnival there and Sugarloaf Mountain, with its tram station, invite recognition. They satisfy the need for a readily recognizable totemic setting. The connotations are variously exotic, glamorous and luxurious, as in the film *A View To A Kill*, where there are killings on both the Eiffel Tower and the Golden Gate Bridge. The British trailer for *Moonraker* promised "the most exotic locations on earth" and extensively featured Rio. In the film, Bond is collected by Rolls Royce at the airport and taken to the president's suite in a luxury hotel, before going to bed with a female assistant, and then going out into the Rio carnival. In *The Spy Who Loved Me*, Bond's Egyptian settings are glamorous. He does not have to search for the submarine tracking device amongst Alexandria's warehouses. Instead, he visits a Cairo casino, the Great Pyramid, the Sphinx, the Temple of Amun at Luxor and, in a totally implausible scene, a desert encampment presided over by a sheikh, Sheik Hossein, who was a Cambridge contemporary, an improbable episode that anticipated the Oxford-educated Afghan leader Kamran Shah in *The Living Daylights*. Thanks to both, the issue of Islamic fervor, especially in the Afghan resistance, is ignored. In *Octopussy*, India is presented as an attractive site for tourism. There is no suggestion of social, ethnic or religious tension within India or of difficulties in the relationship between India/ Indians and outsiders, specifically the former Imperial power, Britain.

The views, interests and existence of the local governments are never mentioned in the African settings. Thus in *Never Say Never Again*, Largo does as he wishes at Palmyra, but so, also, do his opponents: an American submarine shells the fortress. In *The Spy Who Loved Me*, the British and Soviets cooperate in Egypt. There is no role for the local government. The same is true for India in *Octopussy*. Nonalignment means nonexistence for the local government. It is as if these countries are ungoverned, ripe for exploitation by international megalomaniacs, and waiting for the order brought by Western intervention in the shape of Bond. The films (and books) of Bond have imperial attitudes to the exotic. The local population is primarily presented in terms of native color, for example crowded street scenes and festivals, rather than as able to govern itself. Similarly, the Brazilian government, military and police play no role in *Moonraker*.

Drama is an important feature in the settings, especially if the landscape is to be instrumental in the action. This is particularly so with mountain scenes, such as Cortina D'Ampezzo, the Italian alpine resort in *For Your Eyes Only*. The Greek mountains of Meteora are also an important setting in the film, as Gibraltar was at the beginning of

The Living Daylights. Mountains permitted ski chases, the first of which occurred in *On Her Majesty's Secret Service*. They also offer an opportunity for fights, and, in particular, surveillance and escapes, not least because villains classically hide in isolated locations protected in part by the site. This was especially true of Blofeld and Piz Gloria, and of Kristatos at the close of *For Your Eyes Only*.

Mountains are the counterpoint of the other popular setting: underwater. Both offer drama and take the viewer where he or she will rarely go. Both provide the opportunity for hazardous adventures and for the interaction of human and environmental challenges, as when avalanches are set off. The mountains, however, lack sharks, or their equivalent; sharks play an important role in many of the films, as guarantors of evil and terror. The first underwater sequence occurred in *Thunderball*, and it was also the first occasion on which sharks—in this case, the golden grotto sharks—were used by a villain. Sharks also play a major role in *Never Say Never Again* and, most frighteningly, in *License To Kill*, although not in the submarine finale in *The World Is Not Enough*. In contrast to mountainous and subaquatic settings, there has been relatively little use of forests, although one was used extensively in *Dr. No*, and Drax's Brazilian base in *Moonraker* is in deepest Amazonia.

There are also urban escapes, as in *Diamonds Are Forever, A View To A Kill* and *Tomorrow Never Dies*, and pursuits, as in *Octopussy* and *GoldenEye*. However, in general, the cityscape is less menacing than in many spy stories or adventure films. The Harlem scene in the film *Live and Let Die* where Bond is sent by Mr. Big to be "wasted" in a scene of urban desolation is highly unusual.

If urban decay is largely ignored, there is more generally a neglect of the city, although this is far less true of the first two Bronson films. The concentration on the remote reflects an aspect of the escapism so often remarked upon. It offers a predominantly urban and sedentary public a view of something very different.

Tomorrow Never Dies centered on a confrontation in the South China Sea, an area where the modern British presence arose from rule of Hong Kong. *Zero Minus Ten*, a 1997 Bond novel, similarly dealt with Hong Kong, although at the moment of transition. Now little is left if Bond is to be located in the "real" world of British power. Gibraltar has already been used, in both *The Living Daylights* and *Win, Lose or Die*. It was a less exotic set than Hong Kong, and there is a limit to what could plausibly be staged there. The same is true of the Falklands, which are, anyway, a sensitive issue. For similar reasons, hitherto Bond has not been sent to Ulster or employed to track down IRA terrorists outside Britain. He is not allowed to act like a freelance, a fictional equivalent of Sandline, the British company that played a role in overthrowing the military regime in Sierra Leone in 1997.

This leaves few options, unless Bond is to be treated as an international figure, working on behalf of world peace, the path long followed in the films. Addressing American military leaders in the Pentagon on 17 February 1998, President Clinton claimed that Saddam Hussein was part of the "unholy alliance of terrorists, drug traffickers and organized international criminals" who posed the next century's greatest threat to peace, and referred to "the tyrants and terrorists" who will be the "predators of the twenty-first century." Such a prospectus appears to offer Bond a great range of targets. In *The World Is Not Enough* he bested a combination of international anarchism and destructive capitalism, the last in the shape of Elektra King's willingness to kill millions in order to block rival oil routes. Possibly the marked rise in the price of oil in 1999–2000 will encourage further interest in energy sources and control as themes for plots. The films *Diamonds Are Forever, The Spy Who Loved Me* and *Moonraker* indicated that Bond as international savior offers the prospect of incredible adventures in which the fantasy relates to plot as well as the hero's potency. Furthermore, such plots require a cooperation with the Unites States that is sensible in marketing terms but that poses problems for the credibility of British power: Bond himself apart, what can the British offer and why are they involved anyway?—a question cruelly posed by Blofeld in the film *Diamonds Are Forever*.

A second category of internationalism was suggested by mention of the United Nations in the film *On Her Majesty's Secret Service*, but that would not be credible with audiences. The pejorative view of Third World rhetoric presented in the film *Live and Let Die* better captures Anglo-American public attitudes toward an internationalism of this type. The prospect of a benign New World order focused on a Western-led United Nations that was held out at the time of the 1990–91 Gulf War now appears incredible. Bond is unlikely therefore to become a type of man from U.N.C.L.E.

The third form of internationalism would be one focused on the European Union. The process of federalism within Europe indeed poses a challenge, certainly in the long term, for it is unclear how British sovereignty in intelligence, defense and foreign policy would be compatible with a federal superstate. In the short term, European convergence offers possibilities, in that it explains why Bond might be required to act in a wide range of areas. A Europe defined by the Cold War would be replaced by one linked by federalism but still with widespread problems and challenges. Indeed, the range of opponents would be far greater than in the Cold War.

Yet it is difficult at present to see Bond answering to a Spanish M or working with a German Q. Maybe that is the challenge at the political level. How far will Bond have to adapt to governmental changes within Europe? Hitherto, continental European states and their agents had made relatively few appearances in the Bond genre, certainly in comparison with Deighton's interest in Berlin. The world of Royale and Piz Gloria was overshadowed by that of Nassau and Las Vegas. Bond's world became very much that of Britain, North America, the West Indies and Asia. Europe was largely a base where devilish schemes are hatched. For Fleming, Europe seems to have been a somewhat alien continent that he did not understand or sympathize with, as he showed in his comments on Paris.

If he remains quintessentially British, Bond might appear an anachronism, but possibly that is necessary for the foreign and, indeed, domestic market. It is part of the frame of reference that is important to the success of the films, a recognizable frame of reference akin to that of "cult" television series, such as *The Avengers* and *Star Trek*.

Britain itself might well dissolve if independence follows devolution for Scotland. This will leave the irony that Bond for many was created on screen by Sean Connery, in the 1990s a proud and vociferous assertor of the cause of Scottish independence.

The exoticism of the settings was an aspect of the speeded-up character of the films. As the takes became shorter, so the action both speeded up and shifted location, with the view propelled along as if on a roller coaster. There were no longer any troughs and peaks in the action. This was linked to a shift from suspense to spectacle in the plots, seen very clearly in *Tomorrow Never Dies*, where the villain and his plot were revealed from the outset.

Settings in the Bond novels and films are ethnic as well as geographic, although religion does not play a role, except in scams such as in *Live and Let Die* and *The Living Daylights*. It is too contentious, a setting by omission. Ethnicity, however, was readily apparent with *Dr. No* and *Live and Let Die*. In the novel *Dr. No*, Pleydell-Smith, the youngish Cambridge-educated colonial secretary of Jamaica, complained

All they think of nowadays is Federation and their bloody self-importance. Self-determination indeed! They can't even run a bus service. And the colour problem! My dear chap, there's far more colour problem between the straight-haired and the crinkly-haired Jamaicans than there is between me and my black cook.

In the film of *Live and Let Die*, the killing of agents outside the Fillet of Soul restaurant in New Orleans is followed by the exuberant anarchy of a black American funeral procession, with participants of all ages and backgrounds. A different setting for such anarchy is provided by voodoo ceremonies on San Monique, but the implications are that they are related: the black Americans are presented as uncivilized in what can be seen as a racialist film, albeit one lessened by the presence of a black CIA agent, Harry Struther, the victim of the second attack outside the Fillet of Soul, and by Bond's helper, Quarrel Junior. The latter is presented positively and is not frightened of voodoo. Instead, he tells Bond to put a bullet into Baron Samedi. The redneck Louisiana sheriff, J. W. Pepper, refers to a swarm of "Black Russians," a caricature view that is not seconded in the plot and that is mocked by attributing it to the ridiculous Pepper; but the general image of blacks in the film is negative. Rosie Carver, the black CIA agent on San Monique, betrays Bains, the British agent sent there, and then seeks to betray Bond. She is more terrified of voodoo than of Bond. Dr. Kananga's recorded speech attacks the United States, implying that other such attacks also cloaked nefarious purposes. The portrayal of blacks in the film led to accusations of racism. Solitaire, the female lead, had been intended for a black actress, but United Artists pushed successfully for a white for the part.

In the film *Thunderball*, blacks play only minor roles. Although set in the Bahamas, none of Largo's operatives are black, but he does have a black doorman. The native celebrations, the local Mardi Gras, presented in the film, show blacks as exotic, with one girl dancing on hot coals. A black Felix Leiter was an aspect of the novelty of *Never Say Never Again*.

In general, the novels and films find it difficult to accommodate the notion of British villains. Thus Alec Trevelyan is shown to be really a Cossack, and Elektra King in *The World Is Not Enough* makes much of her Azeri background, while in the novel *Goldfinger*, Fleming's portrayal of Red Grant as the product of a "German professional weightlifter" father and a "southern Irish waitress" mother coupling behind a circus bigtop.

There are of course exceptions, such as Peter Franks in the film *Diamonds Are Forever*, a killer who says little, but, on the whole, the villains are not British. Thus, in the film *Thunderball*, Largo's scientist is a Pole, henchmen have names like Vargas, Kutze and Dimitri, and the casting of Luciana Paluzzi for the role of the SPECTRE killer Fiona ensured that she did not seem English. In *Diamonds Are Forever*, Blofeld's laser-refraction man, Dr. Metz, speaks with a Germanic accent, while the two scientists who design Stromberg's submarine tracking system in *The Spy Who Loved Me* have Eastern European names and were cast accordingly. In *Moonraker*, Michael Lonsdale's Drax is portrayed as a foreigner taking what he can from each society. The sinister doctor in *A View To A Kill* is a German. Blofeld himself is confusing, because in *Diamonds Are Forever* he is portrayed by Charles Gray in a stylish fashion that might suggest an English gentleman, although his Mao-style uniform and fondness for cats do not match classic notions of the type. Indeed, he has a self-satisfied, not to say camp, presence.

The meetings between Bond and the villains are the high points of the Fleming novels and the films, and a feature that John Gardner found difficult to emulate successfully. They are important both to the plot and to the atmosphere, and they are crucial to the theatricality of the stories. Crucial to the action and explanation of the plots, the meetings also provided an opportunity for expressing values and establishing the moral status of the central characters. In the film *Octopussy*, General Orlov, a villain held prisoner by Bond, is only briefly bothered that his planned nuclear accident will kill thousands of innocent people. The meeting of the two clearly enables Bond to establish a moral superiority over the callous instrumentality of his opponent. Both hero and villains can be seen as characters from melodrama, for the Bond works are indeed melodrama. A parallel can be drawn with Britain's most successful cult television series, *Dr. Who*. This first appeared in November 1963, a month after the premiere of *From Russia With Love*, and continued until 1989. The villains in this science fiction series were morally inferior, and this frequently led to their failure. The ability of Time Lords to regenerate themselves permitted eight actors to play the doctor.

There is an important element of fantasy in the melodrama of the Bond films. Fantasy can be seen in the notion of criminality represented by Drax and Stromberg, their quest for a new world reflecting a real distaste for human life, and also in SPECTRE: the idea of a secret society of master criminals. The fabulous wealth and power of the villains were also unrealistic.

Melodrama produced for profit. Product placement has become increasingly important for the Bond films. Thus, much fuss was made of the BMWs in the Brosnan films. More typical was the attempt to push sales of Parker Jotter stainless steel ball pens in Britain in early 1997. The publicity offered £2 to those who purchased such a pen and the *GoldenEye* video:

Pay attention Bond fans. The Parker Jotter is the pen that was used by 007 in the film *GoldenEye*. It not only enables you to write with super-smooth efficiency and style, it can also earn you a £2 cash back.

The following winter, Brosnan was used to advertise Omega watches in Britain "as worn by James Bond." The smoothness that was crucial to Bond's style had great commercial appeal, and this shows no sign of changing. Hugh Gaitskell, lover of Ann Fleming as well as leader of the Labour party in 1955–63, wrote to Ian Fleming about the appeal of his novels, "The combination of sex, violence, alcohol and—at intervals—good food and nice clothes is, to one who lives such a circumscribed a life as I do, irresistible." Bond rose to visual prominence in the 1960s, a decade of greatly rising disposable income in Britain and the United States. For societies spending more on clothes, cars, gadgets and foreign travel, Bond set new standards, and made objects such as sports cars and espresso machines stylish and desirable.

At a time when for most Britons a foreign holiday meant Majorca or Benidorm, Bond went to exotic locations, such as the West Indies, India or expensive ski resorts. The world described in the novels presented a wealth fantasy. There was an excitement about luxury cars, air travel or exotic drinks, such as the rum collins Largo hands Bond in the film *Thunderball*, for societies that were starting to adopt them. *Playboy*, the leading magazine of male consumerism, and a stylish American product that sought to define male taste, serialized *On Her Majesty's Secret Service, You Only Live Twice* and *The Man With the Golden Gun* successively in 1963, 1964 and 1965. Bond thus represented a fantasy, but one that was graspable, helping to encourage a large number of parties based on the Bond theme. Too great a contrast with audience experience would have been unacceptable.

Furthermore, Bond acted as an intermediary, showing how affluence and consumerism could be stylish and noble, rather than vulgarly materialistic, translating upper-class mores and practices, such as gambling in casinos and drinking cocktails, for a wider market. Bond lives in economic fantasy, free from concern about mortgages and debts. As part of his escapist world, Bond offers an apparently cost-free style that is attractive both to a more affluent public and to those more obviously indulging escapist fantasies. He exudes a "class" apparently quite unconnected with money or birth. In that sense, perhaps, he is more a cosmopolitan man than a man of class, and his class was a matter of style, not economics. This may help explain his universal appeal. The private income of Fleming's Bond is not mentioned on screen.

Affluence had created, and continues to create, more social insecurity. There were many raw people unsure about how to treat a barman or hotel porter, or how to order dinner. With his social mixing of old and new culture, Bond offered a role model not as far as violence was concerned, nor really sex, although many men desired such a role, but in terms of *savoir faire*: knowing how to behave. *Time* of 24 August 1964 saw Bond as a hero for modern man: "immorality serving the public good, a combination that proved irresistible to an age dedicated to affluence and to being with it." A more caustic response was offered by columnist Paul Johnson:

Our curious post-war society, with its obsessive interest in debutantes, its cult of U and non-U, its working-class graduates educated into snobbery by the welfare state, is a soft market for Mr. Fleming's poison.

Knowing how to behave paralleled an appealing aspect of the Bond corpus: the sense of inside information they contain and convey. This was true from the outset, for example the mention in *Casino Royale* that Bulgarians are kept by the Soviets in Paris for a certain kind of job. Readers and viewers were invited into the sense that they shared privileged information; they were let in on what they would not ordinarily know about—accessible knowledge of the world in every sense. Bond was not the younger son of a duke, like Dorothy Sayers's Lord Peter Wimsey, or a Time Lord like Dr. Who. Bond's wisecracks and the absence of pedigree and social stuffiness made it possible for 1960s audiences to identify with him and to imagine that he was their type of hero.

This enhanced Bond's role as a consumer icon. Indeed, Bond's continued commercial appeal differentiates him from other espionage icons. Licensed Bond merchandise included cars, especially two million toy replicas of the Aston Martin used in *Goldfinger*, toys, towels, clothes, board games, rings, watches, posters and soundtrack albums. Even the spoofs did well. Made at the cost of $9 million, the first *Austin Powers* (1997) movie had earned more than $55 million by July 1998 and sold more than a million videos.

Many of the Bond theme songs did very well in the charts. Shirley Bassey's *Goldfinger* went to eighth on the American charts, setting a pattern for future success. Nancy Sinatra's *You Only Live Twice* theme song rose to eleventh on the UK charts, Paul McCartney and Wings took the song for *Live and Let Die* to second for three weeks in the American charts, and Sheena Easton and *For Your Eyes Only* went to fourth in the American and eighth in the UK charts. The most successful, Duran Duran's title song for *A View To A Kill*, went to first and second places respectively. When in *Moonraker* Q gives Bond darts operated by nerve impulses from his wrist muscles, Bond comments, "very novel, Q. We must get them in the stores for Christmas." The darts did not, in fact, become a Christmas item, but the comment reflected the appeal of gadgetry to scriptwriters, viewers and purchasers.

For the politics of Bond to end on a consumerist note can, in part, be seen as reflecting the end-of-history argument. There is no convincing cause left for the greatest of agents. Furthermore, the grounding in specific details, especially of intelligence organizations, that had been found in Fleming's novels, has gone. In novels such as *From Russia, With Love*, where they admitted responsibility for "strikes in England," the Communists were a damaging threat, but, by the 1990s, the Soviet Union had collapsed, as had European Communism, and the setting and plot of *The World Is Not Enough* reflected the retreat of Russian power. Thanks, however, to the emphasis in the films on timeless themes, and the general move away from specific political contexts, Bond has been detached from this trajectory of global power. This is linked to the escapism that is an important aspect of the films' appeal. Viewers leave nondescript houses on often seedy high streets, go into a cinema, and with eager anticipation are wafted away in an established ritual to an exotic location where a British secret agent sees off the world's nutcases and megalomaniacs and shows that the British do it best after all. The films are popular in Britain in large part because of the element of nostalgia in their appeal. They offer a refuge from the reality of British decline and the decay of traditional British values, a refuge lit by high explosives and colored by the blood of sinister foreigners.

Political detachment, at least in terms of explicit remarks, has an obvious attraction in terms of widening and sustaining Bond's consumer appeal. It also ensures that the explicit political content of the films is limited and has to be searched for very differently from that of the continuation novels, where there are sometimes specific comments.

This wider search for political meanings and echoes in the films need not detract from an appreciation of the adventure. What has been lost in the films, however, is any sense of the past. In part, this is because Bond, although apparently ageless, is not a hero endlessly set at a historical moment, the receding 1950s and 1960s. More generally, there is no sense of the loss of the past that Fleming understood. The presentation of Istanbul in the *The World Is Not Enough* is of a beautiful and very romantic city, but here, from *From Russia, With Love*, is Fleming on Istanbul:

[T]he old European section of Istanbul glittered at the end of the broad half-mile of bridge with the slim minarets lancing up into the sky and the domes of the mosques, crouching at their feet, looking like big firm breasts. It should have been the Arabian Nights, but to Bond, seeing it first above the tops of trams and above the great scars of modern advertising along the river frontage, it seemed a once beautiful theatre-set that modern Turkey had thrown aside in favour of the steel and concrete flat-iron of the Istanbul-Hilton Hotel, blankly glittering behind him on the heights of Pera.

Such a response is difficult to show on screen, but the films did not try. The end of history was not the fall of the Berlin Wall, but the abandonment of Bond's Bentley. The style was to be that of the future, the fascination that of new technology or, at least, gadgets. The formula worked. It left an emptiness and a frenetic cult of action that can come with a loss of the past. However, Bond's presence enabled the continued profitable coining of a film legend for over thirty-five years. The sardonic Fleming would have appreciated the irony.

Appendix:
The Novels and Films

THE FLEMING BOND NOVELS

Casino Royale, 1953

Live and Let Die, 1954

Moonraker, 1955

Diamonds Are Forever, 1956

From Russia, With Love, 1957

Dr. No, 1958

Goldfinger, 1959

For Your Eyes Only (a collection of short stories that includes "For Your Eyes Only"), 1960

Thunderball, 1961

The Spy Who Loved Me, 1962

On Her Majesty's Secret Service, 1963

You Only Live Twice, 1964

The Man With the Golden Gun, 1965

Octopussy, 1966

THE JAMES BOND FILMS 1962-1999*

Dr. No, 1962 (Connery, dir. Terence Young)

From Russia With Love, 1963 (Connery, dir. Terence Young)

Goldfinger, 1964 (Connery, dir. Guy Hamilton)

Thunderball, 1965 (Connery, dir. Terence Young)

You Only Live Twice, 1967 (Connery, dir. Lewis Gilbert)

On Her Majesty's Secret Service, 1969 (Lazenby, dir. Peter Hunt)

Diamonds Are Forever, 1971 (Connery, dir. Guy Hamilton)

Live and Let Die, 1973 (Moore, dir. Guy Hamilton)

The Man With the Golden Gun, 1974 (Moore, dir. Guy Hamilton)

The Spy Who Loved Me, 1977 (Moore, dir. Lewis Gilbert)

Moonraker, 1979 (Moore, dir. Lewis Gilbert)

For Your Eyes Only, 1981 (Moore, dir. John Glen)

Octopussy, 1983 (Moore, dir. John Glen)

A View To A Kill, 1985 (Moore, dir. John Glen)

The Living Daylights, 1987 (Dalton, dir. John Glen)

Licence To Kill, 1989 (Dalton, dir. John Glen)

*There are two "unofficial" Bond films that are not included as they are not Eon Productions—*Casino Royale* (1967) and *Never Say Never Again* (1983).

GoldenEye, 1995 (Brosnan, dir. Martin Campbell)

Tomorrow Never Dies, 1997 (Brosnan, dir. Roger Spottiswoode)

The World Is Not Enough, 1999 (Brosnan, dir. Michael Apted)

Selected Further Reading

ON FLEMING

Amory, Mark, ed. *The Letters of Ann Fleming*. London: Collins Harvill, 1985.

Lycett, Andrew. *Ian Fleming: The Man Behind James Bond*. Atlanta: Turner Publishing, 1995.

McCormick, Donald. *17F: The Life of Ian Fleming*. London: P. Owen, 1993.

Pearson, John. *The Life of Ian Fleming*. London: Cape, 1966; New York: McGraw-Hill, 1966.

ON BOND

Amis, Kingsley. *The James Bond Dossier*. New York: New American Library, 1965.

Barnes, Alan, and Marcus Hearn. *Kiss Kiss Bang! Bang!: The Unofficial James Bond Film Companion* (1997). Published in the United States as *Kiss Kiss Bang Bang: The Secret History of James Bond*. Woodstock, NY: The Overlook Press, 1998.

Bennett, Tony, and Janet Woollacott. *Bond and Beyond: The Political Career of a Popular Hero*. Houndmills, Basingstoke, Hampshire: Macmillan Education; New York: Methuen, 1987.

Benson, Raymond. *The James Bond Bedside Companion*. With an Introduction by Ernest L. Cueno. New York: Dodd, Mead, 1988.

Boyd, Ann S. *The Devil with James Bond*. Richmond, VA: John Knox Press, 1967. (Also, Westport, CT: Greenwood Press, 1975.)

Broccoli, Cubby, with Donald Zec. *When the Snow Melts: The Autobiography of Cubby Broccoli*. London: Boxtreee; Philadelphia: Trans-Atlantic Publications, 1998.

Brosnan, John. *James Bond in the Cinema*, 2nd ed. London: Tantivy Press; San Diego, CA: A. S. Barnes, 1981.

Buono, Oreste Del, and Umberto Eco, eds. *The Bond Affair*. Trans. R. A. Downie. London: Macdonald & Co., 1966.

Cannandine, David. "James Bond and the Decline of England." *Encounter*, November 1979.

Chapman, James. *Licence to Thrill: A Cultural History of the James Bond Films* (1999). Published in the United States as *License to Thrill*. New York: Columbia University Press, 2000.

Johnson, Paul. "Sex, Snobbery and Sadism." *New Statesman*, 5 April 1958.

Lane, Andy, and Paul Simpson. *The Bond Files: The Only Complete Guide to James Bond in Books, Films, TV, and Comics*. London: Virgin Publishing, 1998.

ON ESPIONAGE LITERATURE

Atkins, John. *The British Spy Novel: Styles in Treachery*. London: Calder; New York: Riverrun Press, 1984.

Usborne, Richard. *Clubland Heroes: A Nostalgic Study of Some Recurrent Characters in the Romantic Fiction of Dornford Yates, John Buchanan and Sapper* (1953). Revised ed., London: Barrie & Jenkins, 1974.

ON ESPIONAGE

Andrew, Christopher. *Secret Service* (1985). Published in the United States as *Her Majesty's Secret Service: The Making of the British Intelligence Community*. New York: Penguin Books, 1987.

Andrew, Christopher, and Oleg Gordievsky. *KGB: The Inside Story* (1990). Published in the United States as *KGB: The Inside Story of Its Foreign Operations from Lenin to Gorbachev*. New York: HarperCollins, 1990.

McLachlan, Donald. *Room 39: Naval Intelligence in Action 1939–45*. London: Weidenfeld & Nicolson, 1968.

Richelson, Jeffrey T. *A Century of Spies: Intelligence in the Twentieth Century*. New York: Oxford University Press, 1995.

Stafford, David. *Churchill and Secret Service* (1997). Woodstock, NY: The Overlook Press, 1998.

West, Nigel. *MI6: British Secret Intelligence Service Operations, 1909–45*. New York: Random House, 1983.

Woodward, Bob, *Veil: The Secret Wars of the CIA 1981–1987*. New York: Simon & Schuster, 1987.

Index